THE AI GLOSSARY

Demystifying 101 Essential Artificial Intelligence Terms for Everyone

Richard R. Khan

THE AI GLOSSARY: Demystifying 101 Essential Artificial Intelligence Terms for Everyone

Published by
Richard R. Khan
Toronto Ontario Canada
www.theaiglossary.co

ISBN: 978-1-7383834-2-9

First Edition: version 1.1

The book is accompanied by the following website. The website provides a variety of supplemental material, including slides, blogs and articles, correction of mistakes, and other resources that should be useful to readers.

www.theaiglossary.co

To Ameer and Aruna

Never stop following your dreams

This copy belongs to:

____

Foreword

The field of artificial intelligence (AI) is one of the most fascinating, rapidly evolving areas of study and technology development in the modern world. What began as a fledgling branch of computer science inspired by the imaginings of science fiction writers has blossomed into a vast, multidisciplinary effort spanning neuroscience, psychology, engineering, mathematics, philosophy, and more. Researchers and engineers are making AI systems that can engage in complex decision-making, understand and generate human language, recognize patterns, and even create original content like images, music, and literature.

At the same time, AI has permeated our everyday lives in ways that were unimaginable just a decade or two ago. We rely on AI for internet searches, spam filtering, language translation, recommendation engines for media and shopping, and even for driving directions and autopilot modes in our cars. Machine learning algorithms can outperform humans at many narrowly-defined tasks like playing chess or identifying objects in images. Large language models are generating passages of stunningly fluent and contextually appropriate text. AI is no longer just a curiosity explored in research labs—it is a transformative force impacting industries and societies around the world.

However, the remarkable progress in AI has also given rise to immense challenges and risks that we must grapple with. AI systems can exhibit biases and make counterintuitive mistakes if not designed carefully. There are concerns about privacy, security vulnerabilities, the impact on employment, and the potential existential risks posed by superintelligent AI systems that vastly surpass human cognitive capabilities. Dealing with these challenges while continuing to harvest the immense benefits of AI will require a coordinated, multistakeholder effort grounded in clear communication and a shared understanding of core AI concepts and terminology.

This is where a comprehensive glossary of AI terms can be invaluable. As the public discourse and policy debates around AI grow more intense and widespread, it is crucial that we have a common lexicon to facilitate clear communication. Too often, discussions of AI are hampered by ambiguities and talking past one another due to differences in how key terms and concepts are defined and understood. A shared vocabulary enables experts, policymakers, journalists, students, and others to engage in more productive and substantive dialogues.

This glossary serves as an essential reference guide, demystifying AI jargon and technical terminology through clear, accessible explanations. Its entries cut through the buzz and marketing hype to elucidate fundamental AI concepts like machine learning, neural networks, reinforcement learning, natural language processing, and computer vision. It covers the major techniques and model architectures like deep learning, transformers, generative adversarial networks, and more. And it delves into the different types and applications of AI like narrow vs general AI, symbolic vs statistical AI, and AI for robotics, games, healthcare, and scientific discovery.

It also makes sure that these are not just an alphabetical list but are grouped conceptually. For each term, it also provides key features and examples to help you understand it better. Importantly, the glossary does not stop at just defining individual terms, but weaves together conceptual threads to reveal how the different elements of AI connect and relate to each other. For example, it shows how techniques like supervised learning, unsupervised learning, and reinforcement learning fit into the broader paradigm of machine learning. It illustrates how approaches like convolutional neural networks and recurrent neural networks leverage neural architecture search and transfer learning to tackle different AI tasks like image recognition and language modeling.

Whether you are a technologist, policymaker, entrepreneur, academic, student, or simply someone curious about the remarkable field of AI, this glossary is an indispensable guide. It provides a shared foundation for navigating AI's complex terrain of ideas and technologies. With clear explanations and real-world examples, it bridges gaps in understanding and equips readers to engage in informed discussions about AI's impact on our present and future.

As AI continues its rapid advancement, reshaping industries and societies globally, developing a common vernacular is essential. This glossary is an important step in that vital process of knowledge sharing and mutual understanding. Ultimately, it is a recognition that we all have a stake in the ethical development of transformative AI systems that improve our world while mitigating risks. With a shared AI vocabulary, we can engage in richer dialogues to help steer AI's evolution in a direction that benefits humanity as a whole. This is a document everyone needs to have in their library whether you are a technologist or just new to AI.

Richard Khan has done a tremendous job in compiling this document and is continuously updating this on a daily basis.

Dr. Shalini Gopalkrishnan

Preface

Embarking on the journey into the world of artificial intelligence (AI) and machine learning (ML) can feel like entering a maze—each corner revealing new terms and concepts that can seem daunting. My own journey began with a burning curiosity and a determination to understand the technologies shaping our future. Yet, as I delved deeper, I realized that the complexities of AI and ML weren't just personal challenges—they were barriers faced by many, hindering full engagement with these transformative fields. Recognizing this, I felt a calling to illuminate this path, transforming the maze into a clear trail of exploration and discovery.

Crafting "THE AI GLOSSARY" became my personal mission—a quest to distill the essence of AI and ML into an accessible format for everyone, regardless of background or expertise. I aimed to dismantle the barriers that often deter individuals from delving into these subjects, creating a resource that empowers readers to embark on their own journeys of discovery. This book isn't just about sharing information; it's about empowering you with the tools to navigate the complexities of AI and ML.

As I meticulously examined each term, one question guided me: How can I convey understanding while sparking engagement? From explaining the foundational principles of "Artificial Intelligence" to unraveling the intricacies of "Convolutional Neural Networks," I aimed to craft a narrative that both captivates and educates. By blending clear explanations with real-world examples, I aimed to showcase the tangible impact of these technologies on our lives, igniting a sense of wonder and curiosity.

Yet, "THE AI GLOSSARY" goes beyond definitions—it stands as a testament to the power of human-AI collaboration. Leveraging cutting-edge generative AI, I enhanced my comprehension and creativity, resulting in a glossary that surpasses traditional limitations. This collaboration underscores the potential for fruitful cooperation in addressing complex problems and advancing our collective understanding.

Within these pages, you'll discover more than just words—you'll uncover narratives of innovation, discovery, and the boundless potential of AI and ML. Whether you're a student diving into computer science, a professional expanding your skillset, or simply a curious mind thirsting for knowledge, this book is your companion. It's my aspiration that "THE AI GLOSSARY" serves as a guiding light, illuminating the path ahead and inspiring you to embark on your own journey of exploration and discovery within the captivating realm of artificial intelligence and machine learning.

Welcome to "THE AI GLOSSARY." Let's embark on this adventure together, uncovering the beauty and promise concealed within the ever-expanding landscape of AI and ML.

Acknowledgments

In bringing "THE AI GLOSSARY" to life, I've been blessed with the wisdom and guidance of several key individuals whose insights have been invaluable. Their contributions have ensured the book remains a clear, accurate, and engaging resource for those eager to understand the world of AI and ML.

I am immensely grateful for the insightful reviews and valuable feedback provided by a distinguished group of experts: Sudarshana Bhattacharya's thoughtful perspectives and constructive comments significantly enriched the narrative, making complex topics more relatable and engaging. Peter Rayman's meticulous and incisive critiques were instrumental in refining the content, ensuring that sophisticated concepts are presented in an accessible manner. Uma Maharaj's comprehensive and discerning evaluations added a depth of clarity, helping to fine-tune explanations to resonate more deeply with our audience. Dr. Shalini Gopalkrishnan, with her profound academic insight and deep understanding of AI, played a key role in validating the technical accuracy and reliability of the information presented. Shailendra Mann's contributions, through his keen observations and feedback, have also been invaluable in enhancing the overall quality and readability of the book.

This project also owes a great deal to the advancements in generative AI, particularly the work surrounding models like ChatGPT and DALL-E, and their dedicated teams. These innovations have not only reinvigorated interest in AI but have also provided essential tools and examples that enrich this book's content. ChatGPT's team, with their groundbreaking work in natural language processing, has opened new avenues in conversational AI, offering rich examples and insights that have been pivotal in discussing AI's capabilities and potential. As creators of DALL-E, they have similarly transformed our understanding of AI's creative capacities, illustrating the expansive possibilities of visual content generation by machines.

The collaboration and collective genius of these individuals and teams have been a cornerstone of this project, helping to demystify AI and ML for a broad audience. Their dedication to their respective fields and their willingness to explore and push boundaries have been a source of inspiration and a guiding light throughout the writing process.

To Sudarshana, Peter, Uma, Dr. Gopalkrishnan, Shailendra and the brilliant minds behind ChatGPT, DALL-E, and other generative AI models: your contributions have been instrumental in bridging the gap between complex technological concepts and the curious minds keen on understanding them. This book is a testament to your hard work, innovation, and the transformative impact you've had on the field of AI. Thank you for your invaluable support and for inspiring us all to look deeper into the fascinating world of artificial intelligence.

How to Use this Book

Welcome again to "THE AI GLOSSARY: Demystifying 101 Essential Artificial Intelligence Terms for Everyone". Whether you're a curious beginner, an enthusiastic student, or a professional looking to brush up on the fundamentals, this book is designed to simplify the complex world of Artificial Intelligence (AI) and Machine Learning (ML) for you. Here's how to navigate this resource to maximize your learning and understanding:

Step 1: Begin with the Basics

Start your journey by diving into the Introductory Terms (pg. 1) section. These foundational terms are crucial as it lays the groundwork for understanding AI. It provides detailed descriptions of essential terms, setting the stage for your exploration into this fascinating field. Consider this the first step on your enlightening journey through the realm of AI.

Step 2: Explore at Your Own Pace

After grounding yourself in the basics, proceed to the Alphabetical List of Terms (pg. 14). Here, you have the flexibility to navigate the book in three ways:

Sequential Reading: For a structured approach, read through the terms in alphabetical order. This method ensures you don't miss out on any definitions and can help in building a comprehensive understanding gradually.

Selective Reading: If you're seeking information on specific terms, feel free to jump directly to those entries. This approach is ideal for readers with particular interests or questions, allowing for a customized reading experience.

Random Reading: For an adventurous learning experience, simply choose a term at random and begin your exploration from there. This serendipitous approach allows you to forge your unique path through the AI landscape, stumbling upon intriguing connections and insights along the way. It's a delightful way to cultivate curiosity and discover unexpected relationships between terms.

Step 3: Deepen Your Understanding by Topics

AI is a vast field, with terms often overlapping across different sub-domains. The Terms Grouped by Topic (pg. 207) section categorizes terms by relevant topics, offering you a more nuanced understanding of how these concepts interlink. It's an excellent way to delve deeper into specific areas of interest within AI and ML.

Navigation Tools

Page References and Hyperlinks: Utilize the page references in the print version or hyperlinks in the electronic version to seamlessly navigate between terms and topics. This feature enables you to connect the dots between related concepts, fostering a more integrated understanding of the subject matter.

Mind Maps: Throughout the book, you'll find mind maps that provide a visual overview of the connections between various AI and ML terms. These diagrams serve as valuable tools for visual learners and can help in consolidating your knowledge.

Reference and Continuous Learning

Consider this book not just as a one-time read but as an ongoing reference in your AI learning journey. Whenever you encounter an unfamiliar term or concept, or if you're seeking to reinforce your understanding of a particular topic, you can turn to this glossary. By revisiting terms and exploring related concepts, you'll gradually demystify the complexities of AI and ML, making each term and concept clear and accessible.

By following these guidelines, you'll be well on your way to unlocking the mysteries of Artificial Intelligence and Machine Learning, one term at a time. Enjoy the journey!

Table of Contents

List of Abbreviations

AI	Artificial Intelligence
ANI	Artificial Narrow Intelligence
ANN	Artificial Neural Network
AutoML	Automated Machine Learning
CNN	Convolutional Neural Network
DL	Deep Learning
GNoME	Graph Networks for Material Exploration
LLM	Large Language Model
MDP	Markov Decision Process
ML	Machine Learning
MLM	Masked Language Modeling
NLG	Natural Language Generation
RL	Reinforcement Learning
RNN	Recurrent Neural Network

Introductory Terms

Artificial Intelligence (AI)

To define "Artificial Intelligence (AI)" in a way that's easy to understand, let's start with a simple analogy. Think of AI as a smart robot that can think, learn, and make decisions similarly to a human. However, unlike humans, AI does this through computer systems and algorithms, not a brain. It's like having a virtual assistant that can do a wide range of tasks, from solving complex problems to understanding human language.

In Topic(s): Artificial Intelligence (AI) (pg. 210) | Ethical AI, Social Implications and Cultural Considerations (pg. 235) | Robotics (pg. 260)

Figure 1: An amusing illustration of "Artificial Intelligence (AI)".

What is Artificial Intelligence?

Artificial Intelligence is a branch of computer science that aims to create machines capable of intelligent behavior. In essence, AI is about making computers perform tasks that would normally require human intelligence. This includes things like learning from experience, recognizing objects, understanding and responding to language, making decisions, and solving problems.

Key Concepts in AI:

Learning: Just like humans learn from experience, AI systems learn from data. They identify patterns, make predictions, and improve their performance over time.

Reasoning: AI can make decisions and solve problems, often more quickly and accurately than a human. This involves logical reasoning based on the information it has learned.

Perception: AI systems can interpret the world around them by recognizing objects, speech, and text. This is often used in things like voice assistants and self-driving cars.

Adaptation: AI can adjust its behavior based on new information or changing environments, much like humans adapt to new situations.

Examples of Artificial Intelligence:

Smart Assistants: Devices like Amazon's Alexa or Apple's Siri use AI to understand and respond to your voice commands. They can play music, set alarms, provide weather reports, and even control smart home devices.

Self-Driving Cars: These vehicles use AI to perceive the environment around them, make decisions, and navigate roads without human intervention. They process vast amounts of data from sensors, GPS systems, and cameras to drive safely.

Recommendation Systems: Streaming services like Netflix or e-commerce platforms like Amazon use AI to analyze your past behavior and preferences to recommend movies or products you might like.

Healthcare Diagnosis: AI systems can assist doctors in diagnosing diseases by analyzing medical images or patient data more quickly and accurately than humanly possible.

Remember:

Artificial Intelligence represents a significant leap in the capabilities of computers, enabling them to perform tasks that were traditionally thought to require human intelligence. From simplifying daily tasks to solving complex problems, AI is increasingly becoming a part of our everyday lives. Understanding the basics of AI and its applications helps us appreciate the potential and challenges of this rapidly evolving field.

See also: Agent (pg. 21) | AI Governance (pg. 23) | Artificial General Intelligence (AGI) (pg. 4) | Artificial Narrow Intelligence (ANI) (pg. 6)

Artificial General Intelligence (AGI)

Artificial General Intelligence (AGI) can be likened to a highly skilled and versatile actor who can play any role, from a Shakespearean lead to a modern-day superhero, adapting to different roles with ease and expertise. In the world of Artificial Intelligence (AI), AGI refers to a level of AI development where a machine can perform any intellectual task that a human being can do.

In Topic(s): AI Governance (pg. 208) | Artificial Intelligence (AI) (pg. 210) | Ethical AI, Social Implications and Cultural Considerations (pg. 235) | Future Directions, Trends and Challenges (pg. 243)

Figure 2: An eccentric illustration of "Artificial General Intelligence (AGI)".

What is Artificial General Intelligence?

AGI is a type of AI that has the ability to understand, learn, and apply its intelligence broadly and flexibly, just like a human. Unlike more common forms of AI, which are designed for specific tasks (like voice recognition or playing chess), AGI can adapt to a wide range of tasks and problems without being specially programmed for them.

Key Features of AGI:

Versatility and Adaptability: AGI can tackle various types of tasks and problems, applying its intelligence in different domains, just like a human.

Learning and Reasoning: It possesses the ability to learn from experiences, reason through problems, make judgments, and apply knowledge to new situations.

Autonomous Understanding: AGI can understand and interpret its environment, make decisions, and take actions based on that understanding.

Examples of AGI (Hypothetical):

Medical Research and Diagnosis: An AGI system could read medical texts, research papers, patient records, and clinical trial results, synthesizing this information to diagnose illnesses and suggest treatments.

Complex Problem Solving: AGI could be tasked with solving global challenges like climate change, where it would analyze vast amounts of environmental data, economic models, and scientific research to propose solutions.

Everyday Life Assistance: AGI could serve as a personal assistant, managing schedules, offering advice, learning preferences, and adapting to various tasks, from financial planning to travel arrangements.

Remember:

Artificial General Intelligence represents the ultimate goal of many AI researchers–a machine with the full range of human cognitive abilities. While AGI remains a theoretical concept and not yet realized, understanding its potential helps us appreciate the ambitious scope of AI research and the future direction it might take. AGI would be a transformative leap in AI capabilities, enabling machines to assist with or even lead complex and creative problem-solving across multiple domains.

See also: Artificial Intelligence (AI) (pg. 2) | Artificial Narrow Intelligence (ANI) (pg. 6)

Artificial Narrow Intelligence (ANI)

Artificial Narrow Intelligence (ANI) can be compared to a specialist or an expert in a specific field. Just like a master chess player who excels in chess but might not be skilled in cooking, ANI is designed to perform specific tasks or solve particular problems without possessing the broad range of abilities that a human might have.

In Topic(s): Artificial Intelligence (AI) (pg. 210)

Figure 3: A delightful illustration of "Artificial Narrow Intelligence (ANI)".

What is Artificial Narrow Intelligence?

ANI is a type of Artificial Intelligence (AI) that is focused on a single narrow task. It is programmed to do a specific job and does it very well, but it lacks the general understanding or consciousness that a human has. ANI systems are designed to excel in the tasks they are built for, but they cannot perform outside of their specific domain.

Key Characteristics of ANI:

Task-Specific: ANI systems are tailored to perform specific tasks. They are very good at these tasks but cannot handle tasks they were not designed for.

Limited Understanding: Unlike humans, ANI doesn't have a general understanding of the world. Its 'knowledge' is limited to its specific task area.

Prevalence in Current Technology: Most of the AI systems we interact with today are examples of ANI.

Examples of Artificial Narrow Intelligence:

Voice Assistants: Devices like Siri, Alexa, and Google Assistant are examples of ANI. They can perform tasks like setting alarms, answering questions, or controlling smart home devices, but their capabilities are limited to predefined functions.

Navigation Systems: GPS and navigation apps that provide driving directions and traffic conditions operate with ANI. They are adept at route planning but are limited to this task.

Recommendation Systems: The algorithms used by streaming services like Netflix or shopping websites like Amazon to recommend movies or products are ANI. They analyze your past behavior to make these recommendations but are limited to this context.

Email Spam Filters: The technology that filters out spam from your email inbox is ANI. It can identify and categorize emails as spam based on certain criteria but is limited to this function.

Remember:

Artificial Narrow Intelligence represents the current state of most AI applications. It encompasses systems designed to excel in specific tasks, providing us with efficient solutions in various domains. While ANI lacks the broader cognitive abilities of human intelligence, its specificity and efficiency in particular areas make it a powerful tool in our daily lives and various industries. Understanding ANI helps in recognizing the capabilities and limitations of current AI technologies.

See also: Artificial General Intelligence (AGI) (pg. 4) | Artificial Intelligence (AI) (pg. 2)

ChatGPT (OpenAI)

Imagine having a conversation with someone who is incredibly well-read, knowledgeable about a vast array of topics, and can recall information in an instant. This person isn't just smart; they're also helpful, able to write essays, poems, or even code, based on your requests. This is what interacting with ChatGPT from OpenAI is like. It's a computer program, but one that's designed to converse, inform, and assist in a remarkably human-like way.

In Topic(s): Artificial Intelligence (AI) (pg. 210) | Core Applications (pg. 218) | Cutting-edge Technologies (pg. 221) | Emerging Technologies (pg. 233) | Industry Applications (pg. 247) | Natural Language Processing (NLP) (pg. 254) | Natural Language Understanding (NLU) (pg. 256) | Text and Language Processing (pg. 270)

Figure 4: A charming illustration of "ChatGPT (OpenAI)".

What is ChatGPT?

ChatGPT is a state-of-the-art language model developed by OpenAI. It's designed to understand and generate human language, enabling it to participate in conversations, answer questions, and provide information or creative content. It's trained on a vast array of text data, allowing it to be knowledgeable about a wide range of topics.

Key Features of ChatGPT:

Conversational Abilities: ChatGPT is adept at understanding and generating natural language, making it capable of engaging in conversations that feel surprisingly human-like.

Versatile Information Processing: It can provide explanations, answer questions, write content, and even create code snippets, among other tasks.

Learning from Data: ChatGPT is trained on a large dataset of text, which includes books, articles, and websites, enabling it to have a broad understanding of human knowledge.

Continual Improvement: OpenAI regularly updates ChatGPT, enhancing its abilities and knowledge base.

Examples of ChatGPT in Action:

Educational Assistance: Students can use ChatGPT to get help with homework, understand complex topics, or practice language learning.

Content Creation: Writers and marketers might use ChatGPT to generate ideas, draft content, or even write entire articles or stories.

Programming Help: Programmers can interact with ChatGPT to troubleshoot code, understand programming concepts, or get coding suggestions.

General Queries: Anyone can use ChatGPT to ask questions about various topics, get travel advice, learn about new hobbies, or simply have an engaging conversation.

Remember:

ChatGPT by OpenAI represents a significant advancement in AI, particularly in the field of natural language processing. Its ability to understand and interact in human language makes it a versatile tool for a wide range of applications, from education and content creation to programming and everyday information seeking. Understanding ChatGPT is to appreciate a glimpse into the future of human-AI interaction, where AI can converse, inform, and assist in increasingly sophisticated and helpful ways.

See also: Conversational Agent (pg. 49) | Large Language Model (LLM) (pg. 114) | Natural Language Generation (NLG) (pg. 124)

Generative AI

Think of Generative AI as an imaginative artist who can create new, original pieces of art, music, or even write stories. Just as an artist draws on their knowledge and creativity to produce something new, Generative AI uses data and algorithms to generate new content, often resembling something a human might create.

In Topic(s): Artificial Intelligence (AI) (pg. 210) | Core Applications (pg. 218) | Cutting-edge Technologies (pg. 221) | Emerging Technologies (pg. 233) | Ethical AI, Social Implications and Cultural Considerations (pg. 235) | Future Directions, Trends and Challenges (pg. 243) | Industry Applications (pg. 247)

Figure 5: A delightful illustration of "Generative AI".

What is Generative AI?

Generative AI refers to a type of Artificial Intelligence that focuses on creating new content or data. It can generate realistic images, videos, texts, and sounds that may appear to be created by humans. Unlike traditional AI, which analyzes and interprets data, Generative AI goes a step further by producing new, original output.

Key Features of Generative AI:

Creativity in Machines: Generative AI demonstrates a form of machine creativity, using learned data to create something new and original.

Learning from Data: It learns from existing data, understanding patterns and styles, and then uses this knowledge to generate new, similar data.

Variety of Applications: Generative AI has diverse applications, from art and music creation to developing realistic virtual environments.

Examples of Generative AI in Use:

Art Creation: Generative AI can produce original artworks that mimic the style of famous artists or create entirely new styles.

Music Composition: AI algorithms can compose music in various genres, either imitating existing styles or generating unique compositions.

Writing and Text Generation: Generative AI can write stories, poems, or even news articles. With sufficient training, it can mimic specific writing styles.

Deepfakes: This is a controversial use of Generative AI, where it creates realistic but fake audiovisual content, like altering a video to make it appear that someone said or did something they did not.

Product Design: In industries, Generative AI can assist in designing new products by generating multiple design variations quickly.

Remember:

Generative AI represents a groundbreaking aspect of AI technology, showing the potential for machines not just to analyze data, but to creatively generate new content. While it opens up exciting possibilities in creative fields, it also presents ethical considerations, especially in uses like deepfakes. Understanding Generative AI helps in appreciating the creative potential of AI and its growing impact on various aspects of society and industry.

See also: AlphaFold (pg. 25) | DALL-E (pg. 59)

Machine Learning (ML)

Imagine you're teaching a child to recognize different types of fruits. You show them apples, bananas, oranges, and each time you name the fruit. As you do this, the child learns and starts to identify each fruit on their own. Machine Learning (ML) in the world of computers and Artificial Intelligence (AI) is somewhat similar. It's about teaching computers to learn from data and make decisions or predictions, much like a child learns from examples.

In Topic(s): Artificial Intelligence (AI) (pg. 210) | Core Applications (pg. 218) | Data Science (DS) (pg. 227) | Industry Applications (pg. 247) | Machine Learning (ML) (pg. 250) | Supervised Learning (pg. 266)

Figure 6: A delightful illustration of "Machine Learning (ML)".

What is Machine Learning (ML)?

Machine Learning is a branch of AI that focuses on building systems that can learn from and make decisions based on data. Instead of being explicitly programmed to perform a task, ML systems are trained using large amounts of data, which they use to make predictions or decisions.

Key Features of Machine Learning:

Learning from Data: ML systems learn from past data, identifying patterns and relationships that can be used to make future predictions.

Improving Over Time: As they are exposed to more data, ML systems can improve, making more accurate predictions or decisions.

Wide Range of Applications: ML is used in various fields like healthcare (for disease diagnosis), finance (for predicting stock movements), and technology (like recommendation systems on streaming services).

Different Learning Methods: There are several types of ML, including supervised learning (learning from labeled data), unsupervised learning (learning from unlabeled data), and reinforcement learning (learning through trial and error).

Examples of Machine Learning in Use:

Email Spam Filters: ML is used to identify patterns in emails that are likely to be spam and filter them out of your inbox.

Voice Recognition Systems: Systems like Siri or Alexa use ML to understand and respond to voice commands.

Credit Scoring: Banks use ML to analyze your financial history and determine your credit score, affecting loan approvals.

Medical Imaging: In healthcare, ML helps in analyzing medical images like X-rays or MRIs to identify diseases.

Remember:

Machine Learning is a powerful and increasingly prevalent technology that enables computers to learn from data, much like humans learn from experience. It's a cornerstone of modern AI, empowering a wide range of applications across various industries. Understanding ML is key to appreciating how much of today's technology can adapt, improve, and provide insights and solutions based on the data it processes.

See also: Automated Machine Learning (AutoML) (pg. 37)

Alphabetical List of Terms

Accuracy

Think about playing a game of darts. Your goal is to hit the bullseye, and every time you hit it or get close, you score points. In this game, your accuracy is determined by how many of your throws hit the target area. Similarly, in AI and machine learning, "Accuracy" measures how often the model's predictions are correct.

In Topic(s): Artificial Intelligence (AI) (pg. 210) | Data Analytics (DA) (pg. 223) | Data Science (DS) (pg. 227) | Fundamental Data Concepts (pg. 237) | Fundamental Mathematics and Statistics (pg. 241) | Machine Learning (ML) (pg. 250) | Supervised Learning (pg. 266)

Figure 7: A playful illustration of "Accuracy".

What is Accuracy?

In AI and machine learning, Accuracy is a metric used to evaluate the performance of a model, specifically how often the model makes the correct prediction. It's calculated by dividing the number of correct predictions by the total number of predictions made.

Key Aspects of Accuracy:

Measure of Correctness: Accuracy measures the proportion of correct predictions (both true positives and true negatives) out of all predictions made.

Simple and Intuitive: It's a straightforward way to understand how well a model is performing.

Limitations: While useful, accuracy alone might not always give the full picture, especially if the data is unbalanced (when one class is much more frequent than the other).

Important in Classification Tasks: Accuracy is most commonly used in classification tasks, where the model predicts whether data belongs to certain categories.

Examples of Accuracy in Use:

Email Spam Filter: In a spam filter, accuracy would measure how often the filter correctly identifies an email as spam or not spam.

Medical Diagnosis: In a tool that diagnoses diseases, accuracy would indicate how often the tool correctly identifies the presence or absence of a disease.

Image Recognition: For a model trained to identify animals in photos, accuracy measures how often it correctly identifies the animal.

Remember:

Accuracy is a fundamental metric in AI and machine learning for evaluating how well a model performs, especially in terms of its ability to make correct predictions. It's like the score in a game that tells you how often you're hitting the target, providing a clear and simple way to assess a model's effectiveness. However, it's also important to consider other metrics for a comprehensive evaluation of a model's performance.

See also: Error Minimization (pg. 75) | Evaluation Metric (pg. 80) | Loss Function (pg. 116)

Action Recognition

Imagine watching a video and being able to tell exactly what people are doing in it, like whether someone is dancing, cooking, or playing soccer. This ability to observe and identify actions is similar to what we call Action Recognition in the world of Artificial Intelligence (AI) and Machine Learning (ML). It's about teaching computers to watch a video and understand the actions taking place in it, just as you might when watching a movie or observing people in a park.

In Topic(s): Artificial Intelligence (AI) (pg. 210) | Computer Vision (CV) (pg. 216) | Core Applications (pg. 218) | Image Processing (pg. 245) | Industry Applications (pg. 247) | Robotics (pg. 260) | Sound and Audio Processing (pg. 264) | Supervised Learning (pg. 266) | Video Processing (pg. 274)

Figure 8: A lighthearted illustration of "Action Recognition".

What is Action Recognition?

Action Recognition is a process where AI systems are designed to identify and classify various actions or activities within videos or real-time camera feeds. The goal is to make the computer understand what action or sequence of movements is being performed by objects or people in the visual data it processes.

Key Elements of Action Recognition:

Observation of Movement: The system observes the movements in a sequence of video frames, looking for patterns that represent specific actions.

Learning from Examples: AI models are trained on large datasets of video clips that are labeled with the actions they contain, learning to recognize the distinctive features of different actions.

Temporal Understanding: The AI must understand the temporal sequence of movements, meaning it has to recognize the order and duration of movements to accurately identify the action.

Context Integration: Sometimes, understanding the context or setting is crucial for accurately recognizing an action. For example, the same arm movement might mean something different in a dance class than on a tennis court.

Examples of Action Recognition in Use:

Surveillance and Security: In security camera footage, action recognition can help identify suspicious activities or behaviors, such as someone breaking into a car or a sudden crowd forming, triggering alerts for human operators.

Sports Analysis: Coaches and athletes use action recognition technologies to analyze performance during training or games. It can help in breaking down complex movements, improving techniques, or strategizing based on opponents' actions.

Healthcare and Rehabilitation: For patients undergoing physical rehabilitation, action recognition can monitor their exercises to ensure they're performing them correctly for effective recovery.

Entertainment and Gaming: In interactive video games or virtual reality experiences, action recognition allows the system to respond to the players' physical actions, making the experience more immersive and engaging.

Remember:

Action Recognition is a fascinating area of AI and ML that bridges the gap between the digital world and the dynamic, movement-filled human experience. By enabling machines to understand and classify human actions from visual data, it opens up myriad applications that enhance security, sports, healthcare, and entertainment, among others. Understanding this technology offers a glimpse into how AI is increasingly becoming an integral part of interpreting and interacting with the world around us in intelligent and helpful ways.

See also: Image Recognition (pg. 102) | Video Data (pg. 200)

Activation Function

Let's start by understanding what an "Activation Function" is in the world of Artificial Intelligence (AI) and Machine Learning (ML). To do this, we'll use a simple analogy.

Imagine you're at a party and deciding whether or not to dance. You process several factors: the genre of music, the number of people on the dance floor, your mood, and perhaps even the time of the evening. Based on these inputs, you make a decision: either to start dancing (act) or to remain seated (not act). The process of making this decision is similar to how an activation function works in a neural network, a type of AI model.

In Topic(s): Artificial Intelligence (AI) (pg. 210) | Artificial Neural Networks (ANN) (pg. 214) | Deep Learning (DL) (pg. 231) | Fundamental Data Concepts (pg. 237) | Fundamental Mathematics and Statistics (pg. 241) | Machine Learning (ML) (pg. 250)

Figure 9: A delightful illustration of "Activation Function".

What is an Activation Function?

In the context of neural networks, an activation function is a mathematical function that takes in a set of inputs, processes them, and decides whether a particular neuron should be activated or not. Think of neurons as tiny decision-makers within the network.

Key Points about Activation Functions:

Role in Neural Networks: Each neuron in a neural network processes the inputs it receives and decides whether to send its own signal out to the next layer of neurons. The activation function is the rule that the neuron follows to make this decision.

Binary Decision-Making: Like deciding whether to dance or not, many activation functions make a sort of yes/no decision. They determine whether the information that a neuron has received is important enough to be passed along.

Non-Linearity: Activation functions often introduce non-linear properties to the neural network. This means they allow the network to handle complex patterns, like recognizing faces in images or understanding spoken words.

Examples of Activation Functions:

Step Function: This is like a strict yes-or-no decision. If the inputs to the neuron exceed a certain threshold, the neuron activates (like deciding to dance if your favorite song plays). If not, it stays inactive.

Sigmoid Function: This function is smoother. It's like deciding to dance more energetically as the music gradually shifts to your favorite genre. The neuron's output isn't just on or off; it varies based on how strongly the inputs signal it to activate.

ReLU (Rectified Linear Unit): This function is common in modern neural networks. It's like having a rule where you start dancing only when a certain number of your friends are on the dance floor. Below this number, you won't dance at all, but once this threshold is passed, your enthusiasm (output) increases with more friends joining in.

Remember:

Activation functions in neural networks are like internal decision-makers that determine how a neuron should respond to the inputs it receives. They are crucial for enabling the network to make sense of complex data and perform tasks like recognizing speech, translating languages, or playing games. By introducing non-linearity, they allow neural networks to learn and model intricate patterns and behaviors.

See also: Artificial Neural Network (ANN) (pg. 29) | Neuron (pg. 126)

Agent

Think of a personal assistant, like a secretary or a butler, who performs tasks, makes decisions, and reacts based on your instructions or certain situations. They observe, learn, and act to achieve specific goals or complete tasks. In the realms of Artificial Intelligence (AI) and Machine Learning (ML), an 'Agent' is akin to this personal assistant, but in a digital form.

In Topic(s): Artificial Intelligence (AI) (pg. 210) | Core Applications (pg. 218) | Reinforcement Learning (pg. 259) | Robotics (pg. 260) | Supervised Learning (pg. 266)

Figure 10: A lighthearted illustration of "Agent".

What is an Agent?

An Agent in AI and ML refers to a computer program or software that autonomously performs actions or makes decisions in order to achieve specific objectives. It operates within an environment, gathers information (through sensors or data inputs), processes this information, and then takes actions (via actuators or output mechanisms) that influence the environment.

Key Characteristics of an Agent:

Autonomy: Agents operate without constant human guidance. They make decisions based on their programming and the information they receive.

Reactivity: Agents can perceive their environment and respond to changes in it in a timely manner.

Proactiveness: Agents take initiative to fulfill their objectives, not just react to the environment.

Goal-Oriented: The actions of an agent are directed towards achieving specific goals or objectives.

Examples of Agents in Use:

Virtual Assistants: Like Siri or Alexa, these agents can understand your voice commands, process them, and perform actions like setting reminders, playing music, or providing information.

Online Customer Support Bots: These agents interact with customers, understand their queries, and provide responses or assistance.

Autonomous Vehicles: Self-driving cars are agents that sense their environment (like road conditions, obstacles) and make driving decisions to reach a destination safely.

Recommendation Systems: Agents in recommendation systems analyze your browsing and purchase history to suggest products or content you might like.

Remember:

An Agent in AI and ML is a digital entity designed to perform tasks autonomously in pursuit of specific goals. By interpreting data from their environment and making decisions, these agents can simplify tasks, provide insights, and enhance user experiences across various domains. Understanding agents helps in appreciating the sophistication and practicality of AI in everyday applications, from simplifying routine tasks to handling complex operations.

See also: Artificial Intelligence (AI) (pg. 2) | Reinforcement Learning (RL) (pg. 150)

AI Governance

Imagine you're the captain of a large, sophisticated ship. This ship is not ordinary; it's equipped with the most advanced technologies, capable of navigating itself and making decisions to ensure a smooth voyage. However, as the captain, you must set the rules, guidelines, and frameworks to ensure that this technology is used wisely, ethically, and effectively. This responsibility mirrors the concept of "AI Governance" in the world of Artificial Intelligence (AI) and Machine Learning (ML).

In Topic(s): AI Governance (pg. 208) | Artificial Intelligence (AI) (pg. 210) | Core Applications (pg. 218) | Ethical AI, Social Implications and Cultural Considerations (pg. 235) | Future Directions, Trends and Challenges (pg. 243) | Privacy and Security (pg. 258)

Figure 11: A charming illustration of "AI Governance".

What is AI Governance?

AI Governance encompasses the policies, practices, and frameworks that guide how AI technologies are developed, deployed, and used in society. It's about ensuring that AI works in the best interest of humanity, adhering to ethical standards, respecting privacy, and promoting fairness, accountability, and transparency.

Key Aspects of AI Governance:

Ethical Guidelines: Just as a captain ensures the ship's journey respects maritime laws and ethical standards, AI Governance involves setting ethical guidelines for AI development and use, focusing on fairness, non-discrimination, and the well-being of individuals.

Regulatory Compliance: AI Governance requires adherence to laws and regulations, similar to how a ship must comply with international maritime regulations. This includes data protection laws, privacy regulations, and industry-specific guidelines.

Transparency and Accountability: In AI Governance, there's a push for transparency in how AI systems make decisions and accountability for those decisions, akin to how a ship's log keeps a transparent record of the voyage and decisions made along the way.

Public Engagement: Just as a ship's journey might be influenced by the needs and concerns of its passengers, AI Governance involves engaging with the public, stakeholders, and experts to ensure AI technologies serve the broader interests of society.

Examples of AI Governance in Action:

AI in Healthcare: Implementing AI Governance in healthcare might involve setting strict privacy protections for patient data, ensuring AI diagnostic tools are unbiased and accurate, and clearly explaining AI-assisted decisions to patients and healthcare professionals.

Autonomous Vehicles: For self-driving cars, AI Governance includes establishing safety standards, ensuring the technology can handle ethical dilemmas (like split-second decisions in emergencies), and making the system's decision-making process understandable to regulators and users.

Content Moderation on Social Platforms: AI Governance in this context involves creating guidelines to ensure AI-driven content moderation respects freedom of expression while effectively identifying and mitigating harmful content, with clear avenues for human review and appeals.

Remember:

AI Governance is akin to setting the course for a ship equipped with powerful, autonomous technologies. It's about steering the development and application of AI in a direction that is safe, ethical, and aligned with human values and societal norms. By establishing clear guidelines, regulatory frameworks, and mechanisms for transparency and accountability, AI Governance ensures that the AI "ship" navigates the vast "ocean" of possibilities responsibly, bringing benefits to society while minimizing risks and harms.

See also: Artificial General Intelligence (AGI) (pg. 4) | Artificial Intelligence (AI) (pg. 2)

AlphaFold

Imagine you have a complex puzzle made of thousands of tiny pieces. Each piece represents a part of a protein, an essential molecule in our bodies. The way these pieces fit together determines how the protein functions, much like how the structure of a key determines which lock it can open. For decades, scientists have been trying to figure out how these protein pieces fit together. This is where AlphaFold comes into the picture.

In Topic(s): Artificial Intelligence (AI) (pg. 210) | Core Applications (pg. 218) | Cutting-edge Technologies (pg. 221) | Emerging Technologies (pg. 233) | Future Directions, Trends and Challenges (pg. 243) | Machine Learning (ML) (pg. 250)

Figure 12: An eccentric illustration of "AlphaFold".

What is AlphaFold?

AlphaFold is an artificial intelligence program developed by DeepMind Technologies. Its purpose is to predict the 3D shapes of proteins based solely on their amino acid sequences—the string of molecules that make up the protein. Understanding a protein's shape is crucial because it dictates the protein's function in the body, from fighting off viruses to speeding up chemical reactions.

Key Features of AlphaFold:

Predictive Accuracy: AlphaFold can predict the 3D structure of proteins with a level of accuracy comparable to expensive and time-consuming laboratory methods.

Speed: It can complete predictions in a matter of days, a process that could take scientists years to accomplish through traditional experimental methods.

Wide Application: The technology has implications across many fields, from developing new medicines to understanding diseases better.

Examples of AlphaFold's Impact:

Drug Discovery: By knowing the shape of target proteins involved in diseases, researchers can design drugs that fit perfectly into these proteins, much like a key fits into a lock, to either activate or deactivate their functions.

Understanding Diseases: Many diseases, such as Alzheimer's, are associated with proteins that misfold. AlphaFold's ability to predict protein structures could lead to a better understanding of these conditions and how to treat them.

Enzyme Design: Enzymes are proteins that catalyze chemical reactions. With AlphaFold, scientists can design new enzymes for bioengineering applications, such as breaking down plastic waste more efficiently.

Remember:

AlphaFold represents a monumental leap in the field of biology and bioinformatics. By accurately predicting the 3D structures of proteins, it opens up new avenues for scientific research and practical applications in medicine, environmental science, and more. Understanding AlphaFold and its capabilities helps us appreciate the transformative potential of AI in solving some of the most complex and longstanding challenges in science.

See also: Deep Learning (DL) (pg. 69) | Generative AI (pg. 10)

Anomaly Detection

Consider a security guard at a museum who watches for anything unusual, like someone touching an artwork. They're trained to notice things that don't fit the regular pattern of behavior. In the world of Artificial Intelligence (AI) and Machine Learning (ML), Anomaly Detection is somewhat similar. It involves identifying unusual patterns or behaviors in data that deviate from what is expected or normal.

In Topic(s): Artificial Intelligence (AI) (pg. 210) | Core Applications (pg. 218) | Data Analytics (DA) (pg. 223) | Data Science (DS) (pg. 227) | Future Directions, Trends and Challenges (pg. 243) | Industry Applications (pg. 247) | Privacy and Security (pg. 258) | Supervised Learning (pg. 266) | Unsupervised Learning (pg. 272)

Figure 13: A charming illustration of "Anomaly Detection".

What is Anomaly Detection?

Anomaly Detection is a technique used in AI and ML to identify unusual patterns or outliers in data. These are observations that deviate significantly from the majority of the data and could indicate critical incidents, such as fraud, faults, or errors. The ability to detect anomalies is vital in many domains as it can help in preempting potential problems or discovering new opportunities.

Key Components of Anomaly Detection:

Outlier Identification: This is the process of finding data points that are significantly different from the rest of the data. These outliers could be due to variability in the data or indicate an error or unusual occurrence.

Pattern Recognition: AI systems learn the normal patterns in the data and then use this knowledge to spot deviations.

Alerting Mechanisms: Once an anomaly is detected, the system often triggers an alert for further investigation.

Continuous Learning: AI systems can adapt over time, learning what constitutes normal variations and what might be a true anomaly.

Examples of Anomaly Detection in Use:

Fraud Detection in Banking: Anomaly detection is used to identify unusual transactions in a bank account, such as a large purchase in a foreign country, which could indicate fraud.

Manufacturing Quality Control: In manufacturing, anomaly detection helps in identifying defects in products by recognizing deviations from the standard manufacturing process.

Health Monitoring Systems: In healthcare, monitoring devices use anomaly detection to flag unusual vital signs, potentially indicating a patient's health emergency.

Network Security: In cybersecurity, anomaly detection tools monitor network traffic to identify unusual patterns that could signify a security breach.

Remember:

Anomaly Detection in AI and ML is a critical technique for identifying unusual patterns in data, which can signify important events or issues. It is akin to a vigilant guard that keeps an eye out for anything out of the ordinary, providing an essential layer of intelligence and security in various applications from finance to healthcare. Understanding Anomaly Detection helps in appreciating how AI can be used to safeguard systems and processes, enhance operational efficiency, and prevent potential crises.

See also: Classification (pg. 41) | Unsupervised Learning (pg. 196)

Artificial Neural Network (ANN)

Let's explore "Artificial Neural Networks (ANNs)" in a manner that's straightforward and easy to grasp. Think of ANNs as a team of workers in a company. Each worker specializes in a particular job. They receive information, process it based on their expertise, and pass on their findings. This collaboration allows them to solve complex problems efficiently. ANNs operate in a similar collaborative fashion.

In Topic(s): Artificial Intelligence (AI) (pg. 210) | Artificial Neural Networks (ANN) (pg. 214) | Deep Learning (DL) (pg. 231) | Supervised Learning (pg. 266)

Figure 14: A whimsical illustration of "Artificial Neural Network (ANN)".

What is an Artificial Neural Network?

An ANN is a computer system modeled after the human brain. Just as our brain processes information through a network of neurons, an ANN uses artificial neurons or 'nodes' to process data.

Key Components of Artificial Neural Networks:

Neurons (Nodes): These are the basic building blocks of an ANN. Each neuron processes the information it receives and transmits the output to other neurons.

Layers: There are three types of layers in an ANN.

Input Layer: It receives the initial data, like the first point of contact in a workflow.

Hidden Layers: These are where the data is processed, modified, and analyzed. They're like the various departments in a company that work on the information received from the front desk.

Output Layer: It produces the final result or decision, akin to the company's final product or service.

Weights and Biases: These are parameters within neurons that influence the importance of inputs and the processing of information. They're adjusted during the learning process to improve accuracy.

Activation Function: This determines whether a neuron should 'activate' or contribute to the next layer's input, similar to a decision-making process in a workflow.

Examples of Artificial Neural Networks in Action:

Image Recognition: ANNs are great at identifying objects in pictures. Imagine training an ANN with many photos of different animals. Over time, it learns to recognize various animals in new photos by identifying patterns and features like shapes, colors, and textures.

Speech Recognition: Systems like Siri or Alexa use ANNs to understand spoken words. They analyze sound patterns in your speech and translate them into commands or queries.

Medical Diagnoses: ANNs can assist doctors by analyzing medical images for signs of diseases. For example, they can learn to detect cancerous cells in X-ray or MRI images.

Financial Predictions: In the financial sector, ANNs are used for predicting stock prices or assessing credit risks by analyzing past market data and trends.

Remember:

Artificial Neural Networks are at the heart of many modern AI applications. They replicate aspects of human intelligence and learning, enabling machines to perform complex tasks like recognizing images, understanding speech, or making predictive analyses. Understanding how ANNs work gives us a glimpse into the sophisticated world of AI and its vast potential in various fields.

See also: Convolutional Neural Network (CNN) (pg. 51) | Deep Learning (DL) (pg. 69) | Neuron (pg. 126) | Recurrent Neural Network (RNN) (pg. 146)

Association

Think about your last visit to a grocery store. You may have noticed that bread and butter are often placed near each other. This isn't a coincidence. It's because many shoppers tend to buy them together. This relationship or connection between bread and butter is similar to the concept of "Association" in AI and machine learning.

In Topic(s): Artificial Intelligence (AI) (pg. 210) | Data Analytics (DA) (pg. 223) | Data Science (DS) (pg. 227) | Fundamental Data Concepts (pg. 237) | Fundamental Mathematics and Statistics (pg. 241)

Figure 15: A lighthearted illustration of "Association".

What is Association?

In the context of AI and machine learning, Association refers to the discovery of patterns, correlations, or relationships between variables or data points in large datasets. It's about finding out how the occurrence of one event or item is connected to the occurrence of another.

Key Aspects of Association:

Pattern Recognition: Association involves identifying patterns of co-occurrence or sequences within data.

Correlation, Not Causation: It's important to note that association doesn't necessarily imply causation. It merely indicates that items or events tend to occur together.

Used in Various Domains: Association is a widely used technique in fields like market basket analysis, recommendation systems, and more.

Rule-Based Analysis: Often, association is expressed in terms of rules. For instance, "If a customer buys bread, they are likely to buy butter."

Examples of Association in Use:

Shopping Basket Analysis: Retail stores analyze transaction data to identify products often bought together. This can lead to targeted marketing, such as placing related products near each other or bundling them in promotions.

Movie Recommendation Systems: Streaming platforms use association to recommend movies or shows based on what similar users have watched.

Medical Research: Researchers may find associations between lifestyle choices and the likelihood of developing certain health conditions.

Fraud Detection: In banking, association rules can help identify patterns of transactions that may indicate fraudulent activity.

Remember:

Association is a key concept in AI and machine learning, focusing on finding meaningful relationships and patterns within data. It plays a crucial role in enhancing our understanding of data and aids in decision-making across various industries, from retail to healthcare. Understanding association helps in appreciating how AI can uncover hidden insights in vast amounts of data.

See also: Clustering (pg. 43)

Audio Data

Imagine recording a conversation, the chirping of birds, or a concert on your phone. What you've captured is not just sound but 'audio data'. In the realm of Artificial Intelligence (AI) and Machine Learning (ML), audio data is a crucial component. It's the raw material that AI systems use to understand and interpret sounds, from human speech to environmental noises.

In Topic(s): Fundamental Data Concepts (pg. 237) | Sound and Audio Processing (pg. 264)

Figure 16: A delightful illustration of "Audio Data".

What is Audio Data?

Audio data refers to information captured in the form of sound. This can range from human voices in a conversation, music recordings, environmental sounds like traffic noise, to even the subtle sounds machinery makes. In AI and ML, this data is used to train algorithms to recognize, process, and respond to sound in various ways.

Key Characteristics of Audio Data:

Waveform Representation: Audio data is often visualized as waveforms, which represent the vibration or sound pressure over time.

Digital Format: For use in AI and ML, audio data is usually converted into a digital format, which involves sampling the sound waves at regular intervals and quantifying them.

Frequency and Time Information: Audio data contains information about the frequency (pitch) and time (duration) of sounds.

Examples of Audio Data:

Voice Recognition Systems: Systems like Siri or Google Assistant use audio data of spoken words to understand and execute user commands.

Music Streaming Services: Services like Spotify analyze audio data of songs to make recommendations based on genres, rhythms, and user preferences.

Health Diagnostics: In healthcare, audio data from heartbeats or lung sounds can be used for diagnostic purposes.

Language Translation Tools: Tools that offer spoken language translation process audio data of speech in one language and convert it to another.

Remember:

Audio data in AI and ML is the foundational element that enables systems to interact with the world of sound. From understanding spoken words to recognizing the nuances of music, audio data provides the raw input that AI systems need to interpret and respond to sounds. Its application ranges from simple voice commands to complex tasks like diagnosing health conditions, making it an integral part of modern AI technologies. Understanding audio data is essential for grasping how AI can process and make sense of the diverse sounds in our environment.

See also: Text Data (pg. 178) | Video Data (pg. 200)

Autoencoder

Imagine you have a massive collection of photographs and you need to organize them efficiently. One approach could be to summarize each photo by its key features–maybe the main colors, the presence of people or landscapes, the lighting conditions, and so on. This summary captures the essence of each photo, making it easier to organize and retrieve them. An "Autoencoder" in Artificial Intelligence (AI) and Machine Learning (ML) works on a similar principle, but with data.

In Topic(s): Artificial Intelligence (AI) (pg. 210) | Artificial Neural Networks (ANN) (pg. 214) | Computer Vision (CV) (pg. 216) | Cutting-edge Technologies (pg. 221) | Deep Learning (DL) (pg. 231) | Image Processing (pg. 245) | Machine Learning (ML) (pg. 250) | Self-supervised Learning (pg. 261) | Sound and Audio Processing (pg. 264) | Supervised Learning (pg. 266) | Unsupervised Learning (pg. 272)

Figure 17: A humorous illustration of "Autoencoder".

What is an Autoencoder?

An autoencoder is a type of neural network that is used to learn efficient and compact representations of data, typically for the purpose of dimensionality reduction or feature learning.

Key Components of Autoencoders:

Encoder: This part of the network takes the input data (like a full-size image) and compresses it into a smaller, more compact representation. Think of it like summarizing a detailed report into key points.

Decoder: The decoder takes this compact representation and reconstructs the original input data as closely as possible. It's like using the summary to recreate the full report.

Bottleneck: This is the point in the network where the representation of the data is at its most compressed form. It forces the autoencoder to learn the most important features of the data.

Examples of Autoencoder Applications:

Data Compression: Just like compressing a large file into a zip file, autoencoders can learn to compress data efficiently. For instance, they can be used to compress images or videos while retaining their key features.

Noise Reduction: Imagine having a photograph with some distortions or 'noise'. Autoencoders can be trained to remove this noise, producing a cleaner version of the original image.

Feature Extraction: Autoencoders can identify and isolate the key features from complex data sets. This is particularly useful in fields like bioinformatics where understanding certain patterns in data is crucial.

Anomaly Detection: In industries like finance or manufacturing, autoencoders can learn what 'normal' data looks like and then identify data that deviates from this norm, indicating potential issues or anomalies.

Remember:

Autoencoders are powerful tools in AI for understanding and manipulating complex data sets. By learning to distill data to its most essential features and then reconstruct it, they provide valuable insights and applications across various fields, from image processing to anomaly detection. Understanding autoencoders helps in appreciating how AI can simplify and clarify the complex world of data.

See also: Artificial Neural Network (ANN) (pg. 29) | Deep Learning (DL) (pg. 69) | Dimensionality Reduction (pg. 71) | Feature Engineering (pg. 88)

Automated Machine Learning (AutoML)

Imagine you want to bake a cake, but you're not sure about the exact recipe. You have a smart kitchen that can select the recipe, measure the ingredients, mix them in the right order, and adjust the baking time and temperature based on the type of cake you want. All you have to do is tell the kitchen what kind of cake you're in the mood for, and it takes care of the details, ensuring a delicious outcome. This smart kitchen is akin to Automated Machine Learning (AutoML) in the world of technology.

In Topic(s): AI Governance (pg. 208) | Artificial Intelligence (AI) (pg. 210) | Cutting-edge Technologies (pg. 221) | Data Science (DS) (pg. 227) | Emerging Technologies (pg. 233) | Future Directions, Trends and Challenges (pg. 243) | Machine Learning (ML) (pg. 250) | Supervised Learning (pg. 266)

Figure 18: An amusing illustration of "Automated Machine Learning (AutoML)".

What is Automated Machine Learning (AutoML)?

Automated Machine Learning, or AutoML, is like having a smart assistant in the realm of data science and machine learning. It automates the process of applying machine learning to real-world problems. From selecting the right algorithms and data preprocessing methods to tuning parameters and validating models, AutoML simplifies and speeds up the process of developing and deploying machine learning models, making it accessible even to those without deep expertise in the field.

Key Features of AutoML:

Accessibility: Just as the smart kitchen makes baking accessible to anyone, AutoML opens up machine learning to a broader audience, reducing the need for specialized knowledge.

Efficiency: AutoML can quickly experiment with multiple algorithms and settings to find the best solution, much like trying different recipes and baking techniques in less time.

Optimization: It fine-tunes the parameters of machine learning models, similar to adjusting ingredients and baking conditions for the perfect cake.

Scalability: AutoML can handle a wide range of problems and datasets, adaptable to different tasks just as a smart kitchen can bake anything from a simple sponge to a complex wedding cake.

Examples of AutoML in Use:

Predicting Customer Behavior: Businesses use AutoML to analyze customer data and predict future buying habits, helping tailor marketing efforts and improve sales.

Medical Diagnosis: Healthcare providers use AutoML to develop models that can predict diseases from medical images or patient data, aiding in early diagnosis and treatment planning.

Fraud Detection: Financial institutions employ AutoML to build systems that can detect unusual patterns indicative of fraudulent activity, protecting customers and assets.

Supply Chain Optimization: Companies use AutoML to forecast demand, manage inventory, and optimize logistics, ensuring products are available where and when needed.

Remember:

Automated Machine Learning democratizes the power of machine learning, making it easier and faster to solve complex problems with data. By automating the labor-intensive aspects of model development, AutoML allows more people to leverage machine learning, leading to innovative solutions in various fields. Understanding AutoML is key to appreciating how technology is making advanced data analysis more accessible, enabling better decisions, innovations, and efficiencies across industries.

See also: Machine Learning (ML) (pg. 12)

Big Data

"Big Data" is a term that's become increasingly common, but what does it really mean? Imagine you're at a beach, trying to count every single grain of sand. This task represents the vastness and complexity of big data. It's not just about the sheer volume of data but also its variety, velocity, and the value we can extract from it.

In Topic(s): Artificial Intelligence (AI) (pg. 210) | Data Analytics (DA) (pg. 223) | Data Science (DS) (pg. 227) | Fundamental Data Concepts (pg. 237)

Figure 19: An amusing illustration of "Big Data".

What is Big Data?

Big Data refers to extremely large datasets that are too complex and voluminous to be processed and analyzed by traditional data-processing methods. These datasets can be structured (organized in a specific format) or unstructured (not organized in a specific way, like texts or videos).

Key Aspects of Big Data:

Volume: The sheer size of the data. We're talking about quantities of data that are measured in petabytes or exabytes, far beyond the capacity of a standard database.

Velocity: The speed at which new data is generated and collected. With the advent of the internet and social media, data is being created at an unprecedented rate.

Variety: Data comes in various forms - text, images, videos, audio, sensor data, and more. Managing this diversity is a significant part of handling big data.

Veracity: This refers to the quality and accuracy of the data. Given the vast amount of data, ensuring its reliability and relevance is crucial.

Value: It's not just about having lots of data; it's about deriving meaningful insights and information from it.

Examples of Big Data in Use:

Social Media Platforms: Platforms like Facebook or Twitter generate immense amounts of data every day through user posts, likes, and shares. Analyzing this data helps in understanding user behavior and trends.

Healthcare: Hospitals and healthcare providers collect vast amounts of data, including patient records, treatment plans, and research data. Big data analytics can help in diagnosing diseases, predicting outbreaks, and improving patient care.

E-commerce: Companies like Amazon collect data on customer purchases, preferences, and browsing habits. Analyzing this data helps in personalizing shopping experiences and improving service.

Smart Cities: Sensors and IoT devices in smart cities generate large amounts of data on traffic patterns, energy usage, and public safety. This data can be used to optimize traffic flow, reduce energy consumption, and improve urban living.

Remember:

Big Data represents a paradigm shift in how we collect, analyze, and utilize information. It offers tremendous opportunities for insights and advancements across various fields. However, it also presents challenges in terms of data management, analysis, and ensuring privacy and security. Understanding Big Data is key to navigating the modern landscape of technology-driven decision-making.

See also: Data Lake (pg. 65) | Data Visualization (pg. 67)

Classification

Classification, in the context of Artificial Intelligence (AI) and Machine Learning (ML), is akin to sorting objects into different boxes based on their features. For instance, imagine you have a box for fruits and another for vegetables. When you see a tomato, you decide which box it should go into based on its characteristics. This process of sorting or categorizing items into different groups is what we call classification in AI and ML.

In Topic(s): Artificial Intelligence (AI) (pg. 210) | Core Applications (pg. 218) | Data Analytics (DA) (pg. 223) | Data Science (DS) (pg. 227) | Fundamental Data Concepts (pg. 237) | Fundamental Mathematics and Statistics (pg. 241) | Machine Learning (ML) (pg. 250) | Natural Language Processing (NLP) (pg. 254) | Natural Language Understanding (NLU) (pg. 256) | Supervised Learning (pg. 266) | Text and Language Processing (pg. 270)

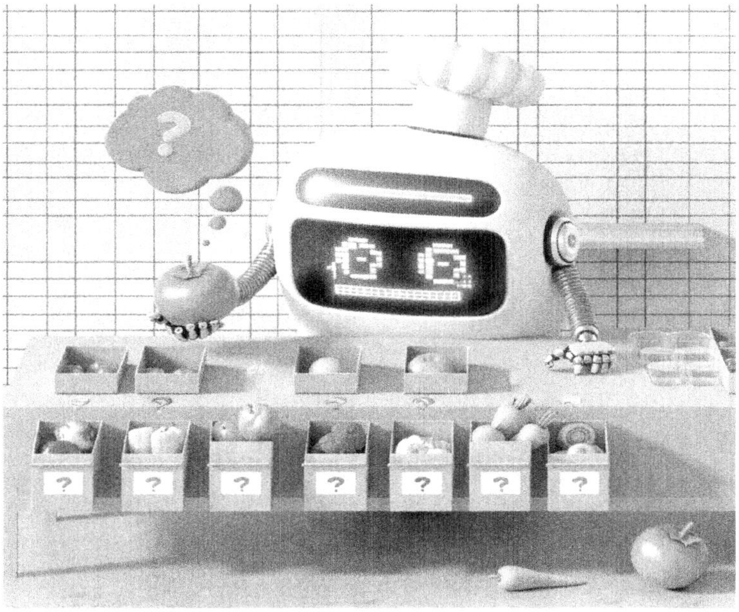

Figure 20: A delightful illustration of "Classification".

What is Classification?

Classification is a type of data analysis used in AI and ML where data is categorized into predefined classes or groups. It's about teaching a computer how to make distinctions between different types of data.

Key Elements of Classification:

Classes or Categories: These are the specific groups into which the data will be sorted. For example, 'spam' and 'not spam' in email filtering.

Features: These are the characteristics or attributes based on which the classification is done. In the case of emails, features might include certain words or the sender's address.

Training Data: This is a dataset used to train the AI model. It includes examples of data and their corresponding categories.

Model Training: The AI system learns from the training data how to classify new, unseen data. It identifies patterns that determine the category of each data point.

Examples of Classification in Use:

Email Filtering: AI systems classify emails as 'spam' or 'not spam' based on their content and sender. The system is trained with many examples of both spam and non-spam emails.

Medical Diagnosis: Classification algorithms can help diagnose diseases by analyzing patient data and categorizing it as indicating different medical conditions.

Credit Scoring: Financial institutions use classification to determine the creditworthiness of individuals. Based on their financial history, people are classified into 'low risk' or 'high risk' for loans.

Image Recognition: In image recognition, AI systems classify images based on what they depict. For example, a system can be trained to identify and classify pictures as 'cats', 'dogs', 'cars', etc.

Remember:

Classification is a fundamental technique in AI and ML that allows for the organization and categorization of data into distinct groups or classes. It plays a crucial role in various applications, from sorting emails to diagnosing diseases, making it a powerful tool for analyzing and making sense of large datasets. Understanding classification helps in appreciating how AI systems can mimic human decision-making and categorization skills.

See also: Clustering (pg. 43) | Regression (pg. 148) | Supervised Learning (pg. 170)

Clustering

Clustering, in the context of Artificial Intelligence (AI) and Machine Learning (ML), can be compared to organizing a vast collection of books in a library without any existing categorization. The goal is to group these books in such a way that books on similar topics are placed together. You might end up with groups like fiction, science, history, and so on, based on the content or features of the books. This process of grouping similar items together is what we refer to as clustering in AI and ML.

In Topic(s): Artificial Intelligence (AI) (pg. 210) | Data Analytics (DA) (pg. 223) | Data Science (DS) (pg. 227) | Fundamental Data Concepts (pg. 237) | Fundamental Mathematics and Statistics (pg. 241) | Machine Learning (ML) (pg. 250) | Unsupervised Learning (pg. 272)

Figure 21: A playful illustration of "Clustering".

What is Clustering?

Clustering is a method of unsupervised learning (a type of machine learning where the model learns from data without being explicitly told the correct answer) used to group a set of objects in such a way that objects in the same group (a cluster) are more similar to each other than to those in other groups.

Key Aspects of Clustering:

No Predefined Labels: In clustering, the groups are not predefined. The algorithm finds patterns and similarities in the data and forms groups based on these.

Similarity Measures: The algorithm determines 'similarity' based on certain criteria or features. For example, in a dataset of animals, similarity could be based on features like size, habitat, or diet.

Different Clustering Algorithms: There are various ways to perform clustering, each with its own method of finding clusters. Some common methods include K-means clustering, hierarchical clustering, and density-based clustering.

Examples of Clustering in Action:

Customer Segmentation: Businesses use clustering to group customers based on purchasing behavior, preferences, or demographics. This helps in targeted marketing and personalized service.

Genetics: In bioinformatics, clustering is used to group genes with similar expression patterns, which might indicate they are involved in similar functions or pathways.

Document Organization: Clustering can be used to organize large sets of documents or text data into groups based on their content, like grouping news articles by topics.

Image Segmentation: In computer vision, clustering can group pixels in an image based on color or texture, which is useful in image recognition and analysis.

Remember:

Clustering is a powerful tool in AI and ML for finding natural groupings in data when we don't have predefined categories. It helps in discovering hidden patterns in data and is widely used across various fields, from marketing to genetics, for insightful data analysis. Understanding clustering gives insight into how AI can make sense of complex, unstructured data sets and reveal meaningful structures within them.

See also: Classification (pg. 41) | Unsupervised Learning (pg. 196)

Code Generation

Imagine you're building a house. Instead of drawing the blueprints by hand, you describe what you want to a smart assistant–how many rooms, the style, special features–and it draws the perfect blueprint for you. In the realm of computer programming, this is similar to what Code Generation in Artificial Intelligence (AI) and Machine Learning (ML) does.

In Topic(s): Core Applications (pg. 218) | Industry Applications (pg. 247) | Supervised Learning (pg. 266)

Figure 22: An eccentric illustration of "Code Generation".

What is Code Generation?

Code Generation refers to the process where an AI system automatically writes new computer code based on certain inputs and requirements. It's like having a smart assistant that can write programming code for you, turning your ideas or requirements into executable computer code.

Key Aspects of Code Generation:

Automated Programming: The AI system creates code automatically, reducing the need for manual coding.

Input-Based Creation: You provide the AI with inputs, like specifications or descriptions, and it generates the appropriate code.

Efficiency and Speed: Code generation can create code faster than a human programmer, which can speed up software development.

Reducing Errors: Since the code is generated by AI, it can potentially have fewer errors than human-written code, assuming the AI is well-designed.

Examples of Code Generation in Use:

Website Development: You tell the AI what features you want on a website, and it generates the HTML, CSS, and JavaScript code to create those features.

Mobile App Creation: An AI takes a description of an app's functionality and automatically writes the code needed for that app.

Data Analysis Scripts: Scientists provide specifications for data analysis, and the AI generates the code to perform this analysis, such as in Python or R.

Game Development: Game developers describe game rules and mechanics, and the AI generates the underlying code that drives the game's operations.

Remember:

Code Generation in AI and ML represents a significant leap in software development, akin to having an intelligent architect for your programming needs. It accelerates the coding process, reduces human error, and can make software development more accessible. This technology is particularly useful in scenarios where speed and efficiency are crucial, and it demonstrates the potential of AI to enhance and streamline creative processes like coding.

See also: Natural Language Generation (NLG) (pg. 124)

Contrastive Learning

Imagine you're trying to understand the difference between two types of apples by closely examining their features: one is red and sweet, the other green and tart. By comparing them, you highlight the differences and similarities, which helps you to better understand and remember each type. This process of learning through comparison and contrast is akin to Contrastive Learning in the realms of Artificial Intelligence (AI) and Machine Learning (ML).

In Topic(s): Cutting-edge Technologies (pg. 221) | Emerging Technologies (pg. 233) | Future Directions, Trends and Challenges (pg. 243) | Machine Learning (ML) (pg. 250) | Self-supervised Learning (pg. 261)

Figure 23: A cheery illustration of "Contrastive Learning".

What is Contrastive Learning?

Contrastive Learning is a technique used in AI to teach models how to understand data by comparing pairs or groups of data points. The goal is to make similar data points come closer together and dissimilar ones move further apart in the model's representation space. Essentially, it's about learning by contrasting differences and similarities.

Key Principles of Contrastive Learning:

Positive and Negative Pairs: The model is presented with pairs of data points. 'Positive' pairs consist of two similar or related data points, while 'Negative' pairs are made up of dissimilar or unrelated data points.

Representation Space: This is where the model 'plots' the data points based on their features. Through training, similar points move closer, and dissimilar points move apart in this space.

Similarity Measure: The model uses a mathematical function to determine how similar or different two data points are. This measure helps in adjusting the distances between points in the representation space.

Learning Objective: The main goal is to adjust the model so that it minimizes the distance between similar points and maximizes the distance between dissimilar points.

Examples of Contrastive Learning in Use:

Facial Recognition: Just as you might distinguish between faces by noting features like eye color or shape, contrastive learning helps models recognize and differentiate faces by comparing various facial features across many images.

Language Understanding: Imagine trying to understand the sentiment of sentences by comparing them. In a similar way, contrastive learning helps AI models understand language nuances by comparing sentences or phrases to grasp their meanings, tones, or sentiments.

Medical Imaging: Like distinguishing between healthy and unhealthy tissue samples by comparison, contrastive learning enables AI models to differentiate between medical images, helping in diagnoses by contrasting healthy and abnormal scans.

Recommendation Systems: Just as you might recommend a book to a friend based on comparing it to books they liked before, contrastive learning can power recommendation systems by comparing user preferences and suggesting similar items or content.

Remember:

Contrastive Learning is a powerful method in AI and ML that leverages the natural human approach of learning by comparison. By focusing on understanding similarities and differences between data points, AI models can develop a nuanced understanding of the data, leading to more accurate and efficient recognition, classification, and prediction capabilities. This approach is fundamental in enabling AI systems to make sense of complex, varied datasets across numerous applications, from enhancing user experiences with personalized content to advancing medical diagnoses with precise imaging analysis.

See also: Self-Supervised Learning (pg. 158)

Conversational Agent

Imagine having a friend who is always available to chat, answer your questions, and help you with tasks, but instead of a person, it's a computer program. This is what a 'Conversational Agent' in the realm of Artificial Intelligence (AI) and Machine Learning (ML) is like. It's a smart software that you can talk to through text or voice, designed to simulate a natural conversation with a human.

In Topic(s): Core Applications (pg. 218) | Emerging Technologies (pg. 233) | Industry Applications (pg. 247) | Natural Language Processing (NLP) (pg. 254) | Natural Language Understanding (NLU) (pg. 256) | Text and Language Processing (pg. 270)

Figure 24: A delightful illustration of "Conversational Agent".

What is a Conversational Agent?

A Conversational Agent is a type of AI designed to communicate with humans in a natural, conversational manner. These agents use AI and ML technologies to understand human language, process it, and respond in a way that mimics human conversation. They can be voice-activated (like talking to someone) or text-based (like texting a friend).

Key Features of Conversational Agents:

Natural Language Understanding: They can understand spoken or written language, interpreting user requests, questions, or commands.

Responsive Interaction: Based on their understanding, these agents can respond in a way that's appropriate to the context of the conversation.

Learning Ability: Many conversational agents learn from interactions, improving their responses and understanding over time.

Versatile Use: They're used in various settings, from customer service chatbots to personal assistants like Siri or Alexa.

Examples of Conversational Agents in Use:

Customer Service Bots: Online, you might chat with a bot that helps you with product inquiries, bookings, or troubleshooting. These are conversational agents assisting customers.

Virtual Personal Assistants: Devices like Amazon's Alexa, Apple's Siri, and Google Assistant are conversational agents that can answer questions, control smart home devices, play music, and more.

Healthcare Assistants: Some conversational agents are designed to provide health-related information, remind patients to take medication, or even offer mental health support through conversation.

Language Learning Apps: Conversational agents in language learning apps help users practice conversation in a new language, providing corrections and suggestions.

Remember:

Conversational Agents in AI and ML represent a blend of technology and human-like interaction, offering a new way for people to engage with digital systems. They're transforming how we access information, perform tasks, and even how we learn, making technology more accessible and conversational. Understanding these agents gives insight into the evolving nature of human-computer interaction, where conversation is a key component.

See also: ChatGPT (OpenAI) (pg. 8) | Virtual Assistant (pg. 204)

Convolutional Neural Network (CNN)

To understand Convolutional Neural Networks (CNNs), let's think of them as specialized detectives in the world of Artificial Intelligence (AI), specifically trained to analyze visual information. Imagine a detective who is an expert in recognizing faces in a crowd or identifying specific patterns in a series of photographs. This detective's skill in analyzing and interpreting visual data is similar to how CNNs function in AI and Machine Learning (ML).

In Topic(s): Artificial Intelligence (AI) (pg. 210) | Artificial Neural Networks (ANN) (pg. 214) | Computer Vision (CV) (pg. 216) | Cutting-edge Technologies (pg. 221) | Data Science (DS) (pg. 227) | Deep Learning (DL) (pg. 231) | Image Processing (pg. 245) | Machine Learning (ML) (pg. 250) | Sound and Audio Processing (pg. 264) | Supervised Learning (pg. 266) | Video Processing (pg. 274)

Figure 25: An amusing illustration of "Convolutional Neural Network (CNN)".

What is a Convolutional Neural Network?

A Convolutional Neural Network is a type of deep learning algorithm primarily used for processing visual data like images and videos. It excels in tasks like image recognition, image classification, and object detection.

Key Elements of CNNs:

Convolutional Layers: These layers are the core building blocks of a CNN. They perform a mathematical operation called convolution, which involves sliding a filter over the input image to extract features such as edges, textures, or specific shapes.

Pooling Layers: Following the convolutional layers, pooling layers reduce the dimensions of the extracted features, simplifying the information without losing important details. This process is similar to summarizing a detailed story into key points.

Fully Connected Layers: At the end of the network, fully connected layers use the simplified and processed information to make decisions or classifications, like deciding if an image contains a certain object.

Examples of CNNs in Action:

Face Recognition: CNNs are used in security systems and smartphones for facial recognition. They analyze facial features to identify individuals accurately.

Medical Image Analysis: In healthcare, CNNs assist doctors by analyzing medical images (like MRIs or CT scans) to detect diseases such as tumors.

Self-Driving Cars: CNNs help autonomous vehicles interpret visual surroundings, like recognizing road signs, pedestrians, and other vehicles, to navigate safely.

Image Classification: In social media, CNNs can automatically tag photos by identifying and classifying objects within them, like distinguishing between a cat and a dog.

Remember:

Convolutional Neural Networks represent a significant advancement in how machines understand and interpret visual information. They mimic aspects of human vision, enabling automated systems to perform complex visual tasks with high accuracy and efficiency. Understanding CNNs provides insight into how AI can not only see but also make sense of the visual world, transforming vast amounts of image and video data into meaningful insights.

See also: Artificial Neural Network (ANN) (pg. 29) | Deep Learning (DL) (pg. 69)

Copilot

Let's think of a scenario where you're writing a novel, and you have a friend who suggests ideas, corrects your grammar, and even helps you overcome writer's block. This friend is like a 'copilot' for your writing process. In the world of AI and ML, 'Copilot' refers to a similar kind of assistance, but in the realm of coding and software development.

Figure 26: A humorous illustration of "Copilot".

What is Copilot?

Copilot in AI and ML is a tool or a system designed to assist software developers by suggesting code, correcting errors, and providing recommendations based on the context of what the developer is writing. It's like having an intelligent assistant that understands coding languages and helps streamline the coding process.

Key Features of Copilot:

Code Suggestion: Copilot can suggest entire lines or blocks of code to help developers write more efficiently. This is based on the context of the existing code and the objective of the program.

Error Correction: It can identify and suggest fixes for errors in code, much like a spell checker for programming.

Learning from Context: Copilot understands the context in which certain functions or commands are used, providing suggestions that are relevant to the specific task at hand.

Adaptability: It adapts to the coding style of the user, making its suggestions more personalized and accurate over time.

Examples of Copilot in Use:

Writing New Code: When a developer starts writing a function, Copilot can automatically suggest how to complete it, based on similar functions written by others.

Debugging: While debugging, Copilot can suggest the most likely causes of bugs and offer solutions.

Learning New Coding Practices: For a developer learning a new programming language or framework, Copilot can accelerate the learning process by providing real-time examples and suggestions.

Optimizing Existing Code: Copilot can suggest more efficient or cleaner ways to write existing code, helping to improve the overall quality of the software.

Remember:

Copilot in AI and ML represents a significant advancement in the field of software development. It acts as an intelligent assistant, enhancing the capabilities of developers by providing real-time assistance and learning from their coding patterns. This tool exemplifies how AI can be used to augment human skills, increasing productivity and efficiency in technical tasks like coding. Understanding Copilot helps in appreciating the practical applications of AI in everyday professional activities, particularly in the rapidly evolving field of software development.

See also: Code Generation (pg. 45)

Co-training

Imagine you're learning to cook, but you have two cookbooks. One book gives you a great overview of flavors and ingredients, while the other offers fantastic step-by-step cooking techniques. By studying both, you get a fuller understanding of how to make delicious dishes because each book teaches you something valuable that the other doesn't cover. In a similar way, Co-training in Artificial Intelligence (AI) and Machine Learning (ML) involves two learning models that teach each other to improve their understanding of the data they're learning from.

In Topic(s): Semi-supervised Learning (pg. 262)

Figure 27: A quirky illustration of "Co-training".

What is Co-training?

Co-training is a technique used in machine learning where two different learning models or algorithms are trained together on the same problem but with different views or subsets of the data. Each model learns and makes predictions independently. Then, they share their most confident predictions with each other. This process allows each model to benefit from the other's strengths, leading to better overall performance, especially when there's limited labeled data available.

Key Principles of Co-training:

Two Views: The data is split into two sets, each providing a different 'view' or perspective. This is like having two different teachers explaining the same concept in different ways.

Independent Learning: Initially, each model learns independently on its respective view of the data. Think of this as each model getting its own lesson from one of the cookbooks.

Sharing Insights: After learning independently, the models share their most confident predictions with each other. This is akin to the two cookbooks 'talking' to each other, filling in gaps the other might have.

Iterative Improvement: With new insights from each other, both models can improve their understanding and make better predictions in the next round. It's like revising your cooking technique based on tips from both books.

Examples of Co-training in Use:

Email Spam Filtering: Imagine one model learns from the email content (text), and another learns from metadata (sender, time sent, etc.). They co-train to better identify spam emails by combining insights from both content and context.

Language Translation: One model could focus on the syntax (sentence structure), and another on semantics (meaning). By sharing their strengths, they can achieve more accurate translations.

Medical Diagnosis: In diagnosing diseases from medical images, one model might learn from visual features (shapes, colors in scans) while another learns from patient history data. Their combined insights lead to more accurate diagnoses.

Sentiment Analysis: For understanding opinions in product reviews, one model might analyze the text, and another could focus on the rating scores. Co-training helps in capturing a more nuanced view of sentiments.

Remember:

Co-training is a collaborative approach in machine learning, where two models learn from different aspects of the data and share their insights, much like learning from two expertly written cookbooks. This method leverages the unique strengths of each model, leading to better performance and more robust learning, especially valuable when dealing with complex problems or when there's a scarcity of labeled data. Understanding co-training helps in appreciating how AI can effectively combine different sources of knowledge to enhance learning and decision-making.

See also: Semi-Supervised Learning (pg. 164)

Cross-Validation

Imagine you've baked several batches of cookies to find the perfect recipe. To be fair in your evaluation, you decide not to just taste-test from one batch. Instead, you try cookies from each batch, ensuring your final verdict on the best recipe isn't based on a single, perhaps anomalous, batch. This method of testing and validating across multiple batches for a reliable outcome is akin to the concept of Cross-Validation in Artificial Intelligence (AI) and Machine Learning (ML).

In Topic(s): Data Science (DS) (pg. 227) | Fundamental Mathematics and Statistics (pg. 241) | Machine Learning (ML) (pg. 250) | Supervised Learning (pg. 266)

Figure 28: A humorous illustration of "Cross-Validation".

What is Cross-Validation?

Cross-Validation is a technique used to assess how well a machine learning model will perform on unseen data. It involves partitioning the available data into several subsets, training the model on some of these subsets, and then testing it on the remaining parts. This process is repeated several times, with different subsets used for training and testing each time. This approach helps ensure that the model's performance is consistent and not dependent on a particular division of the data.

Key Steps in Cross-Validation:

Dividing the Data: The data is split into smaller groups, or 'folds'. Think of this as dividing your cookies into several tasting groups.

Training and Testing: The model is trained (taught) on all but one of these folds, and then tested (evaluated) on the remaining fold to see how well it has learned. This is like using several cookie batches for tasting and leaving one batch out as a final test.

Rotating the Folds: The fold used for testing is rotated so that, over several rounds, each fold has been used as a test set once. It ensures that each part of your data gets the chance to be the 'final test batch'.

Averaging the Results: The performance scores from testing on each fold are averaged to get a final score. This gives a balanced view of how good your cookie recipe is, based on all the tasting rounds.

Examples of Cross-Validation in Use:

Predicting Real Estate Prices: Cross-Validation can help ensure that the model predicting house prices performs well, regardless of variations in the data like location, size, or age of the properties.

Customer Churn Prediction: For models predicting customer churn, Cross-Validation helps verify that the predictions are robust across different segments of the customer base, such as high-value vs. low-value customers.

Disease Diagnosis: In medical diagnostics, Cross-Validation ensures that a model predicting the presence of a disease is reliable, irrespective of variations in patient demographics or disease stages.

Stock Market Forecasting: When forecasting stock prices, Cross-Validation helps in assessing the model's performance across different economic conditions or market sectors.

Remember:

Cross-Validation is a crucial technique in AI and ML that helps in evaluating a model's performance more reliably and robustly. By ensuring that the model is tested across various subsets of data, it helps in identifying potential biases or weaknesses in the model, leading to more accurate and generalizable predictions. Understanding Cross-Validation is essential for anyone looking to grasp how AI models are rigorously tested and validated, ensuring their effectiveness in real-world applications.

See also: Evaluation Metric (pg. 80)

DALL-E

Imagine you're an artist with a magic brush. Whatever you describe, this brush can paint it instantly, no matter how unusual or imaginative the idea. Now, replace the magic brush with a computer program, and you have something very similar to DALL-E.

In Topic(s): Computer Vision (CV) (pg. 216) | Core Applications (pg. 218) | Cutting-edge Technologies (pg. 221) | Emerging Technologies (pg. 233) | Image Processing (pg. 245) | Industry Applications (pg. 247)

Figure 29: A charming illustration of "DALL-E".

What is DALL-E?

DALL-E is an AI program created by OpenAI that generates images from textual descriptions. It's like a highly advanced, intelligent system that can create pictures, artworks, or visual representations from any phrase or combination of words you provide. The name "DALL-E" is a blend of the famous surrealist artist Salvador Dalí and the animated character WALL-E.

Key Features of DALL-E:

Image Generation from Text: You type in a description, and DALL-E creates an image that matches that description.

Creativity and Versatility: It can generate a wide range of images, from realistic to fantastical, based on the creativity of the textual input.

Understanding Complex Concepts: DALL-E can interpret and visualize complex, abstract, or even nonsensical ideas in image form.

Learning from Examples: It has been trained on a diverse set of images and textual descriptions, enabling it to understand and create a wide variety of visual styles.

Examples of DALL-E in Use:

Creating Art: You could ask DALL-E to generate an image of "a two-headed flamingo wearing a top hat in a surreal landscape," and it would produce a corresponding image.

Visualizing Ideas: A writer describes a scene from their story, and DALL-E generates images that visually represent that scene.

Educational Tools: Teachers could use DALL-E to create visual aids for complex subjects by entering descriptions of historical events, scientific concepts, or mathematical theories.

Entertainment and Fun: People use DALL-E to create unique and imaginative images for fun, like "a cat dressed as an astronaut riding a bicycle on Mars."

Remember:

DALL-E represents a significant advancement in AI, bridging the gap between textual descriptions and visual representations. It's like having an incredibly talented artist who can bring any idea, no matter how outlandish or imaginative, to visual life. This technology opens up new possibilities for creativity, education, and entertainment, showcasing the amazing potential of AI to understand and create in ways that were once thought to be exclusively human.

See also: Generative AI (pg. 10) | Large Language Model (LLM) (pg. 114)

Data Cleaning

Imagine your closet is cluttered with clothes, some of which are old, torn, or don't fit anymore. To make your closet functional, you first need to sort through everything, get rid of what you don’t need, and organize the rest neatly. This process is similar to Data Cleaning in the world of Artificial Intelligence (AI) and Machine Learning (ML).

In Topic(s): Core Applications (pg. 218) | Data Analytics (DA) (pg. 223) | Data Science (DS) (pg. 227) | Fundamental Data Concepts (pg. 237) | Machine Learning (ML) (pg. 250) | Privacy and Security (pg. 258) | Supervised Learning (pg. 266)

Figure 30: A charming illustration of "Data Cleaning".

What is Data Cleaning?

Data Cleaning is the process of correcting or removing data in a dataset that is incorrect, incomplete, duplicated, or improperly formatted. This is a crucial step before analyzing data because poor-quality data can lead to inaccurate results and misleading conclusions.

Key Aspects of Data Cleaning:

Removing Inaccuracies: This involves getting rid of data that is wrong. For example, if a person’s age is listed as -30, this is clearly incorrect and needs to be corrected or removed.

Filling in Missing Values: Sometimes data is incomplete. For instance, if some customers’ addresses are missing in a database, you might need to find these addresses or calculate a reasonable substitute.

Eliminating Duplicates: This means removing repeated data, which can skew results. Imagine if a customer is listed twice in a mailing list; they might receive two copies of the same catalog.

Standardizing Data Formats: Ensuring data is consistently formatted, like making sure all dates are in the format YYYY-MM-DD.

Examples of Data Cleaning in Use:

Customer Databases: Cleaning up a customer database by removing duplicate entries, correcting misspelled names, and updating outdated information.

Survey Data: Before analyzing survey results, ensuring all responses are formatted correctly and incomplete answers are addressed.

Healthcare Records: Ensuring patient records are accurate and consistent, with no erroneous entries or duplications.

Financial Reporting: Cleaning financial data to ensure accuracy in reporting and analysis, like correcting wrongly entered transaction amounts.

Remember:

Data Cleaning is a vital step in ensuring the reliability and accuracy of data analysis in AI and ML. It's like tidying up and organizing information so that it's useful and meaningful. Clean data leads to better, more accurate results in data analysis, which is crucial for making informed decisions, whether in business, healthcare, finance, or any other field that relies on data. It's about setting a strong foundation for the analysis that follows.

See also: Data Exploration (pg. 63)

Data Exploration

Imagine you're a detective entering a room to solve a mystery. The room is full of clues–some obvious, some hidden. Your job is to look around, gather these clues, and piece them together to understand what happened. In the world of Artificial Intelligence (AI) and Machine Learning (ML), this detective work is akin to Data Exploration.

In Topic(s): Data Analytics (DA) (pg. 223) | Data Science (DS) (pg. 227) | Fundamental Data Concepts (pg. 237) | Machine Learning (ML) (pg. 250)

Figure 31: A charming illustration of "Data Exploration".

What is Data Exploration?

Data Exploration is the initial step in the data analysis process, where you examine, organize, and understand the available data. It involves looking at the raw data, identifying patterns, spotting anomalies, and gaining insights that help in further analysis or decision-making. It's like the detective carefully examining clues before drawing conclusions.

Key Aspects of Data Exploration:

Understanding the Basics: This includes looking at the size of the data, the types of data (like numbers, dates, text), and basic statistics like averages and ranges.

Visual Analysis: Often, data is visualized using charts, graphs, or plots to see patterns or trends more clearly.

Identifying Relationships: Exploring how different pieces of data relate to each other, like how sales figures might relate to different times of the year.

Finding Anomalies: Spotting anything that looks unusual or unexpected, which could indicate errors in the data or unique insights.

Examples of Data Exploration in Use:

Business Analysis: A company might explore sales data to understand which products are selling well and during which periods sales peak.

Healthcare Research: Researchers explore patient data to find common symptoms or effective treatments for a particular condition.

Market Research: A marketing team analyzes survey data to understand consumer preferences and trends.

Educational Studies: An educator might explore test scores to identify areas where students excel or need more help.

Remember:

Data Exploration is like the foundational detective work in AI and ML. It's about getting to know the data, understanding its characteristics, and uncovering initial insights that guide further analysis. This process is crucial for making informed decisions and building effective AI models, as it helps in identifying what's important, what's unusual, and what might need further investigation. It's the first step in turning a mass of raw data into meaningful, actionable information.

See also: Data Cleaning (pg. 61)

Data Lake

Imagine a vast lake where streams and rivers from various places converge, bringing different types of water together. Some parts of the lake are clear and easily navigable, while others are murky and more mysterious. In the digital world of Artificial Intelligence (AI) and Machine Learning (ML), a 'Data Lake' is quite similar. It's a vast storage repository that holds a significant amount of raw data in its native format until it's needed.

In Topic(s): Data Analytics (DA) (pg. 223) | Data Science (DS) (pg. 227) | Fundamental Data Concepts (pg. 237)

Figure 32: A cheery illustration of "Data Lake".

What is a Data Lake?

A data lake is a centralized storage system that allows you to store all your structured and unstructured data at any scale. It's like a large container where data from various sources is stored in its original form. This data can be anything from text files and images to complex databases.

Key Features of a Data Lake:

Vast Storage Capacity: Data lakes can store massive amounts of data, much like a large lake can hold a vast quantity of water.

Diverse Data Types: Just as a lake contains different types of water bodies, a data lake can store different types of data - structured, unstructured, and semi-structured.

Raw Data Preservation: In a data lake, data is kept in its raw format, similar to how a lake retains water from different sources in its original state.

Flexibility in Usage: Data can be used for various purposes–from data mining to analysis–at any time, much like water can be used from a lake for different needs.

Examples of Data Lakes in Use:

Business Analysis: Companies use data lakes to store all their data. Analysts can later access this data for comprehensive business analysis, identifying trends and insights.

Healthcare Research: In healthcare, data lakes can store patient records, research data, and clinical trial data, providing a rich source for medical research and analysis.

Marketing Insights: Marketers can use data lakes to store various customer data, including social media activity, website visits, and purchase history, to gain insights into customer behavior.

AI and ML Projects: For AI and ML, data lakes provide a vast source of raw data that can be used to train and refine algorithms.

Remember:

A data lake is a vast, flexible repository for storing a wide variety of data in its native format. It's like a big container for all kinds of digital information, ready to be used whenever needed. Understanding the concept of a data lake is important for anyone involved in data management, analysis, and AI, as it provides the foundational infrastructure for large-scale data storage and sophisticated analytics.

See also: Big Data (pg. 39)

Data Visualization

Imagine you have a jar full of different colored beads, representing various types of information. If you wanted to share this information with someone, simply handing them the jar wouldn't be very helpful. Instead, if you sorted these beads by color and arranged them in a pattern or a picture, it would be much easier for them to understand. This process of organizing and presenting information in a visual format is what we call Data Visualization.

In Topic(s): Data Analytics (DA) (pg. 223) | Data Science (DS) (pg. 227) | Fundamental Data Concepts (pg. 237)

Figure 33: An eccentric illustration of "Data Visualization".

What is Data Visualization?

Data Visualization is the technique of representing data in a graphical or pictorial format, like charts, graphs, maps, or other visuals. It transforms complex, numerical data into visual objects, making it easier to understand, interpret, and draw insights from.

Key Aspects of Data Visualization:

Clarity and Simplicity: The aim is to make the presentation of data straightforward and easy to grasp, even for complex data sets.

Visual Elements: This includes the use of bars, lines, colors, and shapes to represent different parts of the data.

Storytelling: Effective data visualization tells a story, highlighting key points and trends in the data.

Tool Use: Various software tools are used to create visual representations, from simple graphs in spreadsheet programs to sophisticated visualizations in specialized software.

Examples of Data Visualization in Use:

Weather Forecasts: Presenting temperature trends and weather patterns using maps and graphs.

Business Reports: Using bar charts or pie charts to show sales data, customer demographics, or market trends.

Health Information: Displaying statistics about health issues or diseases spread using heat maps or line graphs.

Educational Purposes: Teachers using charts and diagrams to explain complex scientific or mathematical concepts.

Remember:

Data Visualization is a crucial aspect of communicating information in the modern world. It helps in transforming raw data into visual stories, making it easier to see patterns, trends, and outliers. Whether in business, education, science, or daily life, data visualization is an essential tool for making sense of the vast amounts of information we encounter and making informed decisions based on that data. It's about turning numbers into pictures to tell the story behind the data.

See also: Big Data (pg. 39)

Deep Learning (DL)

To grasp the concept of Deep Learning, let's compare it to learning a complex skill, like playing a musical instrument. When you first start learning, you begin with the basics, gradually layering on more and more complex skills. Over time, you understand not just the notes, but the nuances and styles of music. Deep Learning in Artificial Intelligence (AI) and Machine Learning (ML) works similarly, where machines learn from basic to increasingly complex patterns.

In Topic(s): Artificial Intelligence (AI) (pg. 210) | Artificial Neural Networks (ANN) (pg. 214) | Core Applications (pg. 218) | Cutting-edge Technologies (pg. 221) | Data Analytics (DA) (pg. 223) | Data Science (DS) (pg. 227) | Deep Learning (DL) (pg. 231) | Emerging Technologies (pg. 233) | Future Directions, Trends and Challenges (pg. 243) | Machine Learning (ML) (pg. 250) | Robotics (pg. 260) | Sound and Audio Processing (pg. 264) | Supervised Learning (pg. 266)

Figure 34: A cheery illustration of "Deep Learning (DL)".

What is Deep Learning?

Deep Learning is a subset of machine learning where algorithms, inspired by the structure and function of the brain (called artificial neural networks), learn from large amounts of data. These algorithms mimic the way humans learn, gradually improving their accuracy and understanding.

Key Features of Deep Learning:

Artificial Neural Networks: The foundation of deep learning is artificial neural networks, consisting of layers of interconnected nodes (similar to neurons in the brain). Each layer can learn different features or aspects of the data.

Layered Structure: In deep learning, there are typically many layers (hence the term 'deep'), and each layer transforms the input data to a more abstract and composite form, allowing for complex learning.

Learning from Data: Deep learning algorithms learn by processing and analyzing vast amounts of data. The more data they process, the better they perform.

Examples of Deep Learning Applications:

Image and Speech Recognition: Tools like facial recognition on smartphones or voice assistants like Siri or Alexa are powered by deep learning, enabling them to recognize images and speech patterns.

Self-Driving Cars: Deep learning is used to enable autonomous vehicles to recognize objects, interpret road signs, and make driving decisions.

Language Translation: Services like Google Translate use deep learning to understand and translate languages in real-time with increasing accuracy.

Healthcare Diagnosis: Deep learning algorithms can analyze medical images like X-rays or MRIs to assist doctors in diagnosing diseases.

Remember:

Deep Learning represents a significant leap in the ability of machines to learn and make decisions. It's like giving a computer a very intricate and nuanced brain, allowing it to recognize patterns and solve complex problems. Understanding deep learning is key to appreciating the advanced capabilities of modern AI technologies and their impact across various industries.

See also: Artificial Neural Network (ANN) (pg. 29) | Convolutional Neural Network (CNN) (pg. 51) | Recurrent Neural Network (RNN) (pg. 146)

Dimensionality Reduction

Imagine walking into a room filled with an overwhelming number of objects. Your challenge is to organize this room in a way that makes it easy to find and understand everything inside. You decide to group similar items together and remove things that aren't really needed. This process of simplifying and organizing for better understanding is akin to dimensionality reduction in Artificial Intelligence (AI) and Machine Learning (ML).

In Topic(s): Artificial Intelligence (AI) (pg. 210) | Data Analytics (DA) (pg. 223) | Data Science (DS) (pg. 227) | Fundamental Data Concepts (pg. 237) | Fundamental Mathematics and Statistics (pg. 241) | Image Processing (pg. 245) | Machine Learning (ML) (pg. 250) | Supervised Learning (pg. 266) | Unsupervised Learning (pg. 272)

Figure 35: A humorous illustration of "Dimensionality Reduction".

What is Dimensionality Reduction?

Dimensionality reduction is a technique used in AI and ML to simplify complex data. It involves reducing the number of variables or features in a dataset while retaining as much of the important information as possible. This is done to enhance the efficiency of data processing and analysis.

Key Aspects of Dimensionality Reduction:

Simplifying Data: The process reduces the number of features (dimensions) in a dataset. For instance, if you have data with hundreds of features, dimensionality reduction might simplify it to just a dozen or so key features.

Removing Redundancy: Often, datasets have features that are either duplicates or highly correlated. Dimensionality reduction helps in eliminating these redundancies.

Improving Model Performance: By reducing the complexity of data, models become more efficient and less prone to problems like overfitting (where a model performs well on training data but poorly on new, unseen data).

Examples of Dimensionality Reduction in Use:

Data Visualization: If you have a dataset with many features, it's hard to visualize. Reducing dimensions can make it possible to plot the data on a 2D or 3D graph.

Image Processing: High-resolution images have vast amounts of data. Dimensionality reduction can compress these images for faster processing without significantly losing quality.

Genomics: In genetics, researchers deal with datasets having thousands of genes. Dimensionality reduction helps in focusing on genes that are most relevant to the study.

Finance: For risk management or investment strategies, financial data can be highly complex. Dimensionality reduction helps in identifying the most crucial factors.

Remember:

Dimensionality reduction is a vital process in AI and ML, enabling easier analysis and processing of complex datasets. It helps in extracting the essence of data by removing unnecessary information, leading to more efficient and effective data-driven decision-making. Understanding dimensionality reduction is key to appreciating how AI systems manage and interpret large volumes of data.

See also: Autoencoder (pg. 35) | Feature Engineering (pg. 88)

Environmental Monitoring

Think about a weather station that collects data like temperature, rainfall, and wind speed to forecast the weather. Similarly, 'Environmental Monitoring' in the context of Artificial Intelligence (AI) and Machine Learning (ML) involves using technology to collect and analyze data about the environment. This helps in understanding and managing environmental conditions and changes.

In Topic(s): Industry Applications (pg. 247)

Figure 36: A delightful illustration of "Environmental Monitoring".

What is Environmental Monitoring?

Environmental Monitoring refers to the systematic collection and analysis of data to understand the condition of the environment. This could include monitoring air and water quality, tracking wildlife populations, or observing climate changes. AI and ML enhance this process by enabling the analysis of large and complex environmental datasets, leading to more accurate and timely insights.

Key Aspects of Environmental Monitoring:

Data Collection: Using sensors and other technologies to gather environmental data such as temperature, pollution levels, or species counts.

Pattern Recognition: AI algorithms analyze the data to identify patterns and trends, like changes in temperature over time or the migration patterns of animals.

Predictive Analysis: ML models can predict future environmental conditions based on historical data, aiding in planning and decision-making.

Real-time Monitoring: Continuous monitoring allows for immediate detection of environmental changes or anomalies.

Examples of Environmental Monitoring:

Climate Change Studies: Using AI to analyze climate data to predict future climate patterns and assess the impacts of global warming.

Wildlife Conservation: ML algorithms can help track animal populations and movements, aiding in conservation efforts.

Air Quality Monitoring: AI systems analyze data from air quality sensors to identify pollution sources and predict pollution levels.

Water Quality Assessment: AI models can predict and detect contamination in water bodies, helping in managing water resources.

Remember:

Environmental Monitoring with AI and ML represents a crucial application of technology in understanding and protecting our natural world. By enabling the processing of vast amounts of environmental data, AI and ML provide valuable insights that can inform policies, drive conservation efforts, and help us respond more effectively to environmental challenges. This field is an excellent example of how technology can be harnessed to foster a sustainable relationship with our environment.

See also: Data Exploration (pg. 63)

Error Minimization

Imagine you're learning to shoot arrows at a target. At first, your arrows might land all over the place, but as you practice, they start hitting closer to the bullseye. Each time you adjust your aim based on where the previous arrow landed, you're essentially minimizing your error. In the realm of Artificial Intelligence (AI) and Machine Learning (ML), 'Error Minimization' follows a similar principle. It's about adjusting an AI model based on its past mistakes to improve its accuracy.

In Topic(s): Fundamental Mathematics and Statistics (pg. 241)

Figure 37: An eccentric illustration of "Error Minimization".

What is Error Minimization?

Error Minimization in AI and ML refers to the process of making adjustments to a model to reduce the difference between its predictions and the actual outcomes. When an AI model is trained, it often starts with many errors - its predictions or decisions don't quite match reality. Through a process of continuous adjustment and learning, the model's 'errors' get smaller, and its predictions or decisions become more accurate.

Key Aspects of Error Minimization:

Learning from Mistakes: Just like learning to shoot arrows accurately, AI models learn from their mistakes. The 'error' is a guide that tells the model how off its predictions are.

Iterative Process: Error minimization is an ongoing process. The model makes a prediction, checks how wrong it is, adjusts, and tries again. This cycle repeats until the error is as small as possible.

Use of Algorithms: AI models use specific algorithms to minimize error. These algorithms adjust the model's parameters (like weights in neural networks) based on the observed errors.

Balance is Key: It's important not to over-minimize error, which can lead to 'overfitting' - where the model is so finely tuned to the training data that it performs poorly on new, unseen data.

Examples of Error Minimization in Use:

Weather Forecasting: An AI model for predicting the weather adjusts its predictions based on past errors, like incorrectly predicted temperatures or rainfall, to improve its future forecasts.

Stock Market Prediction: In financial models, error minimization helps in refining predictions about stock prices by learning from past discrepancies between predicted and actual stock market behavior.

Medical Diagnosis: AI models used for diagnosing diseases learn from past diagnostic errors, improving their ability to accurately identify diseases from medical images or patient data.

Voice Recognition: Error minimization helps voice recognition software become more accurate by learning from instances where it misinterpreted words or phrases.

Remember:

Error Minimization in AI and ML is a critical process where a model progressively improves its accuracy by learning from its past mistakes. It's a fundamental aspect of how AI systems evolve and refine their capabilities, becoming more reliable and effective in tasks ranging from everyday predictions to complex decision-making. Understanding error minimization is key to appreciating the continuous improvement and sophistication of AI technologies.

See also: Evaluation Metric (pg. 80)

Ethical AI Principles

Imagine you're part of a community setting up a neighborhood watch program. Everyone agrees that the safety and well-being of the community are paramount. However, to ensure that the watch program is beneficial and fair to all, the community decides to establish a set of guiding principles: transparency about who is on the watch team and how decisions are made, fairness in treating all community members equally, respect for individuals' privacy, and accountability for actions taken by the watch team. In the realm of Artificial Intelligence (AI), similar guiding principles, known as Ethical AI Principles, are essential to ensure that AI technologies benefit society while minimizing harm and respecting human rights.

In Topic(s): AI Governance (pg. 208) | Ethical AI, Social Implications and Cultural Considerations (pg. 235) | Future Directions, Trends and Challenges (pg. 243) | Privacy and Security (pg. 258)

Figure 38: A whimsical illustration of "Ethical AI Principles".

What are Ethical AI Principles?

Ethical AI Principles are a set of guidelines designed to steer the development, deployment, and governance of AI technologies in a way that upholds human values and ethical standards. These principles aim to ensure that AI systems are developed with consideration for their impact on individuals and society, promoting the common good while mitigating risks and adverse outcomes.

Core Ethical AI Principles:

Transparency: Just as community members have the right to know how the neighborhood watch operates, AI systems should be transparent, with clear explanations of how they work and make decisions. This openness builds trust and understanding.

Fairness: Like ensuring every community member is treated equally by the watch program, AI must avoid bias and discrimination, ensuring that all individuals are treated fairly and equitably, regardless of race, gender, age, or other characteristics.

Privacy: Respecting homeowners' privacy is crucial in a watch program. Similarly, AI must protect individuals' data privacy, ensuring personal information is used appropriately and securely, with consent where necessary.

Accountability: Just as the watch team is accountable for its actions, there must be clear accountability for AI systems' decisions and outcomes, with mechanisms in place to address any negative impacts or errors.

Safety: Ensuring the neighborhood watch doesn't inadvertently cause harm is essential. Likewise, AI systems must be safe, reliable, and secure, minimizing risks and ensuring they perform as intended without causing unintended harm.

Inclusiveness: A watch program should consider the diverse needs and perspectives of all community members. AI should be inclusive, designed with diverse input and considerations to serve a broad spectrum of society effectively.

Examples Illustrating Ethical AI Principles in Action:

Healthcare AI: In developing AI for patient diagnosis, ensuring the algorithms are transparent about how they reach conclusions, use data ethically, and are inclusive to consider diverse patient populations is essential.

Financial Services AI: AI used for credit scoring must be fair, avoiding biases against certain groups, and transparent, so users understand how decisions affecting their financial well-being are made.

Autonomous Vehicles: The safety and reliability of AI systems in self-driving cars are paramount, requiring rigorous testing and clear accountability structures for when things go wrong.

AI in Education: Systems that adapt learning to student needs must respect privacy, be transparent in how they assess and interact with students, and be designed inclusively to cater to diverse learning styles and needs.

Remember:

Ethical AI Principles serve as the moral compass guiding the development and application of AI technologies. By adhering to these principles, we can harness the benefits of AI while safeguarding human rights, promoting societal well-being, and ensuring that technology serves the common good. Understanding these principles helps us appreciate the importance of ethical considerations in the rapidly evolving AI landscape, ensuring that as AI becomes more integrated into our lives, it does so in a way that aligns with our shared values and ethical standards.

See also: Artificial Intelligence (AI) (pg. 2)

Evaluation Metric

Imagine you're a chef who has just tried a new recipe. To know how successful it is, you might ask your guests to rate the taste or you might measure how much they ate. This process of assessing the outcome is similar to what an 'Evaluation Metric' does in the world of Artificial Intelligence (AI) and Machine Learning (ML).

In Topic(s): Data Analytics (DA) (pg. 223) | Data Science (DS) (pg. 227) | Fundamental Mathematics and Statistics (pg. 241)

Figure 39: A delightful illustration of "Evaluation Metric".

What is an Evaluation Metric?

An Evaluation Metric in AI and ML is a standard of measurement used to assess the performance of a model or algorithm. Just like a chef uses feedback to gauge the success of a dish, in AI and ML, various metrics are used to understand how well a model is performing. These metrics help in determining the accuracy, reliability, and effectiveness of AI models.

Key Aspects of Evaluation Metrics:

Performance Indicators: These metrics provide quantifiable measures of how well an algorithm or model is performing.

Model Improvement: They guide developers in refining and improving AI models.

Different Types for Different Tasks: Depending on the task (like classification, regression, clustering), different metrics are used.

Objective Assessment: Evaluation metrics provide an objective way to assess models, which is essential for comparing different models.

Examples of Evaluation Metrics:

Accuracy: In classification tasks, accuracy measures the proportion of correctly identified instances out of the total instances.

Precision and Recall: Used in classification, precision measures how many of the identified items are relevant, while recall measures how many relevant items are identified.

Mean Squared Error (MSE): In regression tasks, MSE measures the average of the squares of the errors between predicted and actual values.

F1 Score: The F1 Score is the harmonic mean of precision and recall, providing a balance between the two in classification tasks.

Remember:

Evaluation Metrics are essential tools in AI and ML for assessing the performance of models. They provide a means to measure and compare the effectiveness of different approaches in various tasks. Understanding these metrics is key to grasping how AI models are developed, refined, and ultimately how their success is determined. It's like having a scorecard that objectively tells you how well your AI 'recipe' turned out.

See also: Accuracy (pg. 15) | Error Minimization (pg. 75)

Exploitation

Imagine you've found a restaurant that serves the best pizza you've ever tasted. Each time you think about dining out, the memory of that delicious pizza tempts you to go back. Choosing this known favorite over trying a new restaurant is a lot like the concept of "Exploitation" in Artificial Intelligence (AI) and Machine Learning (ML).

Figure 40: A charming illustration of "Exploitation".

What is Exploitation?

In the realm of AI, exploitation refers to the strategy of making decisions based on the knowledge already acquired, aiming to maximize rewards based on what's known to work well. It's like sticking with the pizza place you love because you're confident in the enjoyable experience it provides, rather than risking a meal at an untested restaurant.

Key Features of Exploitation:

Reliance on Known Information: Exploitation involves leveraging the data and experiences the AI system has already gathered to make decisions that are likely to lead to positive outcomes.

Maximizing Immediate Reward: The focus is on obtaining the best possible result right now, based on what the system knows works well, much like choosing the pizza that you know will satisfy your hunger and taste buds.

Reduced Risk: By sticking with known strategies or options, exploitation minimizes the risk of encountering negative outcomes, akin to avoiding the disappointment of a bad meal at a new restaurant.

Potential for Stagnation: While exploitation can ensure consistent results, over-relying on it may prevent the discovery of even better options or strategies, similar to never discovering a new favorite dish because you always order the same pizza.

Examples of Exploitation in Everyday AI Applications:

Recommendation Systems: Streaming services like Netflix or Spotify recommend movies or songs based on what you've watched or listened to before, exploiting known preferences to maximize your enjoyment.

Online Shopping: E-commerce platforms display products similar to those you've previously purchased or shown interest in, exploiting past behaviors to encourage further purchases.

Autonomous Vehicles: A self-driving car might choose routes it has taken successfully in the past, exploiting known information to ensure a safe and efficient journey.

Financial Trading Algorithms: In stock trading, an algorithm might exploit known market patterns or strategies that have previously led to gains, focusing on these to maximize profits.

Remember:

Exploitation is a critical strategy in AI, focusing on utilizing existing knowledge to make safe, informed decisions that lead to known positive outcomes. It's the digital equivalent of "better the devil you know than the devil you don't," emphasizing the value of the familiar and tested. While important for achieving immediate goals and ensuring reliability, it's also balanced with exploration to foster learning and discovery, much like occasionally trying a new restaurant to possibly uncover a new favorite. Understanding exploitation helps us appreciate how AI systems navigate decisions, balancing the pursuit of known rewards with the potential of uncharted opportunities.

See also: Exploration (pg. 84)

Exploration

Imagine you're in a city filled with diverse restaurants, each offering a unique culinary experience. While you have your favorite spots where you know the meal will be excellent, the allure of discovering a new favorite cuisine or dish often leads you to try new places. This blend of curiosity and the desire for new experiences mirrors the concept of "Exploration" in Artificial Intelligence (AI) and Machine Learning (ML).

Figure 41: A humorous illustration of "Exploration".

What is Exploration?

In AI, exploration refers to the process where an AI system, often called an agent, ventures into the unknown, trying out new actions or strategies that it hasn't experienced before. This is akin to choosing a new restaurant over a familiar one, not knowing if the meal will be delightful or disappointing. The aim is to gather new information and experiences, which could lead to better decisions and discoveries in the future.

Key Aspects of Exploration:

Seeking the Unknown: Exploration involves the AI agent making choices that are not based on past experiences, stepping into uncharted territory to uncover new knowledge.

Learning and Growth: Through exploration, the agent learns about the effects of various actions, expanding its understanding of the environment and improving its decision-making capabilities over time.

Balancing Act: Exploration is balanced with exploitation (leveraging known strategies for immediate rewards) to optimize learning while still achieving favorable outcomes.

Risk and Reward: Just as trying a new restaurant carries the risk of a less enjoyable meal, exploration in AI involves a degree of risk, as the agent may encounter less favorable results from untested actions.

Examples of Exploration in Everyday AI Applications:

Online Content Discovery: Platforms like YouTube or TikTok might suggest videos outside of your usual viewing habits, encouraging exploration to potentially enhance your content experience.

Product Recommendations: E-commerce sites occasionally show products that are different from your past searches or purchases, inviting you to explore new items that could become new favorites.

Autonomous Exploration: Robots or drones tasked with mapping new terrains or environments, such as Mars rovers, use exploration to gather data on previously uncharted areas.

Personalized Learning: Educational apps might introduce new topics or more challenging materials, encouraging exploration to expand knowledge and foster learning beyond the student's current level.

Remember:

Exploration is a cornerstone of AI, driving systems to venture beyond the safety of known actions and into the potential of the unknown. This process is crucial for learning and adaptation, enabling AI agents to develop a more comprehensive understanding of their environment and the consequences of various actions. Just as exploring new restaurants can lead to the discovery of delightful new dishes, exploration in AI paves the way for innovations and improved decision-making, enriching the AI's repertoire of strategies and responses.

See also: Exploitation (pg. 82)

Facial Recognition

Imagine attending a large family reunion and recognizing relatives by looking at their faces, even those you haven't seen in years. This natural ability of humans to identify and verify individuals by their facial features is mirrored in the technology known as 'Facial Recognition' in Artificial Intelligence (AI) and Machine Learning (ML).

In Topic(s): Computer Vision (CV) (pg. 216) | Core Applications (pg. 218) | Ethical AI, Social Implications and Cultural Considerations (pg. 235) | Image Processing (pg. 245) | Industry Applications (pg. 247) | Supervised Learning (pg. 266)

Figure 42: A humorous illustration of "Facial Recognition".

What is Facial Recognition?

Facial Recognition is a technology that enables computers to identify and verify people based on their facial features. This technology uses AI algorithms to analyze specific features of a person's face—such as the distance between the eyes, the shape of the jawline, and other unique facial landmarks—to identify or authenticate an individual.

Key Components of Facial Recognition:

Facial Detection: The first step is detecting a face in an image or video. The system identifies the human face within a scene or environment.

Feature Analysis: Next, the system analyzes the facial features. This involves measuring various aspects of the face, like the distance between eyes, the shape of the cheekbones, and the contours of the lips.

Faceprint Creation: The analyzed data is used to create a digital representation of the face, often referred to as a 'faceprint', which is as unique as a fingerprint.

Matching and Verification: The faceprint is then compared against a database of known faces for identification or used to verify the identity of an individual.

Examples of Facial Recognition in Use:

Security and Surveillance: Airports and public places use facial recognition for security purposes, identifying and tracking individuals who may pose a threat.

Unlocking Smartphones: Many smartphones now use facial recognition technology to allow users to unlock their devices just by looking at them.

Finding Missing Persons: Law enforcement agencies use facial recognition to identify missing persons or suspects by scanning through surveillance footage.

Personalized Advertising: Some advertising systems use facial recognition to gauge the age or gender of a person and display targeted advertisements.

Attendance Systems: In workplaces and educational institutions, facial recognition is used for verifying attendance without the need for physical IDs.

Remember:

Facial Recognition technology in AI and ML represents a significant advancement in how machines understand and interact with the human world. By automating the identification process, it offers diverse applications, from enhancing security to personalizing user experiences. Understanding facial recognition helps in comprehending how AI systems can interpret and utilize human-like perception in practical and impactful ways.

See also: Image Recognition (pg. 102)

Feature Engineering

Let's think of Feature Engineering in Artificial Intelligence (AI) and Machine Learning (ML) as a chef preparing ingredients for a recipe. Just as a chef carefully selects, cuts, and seasons ingredients to create a delicious dish, Feature Engineering is about selecting, preparing, and transforming data to make it more suitable for machine learning models.

In Topic(s): Artificial Intelligence (AI) (pg. 210) | Core Applications (pg. 218) | Data Analytics (DA) (pg. 223) | Data Science (DS) (pg. 227) | Fundamental Data Concepts (pg. 237) | Image Processing (pg. 245) | Machine Learning (ML) (pg. 250) | Supervised Learning (pg. 266) | Unsupervised Learning (pg. 272)

Figure 43: A cheery illustration of "Feature Engineering".

What is Feature Engineering?

Feature Engineering is the process of using domain knowledge to extract features (characteristics, properties, attributes) from raw data and transform them into formats that are more suitable for machine learning models. This is a crucial step in the data preparation process and can greatly enhance the performance of machine learning algorithms.

Key Aspects of Feature Engineering:

Selection of Relevant Features: This involves identifying which aspects of the data are most relevant to the problem you're trying to solve. It's like picking the right ingredients for a recipe.

Transforming and Creating Features: Sometimes, features need to be modified or combined to make them more effective. This could involve changing the scale, altering the format, or creating new features from existing data.

Improving Model Performance: Properly engineered features can significantly improve the accuracy and efficiency of machine learning models.

Examples of Feature Engineering:

Real Estate Pricing: When predicting house prices, raw data like the age of the house, size, and number of rooms might be transformed into more telling features, such as price per square foot or room-to-bathroom ratio.

Customer Churn Prediction: In predicting whether a customer will leave a service, features like the frequency of service use, customer service interactions, and recent changes in usage patterns might be created and analyzed.

Healthcare Diagnosis: For medical diagnoses, raw patient data could be engineered into features that represent risk factors or symptom combinations that are more indicative of certain conditions.

Image Recognition: In computer vision, raw pixel data of images is often transformed into features that represent various shapes, edges, and textures to help models recognize objects or patterns.

Remember:

Feature Engineering is a critical step in the AI and ML process. It involves creative and insightful transformations of data to make it more usable and effective for machine learning models. This process is akin to preparing and enriching ingredients to ensure that the final dish–or in this case, the AI model–is as good as it can be. Understanding feature engineering is key to recognizing how AI systems effectively learn from and interpret data.

See also: Dimensionality Reduction (pg. 71)

Feature Learning

Imagine you're an artist planning to create a series of paintings about daily life. Instead of focusing on every tiny detail, you decide to highlight certain features that capture the essence of each scene: the warmth of sunlight in a morning landscape, the vibrant colors of a bustling market, or the serene glow of streetlights at night. By emphasizing these key features, you convey the unique atmosphere and emotion of each setting. In the world of Artificial Intelligence (AI) and Machine Learning (ML), there's a similar process known as Feature Learning, where the goal is to automatically identify and utilize the most informative parts or 'features' of data to understand complex patterns or make predictions.

In Topic(s): Computer Vision (CV) (pg. 216) | Data Analytics (DA) (pg. 223) | Data Science (DS) (pg. 227) | Fundamental Data Concepts (pg. 237) | Image Processing (pg. 245) | Sound and Audio Processing (pg. 264) | Unsupervised Learning (pg. 272)

Figure 44: A playful illustration of "Feature Learning".

What is Feature Learning?

Feature Learning is an approach in machine learning where the algorithm autonomously identifies the most relevant features or attributes from raw data that are essential for understanding the data or making accurate predictions. This process helps in simplifying the data, making it easier for models to learn and make decisions, much like how an artist selects key elements to bring a scene to life.

Key Aspects of Feature Learning:

Automatic Discovery: Just as an artist intuitively knows what elements to emphasize, feature learning algorithms automatically detect which aspects of the data are most significant, without being explicitly told what to look for.

Dimensionality Reduction: Similar to an artist choosing not to include every detail in a painting, feature learning often involves reducing the complexity of the data by focusing on the most important aspects, making it easier to work with.

Enhanced Learning: By highlighting the key features, just as the dominant colors and shapes can make a painting more striking, feature learning enables AI models to better understand patterns, making predictions more accurate and efficient.

Examples of Feature Learning in Use:

Facial Recognition: Imagine a system learning to recognize faces by focusing on key features such as the eyes, nose, and mouth, rather than every pixel, much like an artist would in a portrait.

Voice Assistants: Similar to distinguishing a melody in a symphony, feature learning helps voice assistants understand commands by identifying characteristic elements in speech, like tone and rhythm.

Fraud Detection: In banking, feature learning algorithms can identify unusual patterns in transactions that might indicate fraud, focusing on anomalies like large, sudden transfers, akin to spotting a ripple in a calm pond.

Recommendation Systems: For services like online streaming, feature learning helps understand user preferences by focusing on key aspects of content watched, such as genre or actors, similar to how one might recommend a restaurant based on certain favored dishes.

Remember:

Feature Learning is a pivotal process in AI and ML that allows algorithms to automatically uncover and emphasize the most informative aspects of data, enhancing their ability to learn, predict, and make decisions. By focusing on the 'essence' of the data, much like an artist captures the essence of a scene, feature learning facilitates a deeper understanding and more efficient analysis of complex datasets. Grasping the concept of feature learning illuminates how AI models can sift through vast amounts of information to find what truly matters, enabling them to perform tasks with remarkable insight and accuracy.

See also: Deep Learning (DL) (pg. 69)

Function

Imagine you're in your kitchen preparing a recipe, say, a smoothie. You have a process: you take ingredients (fruits, ice, and milk), perform some actions (chop, blend), and get a result (a delicious smoothie). This process is predictable and repeatable; whenever you follow the same steps with the same ingredients, you expect the same tasty outcome. In the world of Artificial Intelligence (AI) and Machine Learning (ML), this process is akin to what we call a "function."

Figure 45: A humorous illustration of "Function".

What is a Function?

In AI and ML, a function is like a recipe for the computer. It's a set of instructions or actions that the computer follows to transform input (like numbers, words, or images) into an output (a result or answer). You can think of a function as a small, specialized machine in a factory line: something goes in, the machine does its work, and something new comes out.

Key Features of a Function:

Input: Just as you start with ingredients for your smoothie, a function begins with input. This could be anything the function needs to do its job, from simple numbers to complex data like pictures or sounds.

Process: This is the set of instructions or steps the function follows, similar to your smoothie recipe. It dictates how the input should be changed or combined to produce the desired result.

Output: The result of the function, like your finished smoothie. Depending on the function's purpose, this could be a number, a decision, a prediction, or any kind of information the function was designed to produce.

Reusability: One of the beauties of a function is that it's reusable. Just like how you can use your smoothie recipe multiple times, a function can be used repeatedly whenever needed, providing consistent results each time.

Examples of Functions in Everyday AI Applications:

Online Calculators: When you use an online calculator to find out your loan payments, there's a function working behind the scenes, taking inputs (loan amount, interest rate, term) and calculating your monthly payment.

Photo Filters: Applying a filter to your photo in an app involves a function that takes the original image, applies certain visual effects, and outputs the altered image.

Voice Assistants: When you ask a voice assistant to play music, it uses a function to interpret your voice command (input), decide on the action needed (process), and start playing your song (output).

Navigation Apps: Functions in these apps take your current location and desired destination as inputs, calculate the best route (process), and provide you with directions (output).

Remember:

Functions are fundamental to making AI and ML systems work. They're the behind-the-scenes workers transforming data, making decisions, and producing results that help these technologies seamlessly integrate into our lives. Understanding functions helps demystify how complex AI systems can perform a wide range of tasks, from simple calculations to recognizing faces, all by following predefined "recipes" tailored to each specific task.

See also: Model (pg. 122)

Function vs. Model

Imagine you're in a kitchen preparing a meal. In this setting, think of a "function" as a kitchen appliance, like a blender or an oven, designed to perform a specific task using a set process. You add ingredients, follow steps, and get a result. Now, envision the "model" as the complete recipe you're following, which might involve using several appliances (functions) and steps to create a dish. The recipe (model) guides you on when and how to use each appliance (function) to achieve the desired meal.

Figure 46: A quirky illustration of "Function vs. Model".

What is a Function?

In the realm of Artificial Intelligence (AI) and Machine Learning (ML), a function is like the kitchen appliance: it's a defined set of operations that takes inputs (like your ingredients), does something with them (blends, bakes), and produces an output (a smoothie, a cake). Functions are the building blocks, the individual tasks that need to be done.

Key Features of a Function:

Input and Output: Just as a blender takes in fruits and ice to produce a smoothie, a function in AI takes in data (input) and transforms it into a result (output).

Specific Task: Each function is designed for a specific task, similar to how a toaster is specifically for toasting bread.

Reusability: Like kitchen appliances, functions can be used multiple times for similar tasks, providing consistent results.

What is a Model?

A model in AI and ML, on the other hand, is more akin to the entire recipe. It's a structured way of using various functions (and sometimes data) to make predictions or decisions, akin to how a recipe guides you through using appliances and ingredients to create a dish. The model encompasses the overall process, from start to finish, to achieve a goal, like a complete meal.

Key Features of a Model:

Combination of Functions: Just as a recipe might require a blender, oven, and stove, a model combines various functions to process data and solve a problem.

Trained with Data: Models are often "trained" with data, learning patterns and making predictions, much like refining a recipe over time to perfect the dish.

Purpose-Driven: Each model is designed with a goal, whether it's to predict weather, recognize faces, or recommend products, similar to how recipes are designed to create specific dishes.

Examples in AI:

Function in AI: A function might be a piece of code that calculates the average value of a list of numbers. It's a straightforward, single-purpose task.

Model in AI: A weather prediction model uses various functions to analyze temperature, humidity, and wind data (among other inputs) to forecast the weather. The model integrates these functions, much like following a recipe, to come up with a prediction.

Remember:

Understanding the difference between a function and a model helps clarify how AI systems operate. Functions are the individual tasks or operations, akin to kitchen appliances, each designed for a specific purpose. Models are the overarching structures or "recipes" that integrate these functions towards achieving complex goals, like predicting outcomes or making decisions. This analogy helps demystify the workings of AI and ML, showing how complex predictions and decisions are built up from simpler, individual tasks.

See also: Function (pg. 92)

Google Colab

Imagine you have a complex math problem to solve, but your calculator isn't powerful enough. Now, imagine a powerful, internet-based calculator that not only solves your problem but also allows you to save, share, and collaborate on your calculations with others. This is similar to what Google Colab, or Colaboratory, offers in the world of Artificial Intelligence (AI) and Machine Learning (ML).

In Topic(s): AI Hardware and Accelerators (pg. 209)

Figure 47: A cheery illustration of "Google Colab".

What is Google Colab?

Google Colab is a free, cloud-based service provided by Google, designed to help you write and execute Python code through your browser. It's particularly popular in AI and ML for several reasons. One of its key features is that it provides free access to powerful computing resources, like Graphics Processing Units (GPUs) and Tensor Processing Units (TPUs), which can process large amounts of data much faster than a typical computer.

Key Aspects of Google Colab:

Accessible Computing Power: It offers high-level computing power that's often necessary for AI and ML tasks, making these fields more accessible to everyone.

Notebook Interface: Colab uses a 'notebook' format, which combines live code, text, and visualizations in a single, interactive document.

Collaboration Features: Similar to Google Docs, it allows real-time collaboration with others on the same document.

Integration with Google Drive: You can easily save your notebooks to Google Drive and access them from anywhere.

Examples of Google Colab in Use:

Learning to Code: Beginners in Python, AI, and ML can experiment and learn by writing and running code without any complex setup.

Data Analysis and Visualization: Professionals and students can use it to analyze large datasets and visualize their data in compelling ways.

AI and ML Projects: Researchers and developers can build and train AI models without needing expensive hardware.

Educational Purposes: Instructors can create interactive tutorials and assignments for students in programming and data science.

Remember:

Google Colab is a powerful, user-friendly platform that brings the sophisticated world of AI and ML within reach of anyone with internet access. By providing free access to advanced computational resources and an easy-to-use interface, it democratizes the ability to analyze data, develop AI models, and collaborate on complex projects. Understanding Google Colab is essential for anyone interested in exploring the vast possibilities of AI and ML without the barrier of costly hardware or software.

See also: Jupyter Notebook (pg. 106)

Graph Networks for Material Exploration (GNoME)

Imagine a world where discovering new materials doesn't take years of trial and error in a laboratory, but instead can be predicted quickly and accurately using advanced computer algorithms. This is the realm of GNoME, short for Graph Networks for Materials Exploration, a groundbreaking AI tool developed by Google DeepMind. GNoME represents a significant leap in how scientists discover new materials, potentially accelerating advancements in various technologies like renewable energy, electronics, and more.

In Topic(s): Cutting-edge Technologies (pg. 221)

Figure 48: A lighthearted illustration of "Graph Networks for Material Exploration (GNoME)".

What is GNoME?

GNoME is a set of sophisticated algorithms that utilizes graph neural networks (GNNs) to predict new materials' structures and properties. Graph neural networks are particularly adept at understanding and modeling complex relationships and structures, making them perfect for exploring the vast, intricate world of material science.

Key Concepts Behind GNoME:

Graph Neural Networks (GNNs): At the heart of GNoME are GNNs, which can process data represented as graphs. This is ideal for materials science, where atoms and their bonds can be thought of as nodes and edges in a graph, respectively.

Material Exploration: GNoME's primary function is to explore and predict new materials by understanding the relationships and patterns within existing materials. It can analyze vast amounts of data to uncover new possibilities that might take humans years to discover.

Predictive Modeling: By predicting the stability and properties of new materials before they are physically made, GNoME can save scientists a tremendous amount of time and resources, focusing only on the most promising candidates for synthesis and testing.

Examples of GNoME in Action:

Discovering New Crystals: GNoME has been used to predict over 2.2 million new crystal structures, including those that could be stable and useful in real-world applications, far surpassing the number of materials discovered through traditional means.

Advancing Technology: The materials discovered by GNoME have the potential to revolutionize several industries, from creating more efficient solar panels and batteries to developing better semiconductors for electronics.

Accelerating Research: With GNoME, the pace of material discovery can significantly accelerate, leading to faster advancements in technology and potentially solving some of the world's most pressing challenges, such as energy storage and generation.

Remember:

GNoME represents a paradigm shift in material science, harnessing the power of AI and graph neural networks to explore the vast, uncharted territory of possible materials. By predicting the structures and properties of materials before they're made, GNoME opens up new avenues for scientific discovery and technological innovation, making the future of materials science more exciting than ever.

See also: Deep Learning (DL) (pg. 69)

Hidden Layer

Imagine a car factory. You see the parts coming in (like metal sheets, tires, and engines) and the finished cars going out, but what happens inside is not visible. Inside, there are multiple stages where these parts are assembled, painted, and checked. In a similar way, in the world of Artificial Intelligence (AI) and Machine Learning (ML), particularly in neural networks, a 'Hidden Layer' is like those internal stages in the factory where a lot of the processing happens, but it's not directly seen from the outside.

In Topic(s): Artificial Neural Networks (ANN) (pg. 214) | Deep Learning (DL) (pg. 231)

Figure 49: An amusing illustration of "Hidden Layer".

What is a Hidden Layer?

In a neural network, a Hidden Layer is a layer of processing units (neurons) that lies between the input layer (where data enters the network) and the output layer (where we get the final result or decision). These Hidden Layers are where the complex computations take place, transforming the input data into something the network can use to make a decision or prediction.

Key Aspects of Hidden Layers:

Internal Processing: Hidden Layers are responsible for extracting and processing features from the input data. Each neuron in these layers performs calculations and transformations on the data.

Depth and Complexity: The number of Hidden Layers (and the number of neurons in each layer) can greatly affect the network's ability to handle complex tasks. More layers generally allow for more complex learning.

Learning Patterns: Hidden Layers enable the network to learn intricate patterns in the data, which is crucial for tasks like image and speech recognition, or complex decision-making.

Not Directly Observable: Unlike input and output, the operations and the exact transformations in the Hidden Layers are not directly observable. We know they're crucial for processing, but we can't see each step like we see the input and output.

Examples of Hidden Layers in Use:

Image Recognition: In recognizing images, the Hidden Layers might first detect edges, then shapes, and then more complex features like textures or specific objects.

Speech Recognition: For recognizing speech, Hidden Layers process audio signals to detect phonemes, words, and then sentences, gradually understanding more complex aspects of speech.

Playing Games: In AI that plays complex games like chess, Hidden Layers analyze different board positions, strategy options, and potential moves to decide the best next move.

Remember:

Hidden Layers in neural networks are essential for the heavy lifting in processing and understanding data. They are where the network learns from the input and makes transformations that lead to accurate outputs or decisions. While we can't see what each neuron in these layers is doing, their collective work is crucial for the AI's ability to perform complex tasks, from recognizing faces to translating languages. Understanding Hidden Layers helps in appreciating the intricate inner workings of AI and ML models.

See also: Artificial Neural Network (ANN) (pg. 29)

Image Recognition

Imagine you're looking at a photo album and recognizing family members, friends, and places. You're able to identify them because you remember their features, like the color of their hair, the shape of their face, or the distinctive landmarks. Image Recognition in Artificial Intelligence (AI) and Machine Learning (ML) is somewhat similar, but instead of a human brain, it uses computer algorithms to identify people, objects, places, and other elements in images.

In Topic(s): Artificial Intelligence (AI) (pg. 210) | Computer Vision (CV) (pg. 216) | Core Applications (pg. 218) | Data Analytics (DA) (pg. 223) | Data Science (DS) (pg. 227) | Image Processing (pg. 245) | Industry Applications (pg. 247) | Supervised Learning (pg. 266)

Figure 50: An eccentric illustration of "Image Recognition".

What is Image Recognition?

Image Recognition is a technology that allows computers to interpret and understand visual information from the world around us. It's a process where AI systems are trained to recognize various elements in images, such as objects, faces, scenes, and actions. This involves analyzing the pixels of images and identifying patterns to understand what is depicted in them.

Key Features of Image Recognition:

Pattern Recognition: AI systems learn to recognize patterns in the visual data, such as shapes, colors, and textures, which correspond to specific objects or features.

Learning from Examples: Like humans, these systems often learn from examples. They are shown thousands (or even millions) of images and learn to identify various elements in these images.

Wide Range of Applications: Image recognition is used in various areas, from security (facial recognition) to healthcare (medical imaging analysis).

Examples of Image Recognition in Use:

Facial Recognition: Used in security systems and smartphones, where the AI identifies and verifies individual faces. For instance, unlocking your phone using facial recognition.

Medical Imaging: In healthcare, image recognition helps in diagnosing diseases by analyzing medical images, such as X-rays or MRIs, to detect abnormalities like tumors.

Autonomous Vehicles: Self-driving cars use image recognition to identify road signs, pedestrians, other vehicles, and road conditions to navigate safely.

Retail: Stores use image recognition for various purposes, like inventory management or to analyze customer behavior. For example, recognizing when a product is taken off the shelf.

Remember:

Image Recognition is a powerful aspect of AI and ML, enabling machines to interpret and respond to the visual world. This technology not only enhances various applications, making them more efficient and intelligent, but also opens up new possibilities for innovation and convenience. Understanding Image Recognition is key to appreciating the remarkable ways in which AI can process and make sense of the vast and complex visual information that surrounds us.

See also: Convolutional Neural Network (CNN) (pg. 51) | Facial Recognition (pg. 86)

Input Layer

Think of making a smoothie. You start by putting ingredients into the blender - fruits, milk, ice, etc. This initial step is crucial because what you put in determines the kind of smoothie you'll get. In Artificial Intelligence (AI) and Machine Learning (ML), specifically in neural networks, an 'Input Layer' is similar to this first step of adding ingredients to the blender. It's where the data enters the system.

In Topic(s): Artificial Neural Networks (ANN) (pg. 214) | Deep Learning (DL) (pg. 231)

Figure 51: A charming illustration of "Input Layer".

What is an Input Layer?

In a neural network, an Input Layer is the first layer that receives the data to be processed. It's the entry point for the information that the neural network will use. Each 'neuron' in this layer represents a feature of the input data. For instance, in image recognition, each neuron might correspond to the pixel intensity of an image.

Key Characteristics of an Input Layer:

Data Reception: The Input Layer is where the neural network takes in the raw data that it will process. This could be anything from numbers and text to pixels in an image.

Size of the Layer: The number of neurons in the Input Layer depends on the dimensions of the input data. For example, if the input is a 28x28 pixel image, the Input Layer will have 784 neurons (since 28x28 = 784).

No Processing: Unlike other layers in the neural network, the Input Layer doesn't do any computation or transformation. It merely passes the data to the next layers.

Foundation for Further Processing: The quality and type of data in the Input Layer are crucial, as they set the foundation for the network's subsequent learning and processing.

Examples of Input Layers in Use:

Recognizing Handwriting: In a handwriting recognition task, the Input Layer takes in pixel data from images of handwritten characters.

Stock Market Prediction: For predicting stock prices, the Input Layer might include neurons representing various market indicators like previous prices, trading volume, etc.

Voice Command Recognition: In recognizing voice commands, the Input Layer receives features extracted from audio data, such as pitch, volume, and duration.

Remember:

The Input Layer in neural networks is the starting point for AI processing and learning. It's where the neural network gets its 'ingredients' - the data it will use to make predictions, recognize patterns, or make decisions. Understanding the Input Layer is crucial for grasping how neural networks function, taking the first step in transforming raw data into insightful outputs.

See also: Artificial Neural Network (ANN) (pg. 29)

Jupyter Notebook

Imagine you have a notebook where you not only write notes but also perform calculations, create graphs, and even run small programs or experiments directly on the pages. This isn't a regular notebook, but a digital one called 'Jupyter Notebook', a tool widely used in the fields of Artificial Intelligence (AI) and Machine Learning (ML).

Figure 52: A playful illustration of "Jupyter Notebook".

What is a Jupyter Notebook?

Jupyter Notebook is an interactive, web-based application that allows you to create and share documents that contain live code, equations, visualizations, and narrative text. It's a powerful tool for data analysis, scientific research, and AI/ML development, combining code, text, and graphics in a single, user-friendly interface.

Key Features of Jupyter Notebook:

Interactive Coding: You can write and execute code (in languages like Python, Julia, R) in small chunks (called 'cells') and see the results immediately.

Data Visualization: Jupyter Notebook makes it easy to create and display graphs and charts, which are essential for analyzing and understanding data.

Documenting Work: You can add explanations, hypotheses, or conclusions alongside your code, making your work more understandable and presentable.

Sharing and Collaboration: Notebooks can be easily shared with others, allowing for collaborative coding and data analysis.

Examples of Jupyter Notebook in Use:

Data Analysis Projects: Data scientists use Jupyter Notebook to explore datasets, perform statistical analysis, and visualize data trends.

Machine Learning Prototyping: ML practitioners can prototype and test machine learning models, experimenting with different algorithms and parameters.

Educational Purposes: Teachers and students use Jupyter Notebook for teaching and learning programming and data science, thanks to its interactive and easy-to-use environment.

Scientific Research: Researchers in fields like physics, chemistry, and biology use Jupyter Notebook to document their experiments, analyze data, and visualize their findings.

Remember:

Jupyter Notebook is a versatile and powerful tool that has revolutionized the way coding, data analysis, and scientific research are done. It combines the practicality of live coding with the clarity of written explanations, making it an invaluable asset in AI, ML, and data science. Understanding Jupyter Notebook is crucial for anyone delving into these fields, as it's not just a tool for coding but also for learning, experimenting, and sharing knowledge.

See also: Google Colab (pg. 96)

Label

Imagine you are sorting a big pile of photographs into different albums based on who is in each photo. You might have an album for family, one for friends, and another for pets. In each case, you're assigning a category or 'label' to the photos based on their content. In Artificial Intelligence (AI) and Machine Learning (ML), a 'label' serves a similar purpose. It's a tag or descriptor that we assign to data, telling the AI system what that data represents.

In Topic(s): Data Analytics (DA) (pg. 223) | Data Science (DS) (pg. 227) | Fundamental Data Concepts (pg. 237) | Machine Learning (ML) (pg. 250) | Supervised Learning (pg. 266)

Figure 53: A lighthearted illustration of "Label".

What is a Label?

In AI and ML, a label is a piece of information assigned to a data point (like a photo, text document, or sound recording) that describes what it is or what it contains. Labels are crucial in supervised learning, a type of machine learning where the model is trained on a dataset that includes both the input data and the correct labels. These labels help the model to learn and make accurate predictions or classifications on new, unlabeled data.

Key Characteristics of Labels:

Descriptive Nature: Labels describe the content or characteristics of the data. For example, in a dataset of animal pictures, each image might be labeled with the type of animal it shows, like 'dog', 'cat', or 'bird'.

Training Supervised Models: Labels are essential for training supervised learning models. The model learns to associate specific features of the data (like shapes in an image) with the corresponding labels.

Accuracy and Consistency: The accuracy and usefulness of a machine learning model heavily depend on the quality and consistency of the labels in the training data.

Variety of Forms: Labels can be in various forms, such as categories (e.g., spam or not spam), numerical values (e.g., the price of a house), or tags (e.g., topics of an article).

Examples of Labels in Use:

Email Filtering: In email filtering systems, emails are labeled as 'spam' or 'not spam'. The AI learns from these labels to classify incoming emails accurately.

Facial Recognition: In facial recognition systems, images of faces are labeled with the names of individuals. The system uses these labels to identify people in new images.

Speech Recognition: For speech recognition, audio recordings are transcribed and labeled with the corresponding text. The AI model uses these labels to learn how to convert speech into text accurately.

Medical Imaging: In medical imaging, scans might be labeled with diagnoses, like 'tumor' or 'no tumor', assisting AI in learning to identify medical conditions from new scans.

Remember:

A label in AI and ML is a critical element, acting as a guidepost for AI systems to learn and make sense of data. It is through these labels that AI models understand what the data represents and how to categorize or respond to new data. Understanding the concept of labels is key to appreciating how AI and ML models are trained and how they apply their learning to real-world scenarios, from sorting emails to diagnosing diseases.

See also: Labeled Data (pg. 112)

Label Propagation

Imagine you're organizing a vast library of books, some of which are meticulously categorized, but many are not. To efficiently sort the uncategorized books, you start placing them next to similar, already categorized books, assuming they likely share the same category. Over time, this approach helps categorize many books based on their 'neighbors,' streamlining the organization process without manually reviewing every single book. This intuitive method mirrors the idea of Label Propagation in Artificial Intelligence (AI) and Machine Learning (ML), where information from 'labeled' data points is spread to 'unlabeled' ones based on similarity, helping to categorize or understand them better.

In Topic(s): Fundamental Data Concepts (pg. 237) | Semi-supervised Learning (pg. 262)

Figure 54: A cheery illustration of "Label Propagation".

What is Label Propagation?

Label Propagation is a technique used in machine learning for classifying data points within a dataset when only a small subset of the data is labeled. It works on the principle that similar data points are likely to share the same label or category. The algorithm 'propagates' or spreads labels from the labeled data to the unlabeled data based on their similarities, like a ripple effect where information flows from known to unknown areas.

Key Principles of Label Propagation:

Similarity: Just as books on similar topics are likely found together, Label Propagation relies on the assumption that data points close to each other or similar in characteristics are likely to belong to the same category.

Network of Data: Imagine all the books in a library connected by a web of similarities. Label Propagation works on a similar network or graph, where data points are connected based on their similarities.

Spreading Labels: Like assigning a genre to a row of books based on the known genres at either end, labels from labeled data points are spread to their unlabeled neighbors, gradually categorizing the entire dataset.

Iterative Refinement: The process isn't one-off; it's repeated, refining the categorization as more unlabeled data receive labels, much like re-evaluating book placements in a library for better organization.

Examples of Label Propagation in Use:

Social Network Analysis: In a social network, Label Propagation can help identify community structures by grouping users based on their connections and interactions, akin to organizing social groups based on shared interests.

Image Classification: For a collection of partially labeled images, Label Propagation can help assign categories to unlabeled images based on visual similarities to labeled ones, similar to sorting a mix of labeled and unlabeled photos into albums.

Text Classification: In a large set of documents, some of which are categorized (e.g., sports, politics), Label Propagation can classify uncategorized documents by their similarity to the categorized ones, much like sorting articles into sections in a newspaper archive.

Biological Data Analysis: In genetics, Label Propagation can help classify unknown genes or proteins based on their similarities to known ones, aiding in the discovery of new biological functions or relationships.

Remember:

Label Propagation is a powerful method in AI and ML that leverages the innate similarities within data to extend categorization from a known subset to an entire dataset, enhancing understanding and organization of the data. By intuitively 'spreading' knowledge from the labeled to the unlabeled, this technique simplifies the task of data classification, especially in scenarios where labeling all data manually is impractical. Understanding Label Propagation helps in recognizing how AI can efficiently make sense of vast, partially known datasets, drawing connections and insights that might otherwise remain hidden.

See also: Semi-Supervised Learning (pg. 164)

Labeled Data

Let's say you're sorting a big pile of photographs into different albums based on who's in the picture. As you sort each photo, you're effectively 'labeling' them–putting them into categories like 'family', 'friends', 'vacations', etc. In the world of AI and ML, this process of categorization is akin to what we call 'Labeled Data.'

In Topic(s): Fundamental Data Concepts (pg. 237) | Machine Learning (ML) (pg. 250) | Supervised Learning (pg. 266)

Figure 55: A charming illustration of "Labeled Data".

What is Labeled Data?

Labeled Data in AI and ML refers to pieces of information (like images, text files, or sound clips) that have been tagged with one or more labels identifying certain properties or classifications. These labels help AI models understand the data and learn from it. Essentially, the labels act as clear, direct explanations of what the data represents.

Key Points about Labeled Data:

Labels as Guides: The labels guide the AI model in understanding what each piece of data represents, which is crucial for the model to learn and make predictions.

Training Data: Labeled data is often used in supervised learning, where the model is 'trained' by being fed data that is already labeled, so it can learn to recognize patterns and make predictions.

Quality and Accuracy: The accuracy of the labels directly impacts the effectiveness of the AI model. Inaccurate or poor-quality labels can lead to incorrect learning and predictions.

Examples of Labeled Data in Use:

Email Spam Filters: In this case, emails are labeled as 'spam' or 'not spam'. The AI model learns from these labels to identify and filter spam emails effectively.

Facial Recognition Systems: Photos are labeled with names of people. The AI uses these labels to learn and later recognize these faces in other photos or videos.

Voice-Activated Assistants: Sound clips are labeled with information about what words are spoken. The AI uses this to learn to recognize voice commands.

Medical Diagnosis: X-rays or MRI scans are labeled with information about whether they show signs of a particular disease. AI models can then learn to identify these signs in unlabeled images.

Remember:

Labeled Data is a cornerstone in many AI and ML applications, especially in supervised learning. It provides the necessary context and meaning to data, enabling AI models to learn, understand, and make accurate predictions or decisions. Understanding Labeled Data is key to appreciating how AI learns from examples, much like how we learn from experience and instruction.

See also: Unlabeled Data (pg. 192)

Large Language Model (LLM)

Imagine you're at a huge international book fair, where millions of books from all around the world are available, covering every topic imaginable. Now, think of a person who has read every single one of these books and remembers everything they've read. This person could answer almost any question you ask or write about any topic. In the realm of Artificial Intelligence (AI) and Machine Learning (ML), a 'Large Language Model' (LLM) is like this incredibly well-read person, but in a digital form.

In Topic(s): Artificial Intelligence (AI) (pg. 210) | Cutting-edge Technologies (pg. 221) | Deep Learning (DL) (pg. 231) | Emerging Technologies (pg. 233) | Ethical AI, Social Implications and Cultural Considerations (pg. 235) | Future Directions, Trends and Challenges (pg. 243)

Figure 56: An amusing illustration of "Large Language Model (LLM)".

What is a Large Language Model (LLM)?

A Large Language Model is a type of AI program that has been trained on enormous amounts of text data. This training allows the model to understand, predict, and generate human language with a high degree of proficiency. LLMs are designed to grasp the nuances of language, including grammar, context, idioms, and even styles of writing, making them extremely versatile in their applications.

Key Features of Large Language Models:

Extensive Training Data: LLMs are trained on vast and diverse text datasets, encompassing everything from literature and websites to scientific papers and social media posts.

Deep Understanding of Language: Because of their extensive training, LLMs can understand context, subtleties, and complexities in language, allowing them to generate coherent and contextually appropriate responses.

Versatility in Applications: LLMs can be used for a variety of tasks, including text completion, translation, summarization, question-answering, and creative writing.

Continual Learning: Many LLMs continue to learn and improve over time, refining their understanding and generation of language as they are exposed to more data.

Examples of Large Language Models in Action:

Virtual Assistants: Virtual assistants in smartphones and smart devices use LLMs to understand user queries and provide relevant responses or perform tasks based on voice commands.

Content Creation: Writers and content creators may use LLMs to help brainstorm ideas, generate draft content, or provide suggestions for improving their writing.

Customer Service Chatbots: Many businesses use chatbots powered by LLMs to handle customer inquiries, providing instant responses that are accurate and contextually relevant.

Language Translation Services: LLMs are behind many advanced language translation tools, providing real-time, accurate translations between various languages.

Remember:

Large Language Models in AI and ML represent a significant leap forward in how machines understand and interact with human language. They are like digital oracles of language, capable of processing and generating text in a way that is remarkably human-like. Understanding LLMs is crucial for appreciating the sophisticated level of interaction and assistance they provide in various sectors, from personal assistance to professional content creation.

See also: ChatGPT (OpenAI) (pg. 8)

Loss Function

Imagine you're practicing archery. Each time you shoot an arrow, you aim for the bullseye, but sometimes you miss. The distance between where your arrow lands and the bullseye can be seen as a score of how 'off' your shot was. In Artificial Intelligence (AI) and Machine Learning (ML), a 'Loss Function' is like this measure of accuracy. It's a way to determine how far off an AI model's predictions are from the actual, desired outcome.

In Topic(s): Deep Learning (DL) (pg. 231) | Fundamental Data Concepts (pg. 237) | Fundamental Mathematics and Statistics (pg. 241) | Machine Learning (ML) (pg. 250) | Supervised Learning (pg. 266)

Figure 57: A playful illustration of "Loss Function".

What is a Loss Function?

A Loss Function in AI and ML is a mathematical function that quantifies the difference between the predicted values by a model and the actual values it was supposed to predict. It's a critical tool in training AI models, as it provides a way to measure how well the model is performing its task.

Key Features of Loss Functions:

Error Measurement: The Loss Function calculates the 'error' or 'loss' - the extent to which the model's predictions deviate from the actual values.

Guide for Improvement: Based on this loss, the model can be adjusted and improved. The aim is to minimize the loss, which means making the model's predictions as accurate as possible.

Variety of Functions: There are different types of Loss Functions for different types of tasks, such as Mean Squared Error for regression tasks and Cross-Entropy for classification tasks.

Critical in Model Training: The process of minimizing the loss, often done through a method called 'gradient descent', is fundamental in training effective AI models.

Examples of Loss Functions in Use:

Predicting House Prices: If an AI model is predicting house prices, the Loss Function would measure how far off each prediction is from the actual house price. The model learns to adjust its predictions to minimize this loss.

Image Classification: In classifying images (like distinguishing cats from dogs), the Loss Function calculates how often the model incorrectly classifies an image and adjusts to reduce these errors.

Medical Diagnosis: For an AI diagnosing diseases from medical images, the Loss Function would quantify the difference between the model's diagnosis and the actual medical diagnosis.

Remember:

The Loss Function in AI and ML is a crucial concept that provides a way to evaluate and improve the accuracy of AI models. It's like a scoring system that tells the model how 'off' its predictions are and guides it towards making more accurate predictions. Understanding the Loss Function is essential for appreciating how AI models learn and improve, aiming to reduce errors in tasks ranging from simple predictions to complex decision-making.

See also: Error Minimization (pg. 75)

Markov Decision Process (MDP)

Imagine you're planning a road trip with multiple destinations along the way. At each stop, you have several choices: you could take a quick break and continue driving, you could stop for a meal, or you could even take a detour to explore a nearby attraction. Each choice leads to different outcomes and sets the stage for your next set of choices. This scenario, where you make decisions at various stages, each influencing your journey's future course, mirrors the concept of a "Markov Decision Process" (MDP) in the realm of Artificial Intelligence (AI) and Machine Learning (ML).

In Topic(s): Artificial Intelligence (AI) (pg. 210) | Fundamental Mathematics and Statistics (pg. 241) | Future Directions, Trends and Challenges (pg. 243) | Machine Learning (ML) (pg. 250) | Reinforcement Learning (pg. 259) | Robotics (pg. 260)

Figure 58: A lighthearted illustration of "Markov Decision Process (MDP)".

What is a Markov Decision Process?

A Markov Decision Process is a mathematical framework used in AI to model decision-making situations where outcomes are partly random and partly under the control of a decision-maker. It's like mapping out your road trip, where each stop represents a state, the routes you can take are your actions, and the places you end up are the outcomes, which also depend on chance events like traffic or weather.

Key Elements of a Markov Decision Process:

States: These are like the various stops or points in your journey, representing the different situations you might find yourself in.

Actions: At each state, you have choices (actions) you can make, like deciding whether to rest, eat, or explore at each stop on your road trip.

Transitions: These are the rules that determine what state you end up in next, based on your current state and the action you choose, much like a road map shows where you'll end up depending on the route you take.

Rewards: Each action you take leads to a reward (or penalty), which could be anything from the enjoyment of a good meal to the time lost in traffic. The goal is often to maximize the total reward over the journey.

How Does MDP Work?

Imagine you're trying to maximize the fun on your road trip (maximize rewards) while dealing with uncertainties like weather and traffic (random outcomes). At each stop (state), you decide what to do next (action), considering how it will affect your trip's enjoyment (reward) and where you might end up next (transition to the next state). The MDP framework helps you systematically think through these decisions to plan the best possible trip given the uncertainties.

Applications of MDP:

Robotics: Robots use MDP to decide how to move and act in an environment where outcomes are uncertain, like navigating through a busy warehouse while avoiding obstacles.

Game Strategy: MDPs can help in developing strategies for games where players must make a series of decisions, each affecting the game's future state and the player's chances of winning.

Resource Management: In environmental management, MDPs can aid in making decisions about resource allocation, like water usage in agriculture, balancing immediate needs with future sustainability.

Healthcare Treatment Plans: MDPs assist in creating treatment plans where each treatment decision (action) leads to different outcomes and future treatment options (states), aiming to maximize patient health (reward).

Remember:

The Markov Decision Process offers a structured way to navigate decision-making in scenarios filled with uncertainties and varying outcomes. By understanding MDPs, we can appreciate how AI systems tackle complex problems, from planning the optimal route for a road trip to devising strategies in games and managing resources efficiently, always aiming to make the best decisions based on current knowledge and possible future states.

See also: Reinforcement Learning (RL) (pg. 150)

Masked Language Modeling (MLM)

Imagine you're reading a thrilling novel, but to add a twist, some words are covered with stickers. Instead of skipping these parts, you use the context from the surrounding sentences to guess the hidden words. Sometimes, you're spot on; other times, you get close. This engaging exercise not only enhances your guessing skills but also deepens your understanding of the language and the story's context. This is akin to the process of Masked Language Modeling (MLM) in the field of Artificial Intelligence (AI) and Machine Learning (ML), where a system learns to understand and use language by filling in intentionally hidden parts of the text.

In Topic(s): Emerging Technologies (pg. 233) | Machine Learning (ML) (pg. 250) | Natural Language Understanding (NLU) (pg. 256)

Figure 59: A charming illustration of "Masked Language Modeling (MLM)".

What is Masked Language Modeling?

Masked Language Modeling is a training technique used in natural language processing (NLP), a branch of AI focused on enabling machines to understand human language. In MLM, random words in a sentence are hidden or 'masked,' and the model's task is to predict these missing words based solely on the context provided by the other words in the sentence. This process helps the AI to grasp language nuances, improve its comprehension, and become better at generating coherent, contextually appropriate text.

Key Elements of Masked Language Modeling:

Masking: Like covering words in a book, certain words in the text are hidden from the model. The model then has to guess these words without seeing them.

Contextual Understanding: The model uses the words around the masked ones to make its guesses, learning how words relate to each other within sentences and broader text, similar to piecing together a story from clues.

Predictive Learning: This method focuses on prediction, encouraging the model to learn a deep understanding of language structure and usage to make accurate guesses, much like solving a crossword puzzle.

Language Comprehension: Through repeated practice, the model becomes proficient at understanding and using language, improving its ability to generate text, translate languages, answer questions, and more.

Examples of Masked Language Modeling in Action:

Content Creation: AI models trained with MLM can assist in writing articles or reports by suggesting contextually appropriate sentences, similar to a co-author suggesting how to fill in gaps in a story.

Language Translation: These models can enhance translation accuracy by understanding the context better, akin to a translator who grasps the nuances of both the source and target languages.

Virtual Assistants: Improved language understanding enables virtual assistants to comprehend and respond to complex queries more effectively, much like a knowledgeable guide providing precise information.

Educational Tools: MLM-trained models can create educational content, such as quizzes or learning materials, by generating questions and masking key terms for students to guess, enhancing the learning experience.

Remember:

Masked Language Modeling is a cornerstone technique in teaching AI the intricacies of human language. By challenging models to fill in the blanks based on context, MLM fosters a deeper understanding of how language operates, equipping AI systems with the ability to comprehend, predict, and generate human-like text. This process is fundamental in advancing AI's role in various applications, from writing assistance to interactive learning platforms, making AI an ever more capable and intuitive companion in our interaction with technology.

See also: Large Language Model (LLM) (pg. 114)

Model

Let's compare a 'model' in Artificial Intelligence (AI) and Machine Learning (ML) to a recipe in cooking. Just as a recipe guides you on how to combine ingredients to create a dish, a model in AI and ML guides the computer on how to combine data and algorithms to make predictions or decisions.

In Topic(s): Artificial Intelligence (AI) (pg. 210) | Machine Learning (ML) (pg. 250)

Figure 60: A lighthearted illustration of "Model".

What is a Model?

A model in AI and ML is essentially a program or set of rules that the computer follows to process data and produce output, such as making predictions or classifying information. It's created by 'training' the model on data, where it learns patterns and relationships within that data.

Key Features of a Model:

Data-Driven: Models are built and improved based on data. They analyze data to learn patterns or trends that can be used for future predictions.

Learning from Examples: Just like learning to cook by trying different recipes, a model in ML learns from examples. It's exposed to large amounts of data to understand and 'learn' from it.

Making Predictions: Once trained, a model can take new data and make predictions based on its training. For example, after seeing many pictures of cats and dogs, it can identify whether a new picture is of a cat or a dog.

Wide Range of Applications: Models are used in numerous applications, from recommending products on a shopping website to predicting weather patterns or diagnosing diseases.

Examples of Models in Use:

Weather Forecasting: A model takes in data like temperature, humidity, and wind speed, and predicts the weather for the coming days.

Speech Recognition: When you talk to voice assistants like Siri or Alexa, a model processes your speech and understands your commands or questions.

Fraud Detection in Banking: Models analyze transaction patterns to detect unusual activities that might indicate fraud.

Image Recognition: Social media platforms use models to automatically tag and recognize faces in photos.

Remember:

A model in AI and ML is like a complex recipe for a computer, guiding it on how to analyze data and make informed decisions or predictions. It's an essential component of AI and ML, allowing machines to learn from data and apply this learning to real-world tasks. From simple applications like filtering emails to complex ones like autonomous driving, models are the heart of what makes AI and ML powerful and increasingly integral in various aspects of life. Understanding models is key to appreciating the capabilities and potential of AI and ML technologies in solving problems, automating tasks, and providing insights.

See also: Function (pg. 92)

Natural Language Generation (NLG)

Imagine you're narrating a story to a child using a mix of your imagination and elements from various tales you know. In a similar manner, 'Natural Language Generation' (NLG) in Artificial Intelligence (AI) and Machine Learning (ML) involves computers creating human-like text or speech. It's about AI not just understanding language, but also producing it coherently and contextually.

In Topic(s): Core Applications (pg. 218) | Industry Applications (pg. 247) | Natural Language Processing (NLP) (pg. 254) | Natural Language Understanding (NLU) (pg. 256) | Supervised Learning (pg. 266) | Text and Language Processing (pg. 270)

Figure 61: A humorous illustration of "Natural Language Generation (NLG)".

What is Natural Language Generation?

Natural Language Generation is the process where AI systems generate human-like text or speech. Unlike humans who use their knowledge of language and the world to compose sentences, NLG systems rely on algorithms and data to produce language. This involves transforming structured data into natural language and constructing sentences that are grammatically correct and contextually relevant.

Key Components of NLG:

Data Interpretation: NLG starts by understanding the input data, which could be numbers, facts, or any structured information.

Content Determination: The system decides what content to include in the text based on the data's significance and relevance.

Text Structuring: Arranging the chosen content into a logical sequence, much like outlining a story.

Sentence Construction: Crafting sentences that are grammatically correct and convey the intended meaning.

Refinement: The text may be further refined for fluency, style, and adherence to linguistic norms.

Examples of NLG in Use:

Weather Reporting: An NLG system can generate weather reports by converting weather data (like temperature, humidity) into a readable forecast narrative.

Financial Reporting: Generating financial summaries or reports from complex datasets, making them easier for investors and stakeholders to understand.

Customer Service Chatbots: Chatbots use NLG to generate responses to customer inquiries in a conversational manner.

Content Creation: NLG tools assist in writing articles or generating content for websites, often starting from a set of data points.

Medical Reporting: Converting patient data and test results into coherent medical reports that can be easily understood by doctors and patients.

Remember:

Natural Language Generation represents a fascinating aspect of AI and ML, where machines are not just passive receivers of human language but active generators of it. By producing language that is coherent, contextually appropriate, and tailored to the intended audience, NLG systems extend the capabilities of AI in fields like journalism, customer service, and analytics. Understanding NLG helps in appreciating the complex interplay of data, algorithms, and linguistics that enable machines to communicate effectively in human language.

See also: ChatGPT (OpenAI) (pg. 8)

Neuron

Consider a busy office worker who receives various pieces of information, processes them, and then passes on the necessary actions or responses to others. This worker acts much like a 'Neuron' in the field of Artificial Intelligence (AI) and Machine Learning (ML).

In Topic(s): Artificial Intelligence (AI) (pg. 210) | Artificial Neural Networks (ANN) (pg. 214) | Deep Learning (DL) (pg. 231) | Image Processing (pg. 245) | Sound and Audio Processing (pg. 264)

Figure 62: A whimsical illustration of "Neuron".

What is a Neuron?

In AI and ML, a neuron is a fundamental unit of a neural network, designed to mimic the function of neurons in the human brain. Just as a neuron in the brain processes and transmits information, an artificial neuron receives input, processes it, and produces output. It is a basic building block that helps the system learn from and make decisions based on data.

Key Aspects of a Neuron:

Input Reception: A neuron receives multiple inputs, which can be raw data or the outputs from other neurons.

Processing: Each input is assigned a 'weight' that signifies its importance. The neuron processes these inputs by summing them up, each weighted by its respective importance.

Activation Function: After processing the inputs, the neuron applies an activation function. This function determines whether the neuron will 'activate' (send its output to other neurons) and how strongly it will do so.

Output Generation: Based on the activation, the neuron produces an output, which can either be a final result or an input to another neuron in the network.

Examples of Neurons in Use:

Image Recognition: In image recognition tasks, neurons process pixel data from images, learning to identify patterns like edges, shapes, and textures.

Voice Recognition Systems: Neurons process sound wave frequencies and learn to identify patterns in speech to recognize words and phrases.

Predictive Typing: In predictive text systems, neurons process sequences of typed letters and learn common patterns to suggest next words.

Fraud Detection: In financial systems, neurons analyze transaction data to learn patterns of normal and fraudulent activities.

Remember:

A neuron in AI and ML is a powerful concept that forms the basis of neural networks, enabling systems to learn from data and make intelligent decisions. By understanding how an artificial neuron works, one can appreciate the complexity and sophistication behind AI technologies that are becoming increasingly integral to various aspects of modern life, from personal gadgets to complex industrial systems.

See also: Artificial Neural Network (ANN) (pg. 29)

Output Layer

Imagine you're using a vending machine. You select a drink, and after processing your choice, the machine delivers your selected beverage. This final step - the delivery of the drink - is akin to the 'Output Layer' in a neural network in the field of Artificial Intelligence (AI) and Machine Learning (ML). Just as the vending machine presents you with the end product, the Output Layer is where the neural network provides its final result or decision based on the input and processing it has done.

In Topic(s): Artificial Neural Networks (ANN) (pg. 214) | Deep Learning (DL) (pg. 231) | Fundamental Data Concepts (pg. 237)

Figure 63: A quirky illustration of "Output Layer".

What is an Output Layer?

In a neural network, the Output Layer is the last layer, responsible for producing the final results or predictions. After the input data has been processed through the hidden layers (if any) of the network, the Output Layer takes over to generate a tangible output, whether that's a classification, a prediction, a decision, or any other form of result.

Key Features of the Output Layer:

Final Results: The Output Layer is where the network outputs its final decision or prediction, based on the data it has received and processed.

Varied Forms of Output: The nature of the output can vary greatly depending on the task - it could be a single value (like a price prediction), a category (like identifying an object in an image), or even a series of values (like a sequence of predicted words).

Activation Functions: This layer often uses specific 'activation functions' to map the processed input into the desired output format. For example, a softmax activation function can be used for classification tasks to represent probabilities of different classes.

Dependent on the Task: The design of the Output Layer, including the number of neurons and the type of activation function, depends heavily on the specific task the neural network is designed to perform.

Examples of Output Layers in Action:

Disease Diagnosis: In a medical diagnosis system, the Output Layer might produce a classification of whether a patient's symptoms indicate a particular disease or not.

Price Forecasting: In stock market prediction, the Output Layer could generate a predicted future price of a stock.

Image Recognition: For an image recognition task, the Output Layer would identify the object present in an image, such as 'cat', 'dog', 'car', etc.

Language Translation: In a language translation model, the Output Layer produces the translated text in the target language.

Remember:

The Output Layer in neural networks is the final stage where all the processing and analysis done by the network culminates in a concrete outcome. It's essential for converting the complex computations of the network into useful and interpretable results. Understanding the Output Layer is key to appreciating how neural networks complete their tasks, providing valuable predictions, classifications, and decisions based on the data they process.

See also: Artificial Neural Network (ANN) (pg. 29)

Overfitting

Think about a comedian who tailors their jokes to a specific audience so well that they get a lot of laughs, but then struggles to make a different audience laugh with the same material. This scenario is similar to 'Overfitting' in Artificial Intelligence (AI) and Machine Learning (ML).

In Topic(s): Machine Learning (ML) (pg. 250)

Figure 64: A charming illustration of "Overfitting".

What is Overfitting?

Overfitting occurs when an AI or ML model learns the details and noise in the training data to the extent that it negatively impacts the performance of the model on new data. It's like memorizing the answers to specific questions in a test rather than understanding the subject broadly. When faced with new questions, the memorized answers aren't as effective.

Key Points about Overfitting:

Too Specific to Training Data: The model performs well on its training data but poorly on any new, unseen data because it has learned the training data too closely, including its errors and random fluctuations.

Lack of Generalization: The main issue with overfitting is that the model fails to generalize from the training data to broader, real-world situations.

Complex Models: Overfitting is more common in highly complex models that have too many parameters relative to the amount of training data.

Examples of Overfitting in Use:

Stock Market Prediction: If a model is trained on past stock market data and picks up on random fluctuations as patterns, it may fail to predict future market trends accurately.

Sports Prediction: A model that learns the outcomes of specific games in detail might fail to predict the outcome of new games because it hasn't learned the broader trends and rules of the game.

Medical Diagnosis: If a diagnostic tool is trained on a small set of patient data, it might perform excellently on that specific data but poorly on other patients because it has learned the peculiarities of the initial group too well.

Strategies to Prevent Overfitting:

Use More Data: More data can help the model learn the general patterns rather than the specifics of a small dataset.

Simplify the Model: Reducing the complexity of the model can prevent it from picking up and learning noise in the data.

Cross-Validation: This involves dividing the data into parts, training the model on some parts and validating it on others to ensure it generalizes well.

Regularization: Techniques like L1 or L2 regularization can discourage the model from becoming too complex and focusing too much on the training data.

Remember:

Overfitting is a common challenge in AI and ML, where a model becomes so attuned to its training data that it performs poorly in real-world scenarios or on new data. Understanding overfitting is crucial for developing effective AI and ML models, as it highlights the importance of building models that not only learn well but also generalize well to new, unseen data.

See also: Underfitting (pg. 190)

Policy Function (Q-function)

Imagine you're playing a video game where you're navigating through a maze to find treasure. At each intersection, you must decide whether to go left, right, forward, or back, based on which direction you think will lead you to the treasure the quickest. In this scenario, the "Policy Function," often referred to as the Q-function in the context of Artificial Intelligence (AI) and Machine Learning (ML), is like an internal guide or map that helps you make the best decision at each point based on your current situation and your past experiences in similar mazes.

In Topic(s): Fundamental Mathematics and Statistics (pg. 241) | Reinforcement Learning (pg. 259)

Figure 65: An amusing illustration of "Policy Function (Q-function)".

What is a Policy Function (Q-function)?

In AI, especially in areas dealing with decision-making like Reinforcement Learning, a Policy Function (or Q-function) is a mathematical tool that helps an AI agent (like a character in a video game) decide the best action to take in a given situation to achieve its goal. The "Q" stands for "quality," and this function evaluates the quality or usefulness of taking a certain action in a particular state, considering the long-term benefit of that action.

Key Elements of a Policy Function (Q-function):

States: These are the different situations or configurations the agent can find itself in, like the various intersections in the maze.

Actions: These are the choices available to the agent in each state, such as turning left or right at an intersection.

Rewards: After taking an action, the agent receives feedback in the form of rewards (or penalties), which indicate how good a decision was in the context of reaching the goal.

Quality Value: The Q-function assigns a value to each action in each state, representing the expected future rewards. This helps the agent predict which actions will bring it closer to its goal.

Examples of Policy Function (Q-function) in Use:

Video Games: In a strategy game, the AI uses a Q-function to decide its moves based on the current state of the game, aiming to maximize its chances of winning.

Robot Navigation: A robot in a warehouse uses a Q-function to determine the most efficient path to pick and deliver items, learning from past trips to optimize its routes.

Financial Trading: Trading algorithms use Q-functions to decide when to buy or sell assets, based on historical and real-time market data, to maximize profit.

Personalized Recommendations: AI systems in streaming services use versions of Q-functions to decide which movies or songs to recommend, aiming to maximize viewer or listener satisfaction.

Remember:

The Policy Function (Q-function) in AI and ML is a fundamental concept that underpins how intelligent agents learn to make decisions that lead them to achieve their goals effectively. By evaluating the potential long-term rewards of actions in various situations, the Q-function guides agents through complex environments, whether they're virtual characters in a game, robots in a factory, or algorithms managing investments, helping them learn from their experiences to improve their performance over time.

See also: Reinforcement Learning (RL) (pg. 150)

Predictive Coding

Imagine you're watching your favorite TV series, and over time, you've become so familiar with the characters and plot twists that you often predict what's going to happen next. Sometimes, your predictions are spot on, and other times, the show surprises you, but each guess and its outcome teach you more about the storyline's patterns. This process of making predictions based on patterns and adjusting your expectations based on the actual outcomes is similar to the concept of Predictive Coding in Artificial Intelligence (AI) and Machine Learning (ML).

Figure 66: An eccentric illustration of "Predictive Coding".

What is Predictive Coding?

Predictive Coding is a theory and methodology used in neuroscience, psychology, and more recently, in AI and ML, where it's believed that the brain (or an AI system) constantly tries to predict sensory input (like sights and sounds) based on past experiences. When actual input differs from these predictions, the system updates its internal models to better predict future inputs. In AI and ML, this concept is applied to develop models that can predict outcomes based on data patterns and then refine their predictive capabilities over time through feedback.

Key Principles of Predictive Coding:

Prediction: Just as you might anticipate plot developments in a TV series, predictive coding models make predictions about incoming data based on learned patterns.

Error Correction: When the actual data differs from the prediction (a surprise twist in the plot, for example), the model notes the 'prediction error.'

Model Updating: The model uses these errors to adjust and improve its predictions for the future, much like you refine your series plot predictions over time.

Efficiency: Over time, the model becomes more efficient, reducing prediction errors and becoming better at forecasting future data, mirroring how your series predictions improve with each episode.

Examples of Predictive Coding in Use:

Speech Recognition: Predictive coding helps improve speech recognition systems by predicting the next words or sounds in speech, making these systems more accurate and efficient, much like predicting dialogue in a conversation.

Medical Diagnosis: In healthcare, predictive coding models can forecast potential health issues based on patient data trends, similar to anticipating health outcomes based on symptoms and history.

Market Forecasting: In finance, predictive coding can be used to anticipate market trends and movements based on historical data, akin to predicting plot twists in a financial thriller.

Autonomous Vehicles: Predictive coding aids self-driving cars in anticipating the movements of other road users, improving safety and efficiency, much like predicting the next moves in a high-speed chase scene.

Remember:

Predictive Coding is a sophisticated approach that mirrors the human tendency to predict based on past experiences, applied in the realm of AI and ML to enhance the ability of machines to forecast and adapt to new information. By continuously refining its predictions through feedback, an AI system becomes more adept at understanding and interacting with the world, much like we become more perceptive viewers of our favorite TV series. This concept not only helps demystify how AI learns from the environment but also highlights the potential for creating more intuitive and adaptive technological solutions.

See also: Self-Supervised Learning (pg. 158)

Pretext Task

Imagine you're trying to become a master chef. Before tackling complex dishes, you start with basic exercises like chopping vegetables, measuring ingredients precisely, and managing the heat of your stove. These foundational tasks aren't just random chores; they're carefully chosen to build the skills you'll need for more advanced cooking. In the world of Artificial Intelligence (AI) and Machine Learning (ML), there's a similar strategy known as Pretext Tasks. These are simpler, foundational tasks designed to teach AI models crucial skills and knowledge that will be useful for tackling more complex, real-world problems later on.

In Topic(s): Self-supervised Learning (pg. 261)

Figure 67: A lighthearted illustration of "Pretext Task".

What is a Pretext Task?

A Pretext Task is an initial task or set of tasks that an AI model is trained on to learn useful features, patterns, or representations from data, which can then be applied to perform more complex tasks. These tasks are called 'pretext' because they are not the end goal but a means to an end, helping the model to develop a deeper understanding of the data before applying it to the main problem or 'target task'.

Key Aspects of Pretext Tasks:

Skill Building: Just as basic cooking exercises hone essential culinary skills, pretext tasks help AI models learn fundamental patterns and features within the data.

Data Understanding: Through pretext tasks, models get acquainted with the nuances of the data, similar to how a chef becomes familiar with ingredients' flavors and textures.

Transferability: The knowledge gained from pretext tasks is designed to be transferable, meaning it can be applied to more complex tasks later on, much like foundational cooking skills used to create a wide array of dishes.

Examples of Pretext Tasks in AI:

Image Processing: In teaching an AI to understand images, a common pretext task might be to rotate images and have the model predict the rotation angle. This helps the model learn about object shapes and spatial orientations, useful for more complex image recognition tasks.

Language Understanding: An AI model might be trained to predict missing words in sentences, helping it grasp grammar, context, and vocabulary. This foundational knowledge is crucial for tasks like language translation or sentiment analysis.

Sound Recognition: A pretext task could involve distinguishing between different types of background noise in audio clips, which helps the model learn to focus on relevant sounds, a skill useful in voice recognition or music classification.

Social Network Analysis: An AI might be tasked with predicting which nodes (people, pages, etc.) in a network are connected. Understanding these relationships helps the model tackle more complex tasks like community detection or recommendation systems.

Remember:

Pretext Tasks are a strategic step in training AI models, serving as the groundwork for understanding complex data and performing intricate tasks. By mastering simpler, foundational tasks, AI models develop a robust set of skills and knowledge that can be applied to a wide range of real-world applications, much like a chef uses basic culinary skills to craft a diverse menu of dishes. Understanding the role and design of pretext tasks sheds light on the meticulous and thoughtful process behind training AI, ensuring models are well-prepared to tackle the complexities of the tasks they're ultimately designed for.

See also: Self-Supervised Learning (pg. 158)

Pseudo-labelling

Imagine you're trying to learn the names of various plants in your garden, but you only know a few of them. To speed up the learning process, you start by labeling those few you're confident about. Then, you make educated guesses about the rest based on similarities to the ones you know, tagging them with tentative names. Over time, as you learn more about each plant, you refine these guesses, gradually improving your garden's overall labeling. This approach of starting with what you know and expanding through educated guesses mirrors the idea of Pseudo-Labeling in the realm of Artificial Intelligence (AI) and Machine Learning (ML).

In Topic(s): Self-supervised Learning (pg. 261) | Semi-supervised Learning (pg. 262)

Figure 68: A playful illustration of "Pseudo-labelling".

What is Pseudo-Labeling?

Pseudo-Labeling is a technique used to enhance the learning process of AI models, particularly when there's a limited amount of labeled data (data where the correct answer is known). The model initially learns from this small set of labeled data. Then, it applies what it's learned to make predictions on unlabeled data. These predictions, although not verified by humans, are treated as 'pseudo-labels' and are used to further train the model, expanding its learning base as if it had a larger set of true labels from the start.

Key Features of Pseudo-Labeling:

Leveraging Unlabeled Data: Like guessing the names of unknown plants, pseudo-labeling allows AI models to learn from data that hasn't been manually labeled, significantly increasing the amount of data the model can learn from.

Iterative Learning: The process is cyclical - the model makes predictions, learns from these pseudo-labels, and then makes better predictions, similar to refining your guesses about plant names as you gain more knowledge.

Self-improvement: Over time, as the model's predictions improve, the quality of the pseudo-labels also improves, leading to a virtuous cycle of continuous learning and enhancement.

Examples of Pseudo-Labeling in Action:

Image Recognition: In teaching an AI to identify different breeds of dogs in photos, it might start with a small set of images where the breeds are known. It then uses these to make educated guesses on a much larger set of unlabeled images, gradually improving its breed recognition capabilities.

Sentiment Analysis: An AI model could begin by understanding the sentiment (positive, negative, neutral) of a small batch of social media posts. It then applies this knowledge to predict the sentiments of a vast number of unlabeled posts, using these predictions to enhance its understanding.

Speech Recognition: Starting with a small dataset of labeled audio recordings, an AI model can learn basic patterns of speech. It then listens to unlabeled recordings, guesses the transcriptions, and uses these guesses to further refine its speech recognition abilities.

Fraud Detection: Initially trained on a small set of transactions labeled as 'fraudulent' or 'legitimate,' a model can then assess a larger pool of unlabeled transactions, applying pseudo-labels to them, and thereby enhancing its ability to detect fraud patterns.

Remember:

Pseudo-Labeling is a clever strategy that empowers AI models to extend their learning beyond the confines of limited labeled data, using their own predictions to boost their training. This technique embodies the principle of learning by doing, allowing models to improve iteratively by engaging with unlabeled data and refining their understanding and predictions over time. Understanding pseudo-labeling illuminates how AI can effectively leverage vast amounts of available data, even when explicit knowledge (labels) is scarce, driving continuous improvement and expanding the model's capabilities in a cost-effective manner.

See also: Semi-Supervised Learning (pg. 164)

Python

Imagine a versatile tool, like a Swiss Army knife, that can perform a wide range of tasks from opening a bottle to cutting a piece of string. In the world of computer programming, especially in Artificial Intelligence (AI) and Machine Learning (ML), 'Python' is akin to such a multi-purpose tool.

Figure 69: A lighthearted illustration of "Python".

What is Python?

Python is a popular programming language known for its simplicity and readability, making it accessible to beginners, yet powerful enough for experts. It's like a language that, once learned, allows you to communicate a wide array of instructions to a computer.

Key Features of Python:

Easy to Learn: Python's syntax (its set of rules) is clear and easy to understand, making it a favorite for beginners.

Versatile: It can be used for a wide range of tasks, from web development to data analysis and AI.

Rich Libraries: Python has a vast collection of pre-written codes (libraries) which can be used to perform complex tasks without needing to write code from scratch. For AI and ML, libraries like TensorFlow, PyTorch, and scikit-learn are particularly valuable.

Community Support: A large community of developers contributes to Python's growth, offering support, sharing knowledge, and creating useful tools.

Examples of Python in Use:

Web Development: Websites like Reddit and Instagram use Python for their back-end development.

Data Analysis: Python is extensively used in analyzing large datasets, visualizing data, and drawing insights from it.

AI and ML Projects: Python is a go-to language for developing AI models, due to its simplicity and the powerful libraries available.

Automation: Simple Python scripts can automate repetitive tasks like file organization, sending emails, or scraping information from websites.

Why is Python Important?

Accessibility: Its simplicity makes it accessible to a wide range of people, from hobbyists to professional developers.

Flexibility: Python's versatility means it can be applied in almost any area of technology.

Remember:

Python in AI and ML is like a bridge that makes it easier to translate human ideas into instructions that computers can understand and act upon. It is an essential tool in modern computing, enabling the creation and implementation of complex algorithms and systems in a user-friendly manner. Understanding Python is key to navigating the world of technology, particularly in areas related to AI and ML.

See also: Jupyter Notebook (pg. 106)

PyTorch

Imagine you're an artist about to start on a grand canvas, but instead of traditional paint, your medium is data, and your goal is to create a masterpiece that can learn from its surroundings and improve over time. In this digital artistry, "PyTorch" is akin to a sophisticated palette, offering a wide array of colors (tools and functions) that allow you to blend, mix, and apply data in creative ways to bring your intelligent creations to life.

In Topic(s): AI Hardware and Accelerators (pg. 209)

Figure 70: A delightful illustration of "PyTorch".

What is PyTorch?

PyTorch is a popular open-source machine learning library for Python, known for its flexibility, ease of use, and dynamic computational graph. It provides the essential tools for building and training machine learning models, akin to the brushes, colors, and techniques in an artist's toolkit. PyTorch is particularly favored for research and development due to its intuitive design and ability to perform complex tensor computations with automatic differentiation, making the process of creating and refining learning algorithms as fluid as painting on a canvas.

Key Features of PyTorch:

Dynamic Computational Graph: PyTorch allows you to modify and adjust your model architecture on-the-fly, much like how an artist might change their technique or approach as their vision evolves.

Ease of Use: Its straightforward and Pythonic design makes PyTorch accessible, allowing both novice and experienced data scientists to bring their models to life with relative ease.

Rich Ecosystem: PyTorch is supported by a vast ecosystem of tools and libraries for machine learning, data analysis, and visualization, offering a comprehensive set of instruments for the modern data artist.

Strong Community: With a large and active community, PyTorch users have access to extensive resources, tutorials, and pre-trained models, similar to an artist being part of a vibrant and supportive art collective.

Examples of PyTorch in Use:

Image Recognition: PyTorch's tools can be used to train models that recognize and classify images, much like teaching your canvas to understand and interpret different scenes and objects.

Natural Language Processing: It's used to develop models that can understand and generate human language, enabling applications like chatbots and translators to communicate naturally.

Predictive Analytics: PyTorch can analyze historical data to make predictions about future events, akin to giving your painting the foresight to anticipate changes in the landscape.

Generative Art: With PyTorch, you can create models that generate new content, from artwork to music, learning from existing styles and patterns to create something entirely new.

Remember:

PyTorch is like a versatile and dynamic palette for the data artist, offering the tools and flexibility needed to explore the realms of machine learning and artificial intelligence creatively. Whether you're crafting intricate models that mimic human perception or devising algorithms that predict the ebb and flow of financial markets, PyTorch empowers you to turn the vast and complex world of data into intelligent systems capable of learning, adapting, and evolving. Understanding PyTorch opens up a world of possibilities for creating advanced AI models, making it an essential tool in the modern data scientist's toolkit.

See also: TensorFlow (pg. 176)

Recommendation Engine

Imagine you're at a large, bustling market with countless stalls, each offering a myriad of items. It's overwhelming to decide where to look or what to buy. Now, picture a friendly guide who, after getting to know your tastes and preferences, leads you to specific stalls with items that perfectly match what you love. This guide is like a "Recommendation Engine" in the digital world, a smart assistant that helps you navigate through the vast expanse of options online, be it movies, books, music, or products, by suggesting choices tailored just for you.

In Topic(s): Core Applications (pg. 218) | Data Analytics (DA) (pg. 223) | Industry Applications (pg. 247)

Figure 71: A whimsical illustration of "Recommendation Engine".

What is a Recommendation Engine?

A Recommendation Engine is a sophisticated system that analyzes your past behavior, preferences, and interactions to suggest relevant items or content you might enjoy or find useful. It's like having a personal shopper who knows your taste better with each choice you make, constantly refining its suggestions to better match your preferences. These engines power the "Recommended for You" sections on platforms like Netflix, Amazon, Spotify, and many others, making it easier for you to discover content or products you're likely to enjoy.

How Does a Recommendation Engine Work?

Data Collection: The engine gathers data about your interactions, such as your purchases, views, likes, and ratings, to understand your preferences.

Analysis: It analyzes this data, often using sophisticated AI and ML algorithms, to find patterns, similarities, and trends.

Matching: Based on this analysis, the engine identifies items that match your profile, considering factors like what others with similar tastes have enjoyed.

Personalization: The recommendations become more personalized over time as the engine learns more about your preferences through your ongoing interactions.

Types of Recommendation Engines:

Content-Based Filtering: This type suggests items similar to what you've liked before, focusing on the properties of the items themselves.

Collaborative Filtering: Here, the engine recommends items liked by other users who have a history or profile similar to yours.

Hybrid Systems: Many modern engines combine both approaches, along with other techniques, to provide more accurate and diverse recommendations.

Examples of Recommendation Engines in Everyday Life:

Streaming Services: Netflix uses a recommendation engine to suggest movies and shows you might like, based on your viewing history and ratings.

E-commerce Websites: Amazon's "Customers who bought this item also bought" feature is powered by a recommendation engine that analyzes shopping patterns to suggest related products.

Music Streaming: Spotify recommends playlists and songs by understanding your music preferences and what similar listeners enjoy.

Social Media: Platforms like Facebook and Instagram recommend friends to add or content to view, based on your interactions and the network of connections.

Remember:

Recommendation Engines are like digital guides that help us navigate the vast and often overwhelming world of online content and products. They enhance our digital experiences by making personalized suggestions, saving us time, and introducing us to items and content we might not have discovered on our own. Understanding how these engines work illuminates the increasingly personalized nature of our digital interactions, showcasing the power of AI and ML in making our online journeys more relevant and enjoyable.

See also: Machine Learning (ML) (pg. 12)

Recurrent Neural Network (RNN)

Think about watching your favorite TV series. To understand the story in the current episode, you rely on remembering what happened in the previous episodes. This process of retaining past information to make sense of the current context is similar to how a 'Recurrent Neural Network' (RNN) functions in Artificial Intelligence (AI) and Machine Learning (ML).

In Topic(s): Artificial Neural Networks (ANN) (pg. 214) | Deep Learning (DL) (pg. 231) | Sound and Audio Processing (pg. 264)

Figure 72: A cheery illustration of "Recurrent Neural Network (RNN)".

What is a Recurrent Neural Network (RNN)?

A Recurrent Neural Network is a type of AI model designed to recognize patterns in sequences of data, such as text, genomes, handwriting, or spoken words. Unlike traditional neural networks, which assume that all inputs (and outputs) are independent of each other, RNNs have 'memory' about previous inputs. This allows them to make decisions based on the entire context, not just the current input.

Key Features of RNNs:

Memory: RNNs have loops that allow information to persist. In essence, they have a form of memory that captures information about what has been calculated so far.

Sequential Data: They are well-suited for sequential data, where the order of data points is important (like in a sentence where the arrangement of words affects the meaning).

Applications: RNNs are used in language modeling, text generation, speech recognition, and even in generating image descriptions.

Examples of RNN in Use:

Language Translation: Translating a sentence from one language to another while maintaining its grammatical structure and meaning.

Voice Recognition Systems: Converting spoken words into text by understanding the sequence and context of spoken language.

Text Prediction: When you type a message on your phone, and it suggests the next word, an RNN could be at work.

Why are RNNs Important?

Contextual Understanding: RNNs are capable of understanding the context in sequences of data, which is crucial for many AI applications like language translation and speech recognition.

Dynamic Inputs and Outputs: They can handle inputs and outputs of varying lengths, unlike traditional neural networks that require fixed-length inputs and outputs.

Remember:

Recurrent Neural Networks represent a significant advancement in AI, particularly in handling and making predictions based on sequential data. Their ability to remember past inputs allows them to understand context and sequence, making them particularly useful in language-related tasks and other areas where the sequence of data points is critical. Understanding RNNs is key to appreciating how AI can process and analyze data that changes over time or has an inherent order.

See also: Artificial Neural Network (ANN) (pg. 29)

Regression

Imagine you're a farmer trying to predict how much crop you'll harvest based on the amount of rainfall. You notice that as the rainfall increases, so does your crop yield, up to a certain point. This relationship between rainfall and crop yield is an example of what's called 'Regression' in the world of AI and ML.

In Topic(s): Data Analytics (DA) (pg. 223) | Data Science (DS) (pg. 227) | Fundamental Data Concepts (pg. 237) | Fundamental Mathematics and Statistics (pg. 241) | Industry Applications (pg. 247) | Machine Learning (ML) (pg. 250) | Supervised Learning (pg. 266)

Figure 73: A humorous illustration of "Regression".

What is Regression?

Regression is a method used in AI and ML for understanding the relationship between variables. It's about predicting a specific value (like crop yield) based on the values of other variables (like rainfall). In simpler terms, regression helps in predicting one thing based on other things.

Key Aspects of Regression:

Predicting Values: The main goal of regression is to predict the value of a 'dependent' variable based on the values of 'independent' variables.

Finding Relationships: It involves finding out how the dependent variable changes when any of the independent variables are varied.

Types of Regression: There are various types, like linear regression (where the relationship between variables is a straight line) and nonlinear regression (where the relationship is more complex).

Examples of Regression in Use:

Real Estate Prices: Predicting the price of a house based on factors like its size, location, and age.

Healthcare: Estimating a patient's recovery time based on variables like age, treatment type, and medical history.

Sales Forecasting: Predicting future sales based on current spending trends and economic conditions.

Academic Performance: Assessing how factors like study time, class attendance, and sleep impact a student's grades.

Climate Change Studies: Estimating changes in temperature or sea level based on greenhouse gas emissions.

Remember:

Regression is a powerful tool in AI and ML for making predictions and understanding the relationships between different variables. It's used in various fields to analyze trends, forecast future scenarios, and make informed decisions. Understanding regression is crucial for appreciating how we can use data to predict outcomes and uncover patterns in the world around us.

See also: Classification (pg. 41)

Reinforcement Learning (RL)

Imagine you're teaching your dog a new trick. You reward him with a treat when he does it right and give no treat when he doesn't. Gradually, he learns to perform the trick correctly more often to get more treats. This process of learning through rewards and penalties is similar to 'Reinforcement Learning' in AI and ML.

In Topic(s): Artificial Intelligence (AI) (pg. 210) | Core Applications (pg. 218) | Cutting-edge Technologies (pg. 221) | Data Analytics (DA) (pg. 223) | Data Science (DS) (pg. 227) | Emerging Technologies (pg. 233) | Ethical AI, Social Implications and Cultural Considerations (pg. 235) | Future Directions, Trends and Challenges (pg. 243) | Industry Applications (pg. 247) | Machine Learning (ML) (pg. 250) | Reinforcement Learning (pg. 259) | Robotics (pg. 260) | Supervised Learning (pg. 266)

Figure 74: A delightful illustration of "Reinforcement Learning (RL)".

What is Reinforcement Learning?

Reinforcement Learning (RL) is a type of machine learning where an AI 'agent' learns to make decisions by performing actions and receiving feedback in the form of rewards or penalties. The goal is to learn a strategy, called a policy, that will earn the most reward over time.

Key Features of Reinforcement Learning:

Trial and Error: The AI agent learns from the consequences of its actions, rather than from being told explicitly what to do.

Rewards and Penalties: Positive feedback (rewards) encourages the agent to repeat certain actions, while negative feedback (penalties) discourages others.

Learning a Policy: The agent develops a policy, which is a strategy for choosing actions based on the current state and the learned experiences.

Examples of Reinforcement Learning in Use:

Video Games: An AI agent learns to play a game, making moves and learning from winning or losing points.

Robotics: Robots learn to perform tasks, like picking up objects, by trying different methods and learning from successful outcomes.

Self-Driving Cars: These vehicles use RL to make decisions on the road, learning from various driving scenarios and outcomes.

Personalized Recommendations: Online platforms use RL to learn user preferences and improve content recommendations.

Finance: RL is used in algorithmic trading, where the system learns to make profitable trades based on market feedback.

Remember:

Reinforcement Learning is a dynamic and powerful approach in AI and ML, where learning is driven by interaction with the environment and feedback in terms of rewards and penalties. It mimics the way humans and animals learn from experience, making it a fascinating and effective method for teaching machines to make complex decisions and solve problems. Understanding RL is key to appreciating the adaptability and potential of AI in various challenging and dynamic applications.

See also: Agent (pg. 21)

Reward Signal

Imagine you're training your dog to perform a new trick, such as rolling over. Each time your dog successfully completes the trick, you give it a treat. This treat acts as a positive reinforcement, signaling to your dog that it has done something right, encouraging it to repeat the behavior. In the realm of Artificial Intelligence (AI) and Machine Learning (ML), particularly in an area called reinforcement learning, a similar concept is employed, known as a "Reward Signal."

In Topic(s): Fundamental Mathematics and Statistics (pg. 241) | Reinforcement Learning (pg. 259)

Figure 75: A whimsical illustration of "Reward Signal".

What is a Reward Signal?

A Reward Signal is a form of feedback given to an AI system, indicating how well it is performing a given task. It's like the treat you give your dog; it tells the AI whether the actions it took were beneficial or detrimental towards achieving its goal. The AI uses these signals to adjust its behavior, learning over time which actions lead to positive outcomes and which do not, thereby improving its performance on the task at hand.

Key Features of Reward Signals:

Feedback Loop: Just as your dog uses your feedback (treats or no treats) to guide its learning, an AI system relies on reward signals to understand the consequences of its actions, forming the basis of its learning process.

Positive and Negative Reinforcement: Reward signals can be positive (like a treat for your dog, indicating a good action) or negative (like withholding a treat, indicating an undesirable action), guiding the AI towards more favorable behaviors.

Goal-Oriented Learning: The ultimate purpose of reward signals is to align the AI's actions with a specific goal or task, much like training your dog to perform a specific trick.

Examples of Reward Signals in Use:

Video Games: In training AI to play video games, a reward signal might be the game score. Positive actions (like defeating an enemy) increase the score, while negative actions (like losing a life) decrease it. The AI learns to maximize its score by taking more beneficial actions.

Autonomous Vehicles: For a self-driving car, staying within the lane and maintaining a safe distance from other vehicles might generate positive reward signals, while veering off course or braking too hard might produce negative ones. The car learns safe driving behaviors by seeking to maximize these positive rewards.

Robotics: A robot learning to navigate a maze might receive positive rewards for moving closer to the exit and negative rewards for hitting walls. Over time, it learns the most efficient path through the maze by following the trail of positive rewards.

Personalized Recommendations: An AI system recommending movies or products might receive positive reward signals when a user accepts a recommendation and negative signals when a recommendation is ignored, helping it to refine its understanding of user preferences over time.

Remember:

Reward Signals are a crucial component of reinforcement learning in AI, serving as the guiding feedback that teaches systems how to behave or perform tasks more effectively. By understanding the role of reward signals, we can appreciate how AI systems learn from their interactions with the environment, continually adjusting and improving their actions to achieve their goals, much like a pet learning a new trick through the reinforcement of treats. This concept highlights the dynamic, interactive nature of learning in AI, where each action and its outcome contribute to the system's growing knowledge and capabilities.

See also: Reinforcement Learning (RL) (pg. 150)

Rotation Prediction

Imagine you're holding a photograph in your hand, and for some reason, it's been flipped upside down. Your brain effortlessly recognizes that the image is rotated and instinctively knows how to turn it to view it correctly. This ability to detect and correct the orientation of objects is not just a human skill; it's also a task we can teach machines, especially in the realm of Artificial Intelligence (AI) and Machine Learning (ML), through a process known as Rotation Prediction.

In Topic(s): Computer Vision (CV) (pg. 216) | Image Processing (pg. 245)

Figure 76: A playful illustration of "Rotation Prediction".

What is Rotation Prediction?

Rotation Prediction is a task we give to AI systems to help them understand and learn about the visual world. In this task, images are intentionally rotated by various degrees, and the AI's job is to predict how much the image has been rotated to bring it back to its original, upright position. This process is not just about recognizing angles; it's a way for the AI to deeply analyze the content of the image, understand its structure, and learn about the objects it contains by observing them from different perspectives.

Key Aspects of Rotation Prediction:

Visual Understanding: Just as you intuitively know how to orient a photograph correctly, Rotation Prediction helps AI systems develop a deeper understanding of images, enhancing their ability to recognize and interpret visual data.

Learning from Different Perspectives: By analyzing rotated images, AI learns that objects and scenes can appear differently depending on the viewpoint, much like recognizing a friend even when they're standing on their head.

Feature Learning: This task encourages the AI to pay attention to important visual features within images, such as edges, shapes, and textures, which are crucial for understanding and recognizing objects, regardless of orientation.

Examples of Rotation Prediction in Use:

Image Sorting and Organization: For photo management software, Rotation Prediction can automatically correct the orientation of uploaded images, ensuring that all photos are displayed correctly without manual adjustment.

Augmented Reality (AR) Applications: In AR, understanding the orientation of objects is crucial for accurately overlaying digital information onto the real world. Rotation Prediction helps AR systems comprehend the 3D structure of the environment.

Robotics: Robots equipped with cameras use Rotation Prediction to understand their surroundings better, allowing them to navigate and interact with objects effectively, even when their view is obstructed or unusual.

Medical Imaging: In analyzing medical scans, Rotation Prediction can help in automatically adjusting the orientation of images for better readability and diagnosis, ensuring that scans are consistently presented to medical professionals.

Remember:

Rotation Prediction is a fascinating and practical task in AI and ML, teaching systems to understand and interpret the visual world by recognizing and adjusting the orientation of images. This capability not only enhances the AI's ability to analyze and interact with images but also serves as a foundation for more complex visual understanding tasks, from organizing photos to enabling sophisticated robotics and AR experiences. By learning how to predict and correct rotations, AI systems gain a more nuanced understanding of the visual cues that define our world, making them more adept at navigating and interpreting the vast array of visual information they encounter.

See also: Self-Supervised Learning (pg. 158)

Scikit Learn

Imagine you have a vast collection of recipes from all over the world, and you want to organize them in a way that helps you decide what to cook based on the ingredients you have, the cuisine you're craving, and the cooking time you're willing to commit. You could sort them manually, but that would take forever. Instead, you use a sophisticated recipe organizer that automatically categorizes your recipes, suggests dishes based on your preferences, and even learns from your past choices to make better recommendations in the future. This organizer is akin to Scikit-learn, a powerful tool used in the realm of data science and machine learning.

Figure 77: A delightful illustration of "Scikit Learn".

What is Scikit-learn?

Scikit-learn is a free software library for the Python programming language that's used to understand and analyze data. It's like a Swiss Army knife for data scientists, packed with tools for performing various machine learning tasks, such as classifying data, predicting outcomes, and organizing information.

Core Features of Scikit-learn:

Versatility: Scikit-learn provides a wide array of algorithms for different tasks, much like how a versatile kitchen appliance can blend, chop, and puree.

Ease of Use: The library is designed to be accessible, allowing you to perform complex data analysis and predictive modeling with relatively simple commands, similar to using a smart appliance with user-friendly controls.

Integration: It works well with other Python libraries used for data manipulation and analysis, such as NumPy and pandas, akin to how different kitchen gadgets might work together seamlessly in preparing a meal.

Examples of Scikit-learn in Action:

Spam Detection in Emails: Just as a mail organizer separates junk mail from important letters, Scikit-learn can be used to train a computer to distinguish between spam and non-spam emails.

Customer Segmentation: Imagine a store wanting to group customers based on their shopping habits to tailor marketing strategies. Scikit-learn can analyze customer data and segment them into distinct groups, much like sorting a mixed bag of groceries into categories.

Real Estate Price Prediction: If you're looking to buy a house and want to know if a listing is priced right, Scikit-learn can use information from past sales to predict the price of a house based on its features, like location, size, and number of bedrooms.

Image Recognition: Scikit-learn can help in identifying objects in images, similar to how a photo organizer might tag and sort your pictures based on the people or objects in them.

Why Scikit-learn Stands Out:

Community Support: It has a large and active community, ensuring the library is constantly updated, improved, and well-documented, much like a popular cooking app that's regularly updated with new recipes and features.

Educational Value: Scikit-learn is not just a tool for professionals; it's also a learning resource for those new to data science, offering extensive documentation and tutorials, akin to a cookbook with detailed recipes and cooking tips for beginners.

Remember:

Scikit-learn is a cornerstone in the field of machine learning, offering a comprehensive toolkit for data analysis and predictive modeling. It simplifies the process of extracting insights from data, making it accessible not just to experts but to anyone with an interest in understanding the patterns and predictions hidden within their data. Just as a well-organized recipe collection can inspire and facilitate great cooking, Scikit-learn empowers users to make informed decisions, uncover hidden insights, and create innovative solutions across various domains.

See also: Machine Learning (ML) (pg. 12)

Self-Supervised Learning

Imagine you're a detective trying to solve a mystery without any direct clues. You don't have a clear list of suspects or evidence to guide you, but you do have some subtle hints scattered around the crime scene. Your task is to piece together these clues and gradually uncover the truth. This process of solving the mystery using the available hints is somewhat akin to how Self-Supervised Learning works in the world of Artificial Intelligence (AI) and Machine Learning (ML).

In Topic(s): Artificial Intelligence (AI) (pg. 210) | Cutting-edge Technologies (pg. 221) | Emerging Technologies (pg. 233) | Future Directions, Trends and Challenges (pg. 243) | Machine Learning (ML) (pg. 250) | Self-supervised Learning (pg. 261)

Figure 78: A lighthearted illustration of "Self-Supervised Learning".

What is Self-Supervised Learning?

In the realm of AI and ML, Self-Supervised Learning is a type of learning where a model learns to understand and represent the underlying structure of the data without explicit supervision or labeled examples. Instead of relying on labeled data provided by humans, the model generates its own labels or objectives from the input data itself.

Key Aspects of Self-Supervised Learning:

Generating Labels from Data: In Self-Supervised Learning, the model creates its own labels or tasks based on the available input data. These tasks are designed to encourage the model to learn meaningful representations of the data without needing human-labeled examples.

Unsupervised-like Learning: While Self-Supervised Learning doesn't rely on human-labeled data, it shares some similarities with unsupervised learning, where the model learns to find patterns or structure in unlabeled data. However, in Self-Supervised Learning, the model typically generates its own 'pseudo-labels' to guide the learning process.

Example-based Learning: Even though Self-Supervised Learning doesn't require human-labeled data, it still learns from examples. These examples are often generated from the input data itself, using techniques like data augmentation or context prediction.

Examples of Self-Supervised Learning in Use:

Image Representation Learning: In image processing tasks, Self-Supervised Learning can be used to learn useful representations of images without explicit labels. For example, the model might be trained to predict the rotation angle of an image patch based on the original image, forcing it to capture meaningful features like edges and textures.

Natural Language Understanding: In Natural Language Processing (NLP), Self-Supervised Learning techniques can be applied to learn word embeddings or sentence representations. For instance, the model might be trained to predict the missing word in a sentence based on the surrounding context, leading to the acquisition of rich semantic representations.

Video Analysis: Self-Supervised Learning can also be employed in video analysis tasks. For instance, a model might be trained to predict the next frame in a video sequence based on preceding frames, helping it to capture temporal dependencies and learn about motion and dynamics in videos.

Remember:

Self-Supervised Learning is a powerful approach in AI and ML where models learn to understand the structure of data without explicit human supervision. By generating their own labels or objectives from the input data, these models can effectively capture meaningful representations, making them versatile and adaptable across various domains and tasks. It's an innovative technique that leverages the inherent information present in the data itself to drive the learning process, leading to more autonomous and intelligent systems.

See also: Semi-Supervised Learning (pg. 164)

Self-training

Imagine you're learning to play a new musical instrument, like the guitar. Initially, you might start with a few basic chords and songs, practicing them until you're comfortable. As you get better, you challenge yourself with more complex pieces, using the skills you've mastered as a foundation to tackle harder challenges. This process of building upon your own learning and gradually increasing the difficulty is akin to the concept of Self-Training in Artificial Intelligence (AI) and Machine Learning (ML).

Figure 79: A quirky illustration of "Self-training".

What is Self-Training?

Self-Training is a technique in machine learning where a model, initially trained with a limited set of labeled data (data for which we know the correct outcome), begins to use its own predictions to further train and improve itself. The model starts by making predictions on unlabeled data (data without known outcomes). Then, it selects some of these predictions it's most confident about to use as new training examples, effectively learning from its own activity.

Key Elements of Self-Training:

Initial Learning Phase: Just like learning the basic chords on a guitar, the model first learns from a small, labeled dataset to understand the basics of the task at hand.

Prediction on Unlabeled Data: The model then applies what it has learned to make predictions on unlabeled data, similar to playing a new song by ear based on your understanding of music.

Confidence Assessment: The model evaluates how confident it is in its own predictions. This is akin to listening to yourself play and deciding if it sounds right.

Incorporating Self-Predictions: The most confident predictions are treated as new truths (labeled data) and added to the training set. It's like adding more songs to your repertoire that you've learned by yourself.

Iterative Improvement: The process repeats, with the model continuously learning from its own predictions, gradually improving over time, much like how your guitar skills improve as you learn from your own practice.

Examples of Self-Training in Use:

Language Translation: A translation model might start with basic translations and then use self-training to improve its ability to translate more complex sentences, learning from its own successes.

Speech Recognition: Initially trained on a small set of voice commands, a speech recognition system can use self-training to expand its understanding and accurately recognize a wider variety of phrases and accents.

Image Classification: An image classifier might begin by recognizing simple objects and then employ self-training to refine its ability to identify more complex scenes or objects with subtle distinctions.

Sentiment Analysis: A model trained to understand basic positive or negative sentiments in text can use self-training to grasp more nuanced emotions or sarcasm in a broader array of text sources.

Remember:

Self-Training in AI and ML is a powerful method that allows models to enhance their learning beyond the initial training phase, using their own predictions to expand their knowledge and capabilities. This approach not only makes efficient use of available unlabeled data but also enables models to adapt and improve continually, much like a musician mastering their instrument by building on their own learning and practice. Understanding self-training helps illuminate how AI systems can grow more sophisticated and accurate over time, reflecting a self-sustained learning journey that mirrors our own ways of learning and improving in various skills.

See also: Semi-Supervised Learning (pg. 164)

Semi-Structured Data

Imagine you're organizing a collection of documents, some of which are neatly labeled and organized into folders, while others are more like a pile of papers scattered on a desk. The neatly labeled documents are easy to categorize and understand, while the scattered papers may have some order but lack a clear structure. Semi-structured data is similar

–it has some organization, but it's not as rigidly structured as traditional databases or spreadsheets.

In Topic(s): Data Science (DS) (pg. 227) | Fundamental Data Concepts (pg. 237)

Figure 80: A delightful illustration of "Semi-Structured Data".

What is Semi-Structured Data?

Semi-Structured Data is information that doesn't fit neatly into traditional rows and columns like in a spreadsheet, but it's not entirely unstructured either. It contains some organization or hierarchy, often in the form of tags, labels, or key-value pairs, but it doesn't adhere to a strict schema or predefined data model.

Key Aspects of Semi-Structured Data:

Flexibility: Unlike structured data with fixed schemas, semi-structured data allows for more flexibility in how information is represented and stored. New attributes or fields can be added without requiring changes to the entire dataset.

Hierarchy: Semi-structured data often exhibits a hierarchical structure, where data elements are organized into nested levels or categories. This hierarchical organization provides a way to group related information together.

Variety of Formats: Semi-structured data can exist in various formats, including JSON (JavaScript Object Notation), XML (eXtensible Markup Language), YAML (YAML Ain't Markup Language), and others. These formats provide ways to represent complex data structures with nested relationships.

Examples of Semi-Structured Data:

JSON Data: JSON (JavaScript Object Notation) is a common format for semi-structured data used in web applications and APIs. It consists of key-value pairs enclosed in curly braces, allowing for nested structures and flexible data representation.

XML Documents: XML (eXtensible Markup Language) is another format for semi-structured data commonly used for representing hierarchical data with nested elements.

Web Page Content: Web pages often contain semi-structured data in the form of HTML (Hypertext Markup Language). While HTML provides structure for organizing content (e.g., headings, paragraphs), it also allows flexibility in how content is presented and formatted.

Remember:

Semi-Structured Data is a flexible and hierarchical form of information that falls somewhere between structured and unstructured data. It allows for varying degrees of organization and can be represented in different formats like JSON, XML, or HTML. Understanding semi-structured data is essential for effectively managing and analyzing diverse data sources, especially in modern web applications and data-driven systems.

See also: Structured Data (pg. 168)

Semi-Supervised Learning

Let's say you're learning to identify different types of trees. You start with a few trees that an expert has already identified for you. Using this knowledge, you then try to identify other trees on your own, even those you haven't seen before. This approach of learning with a mix of known (labeled) and unknown (unlabeled) examples is what we call 'Semi-Supervised Learning' in AI and ML.

In Topic(s): Machine Learning (ML) (pg. 250) | Semi-supervised Learning (pg. 262)

Figure 81: A playful illustration of "Semi-Supervised Learning".

What is Semi-Supervised Learning?

Semi-Supervised Learning is a method in AI and ML where the learning process uses a combination of a small amount of labeled data (data where the answer is known) and a larger amount of unlabeled data (data where the answer is not known). It's a middle ground between supervised learning (where all data is labeled) and unsupervised learning (where no data is labeled).

Key Elements of Semi-Supervised Learning:

Combining Labeled and Unlabeled Data: The algorithm learns from both the labeled data provided and the patterns it finds in the unlabeled data.

Cost-Effective Learning: Since labeling data can be expensive and time-consuming, using a larger amount of unlabeled data can be more cost-effective.

Enhancing Learning Accuracy: The combination of both types of data can improve the accuracy and robustness of the learning process.

Examples of Semi-Supervised Learning in Use:

Image Recognition: An AI system is trained with some labeled images (e.g., pictures of cats with a label 'cat') and then uses a large set of unlabeled images to further refine its ability to recognize cats.

Web Content Classification: A model is initially trained with a small set of web pages that have been categorized and then uses a much larger set of uncategorized pages to improve its classification skills.

Speech Analysis: An AI system learns from a small amount of transcribed audio (labeled) and then applies this knowledge to a larger set of untranscribed audio (unlabeled) to improve its speech recognition capabilities.

Remember:

Semi-Supervised Learning is an effective approach in AI and ML, especially when it's difficult or impractical to obtain a large set of labeled data. By leveraging the strengths of both labeled and unlabeled data, it provides a balanced and efficient way for machines to learn and improve their accuracy. Understanding this concept is key to recognizing how AI models can be trained effectively, even with limited direct information.

See also: Self-Supervised Learning (pg. 158)

Smart Contract

Imagine you're setting up a vending machine. You program it so that whenever someone inserts the correct amount of money and selects an item, the machine automatically dispenses that item. There's no need for a shopkeeper to check the money or hand you the item; the machine handles the transaction based on the rules you've set up. This self-executing process, driven by predefined rules and conditions, closely resembles the concept of a "Smart Contract" in the digital world.

In Topic(s): AI Governance (pg. 208) | Ethical AI, Social Implications and Cultural Considerations (pg. 235) | Industry Applications (pg. 247) | Privacy and Security (pg. 258)

Figure 82: A lighthearted illustration of "Smart Contract".

What is a Smart Contract?

A Smart Contract is a self-executing contract with the terms of the agreement directly written into lines of code. These contracts are stored and replicated on a blockchain system, making them secure and tamper-proof. Just like the vending machine automatically completes a transaction based on predefined rules, a Smart Contract automatically enforces and executes the terms of a contract when certain conditions are met, without the need for intermediaries.

Key Features of Smart Contracts:

Self-Executing: Once the conditions of the contract are met, it automatically executes the agreed-upon actions, like transferring funds or issuing a ticket.

Tamper-Proof: Stored on a blockchain, Smart Contracts are secure and cannot be altered, ensuring that the terms of the agreement are upheld.

Transparent: The terms of the Smart Contract are visible to all relevant parties, ensuring clarity and trust in the agreement.

Efficiency and Speed: By eliminating intermediaries and automating execution, Smart Contracts can significantly reduce processing times and costs.

Examples of Smart Contracts in Use:

Real Estate Transactions: Imagine buying a house where, upon receiving your payment, the ownership of the property is automatically transferred to you, without the need for lawyers or real estate agents to verify and process the paperwork.

Supply Chain Management: In a supply chain, a Smart Contract could automatically release payment to a supplier once a tracking system confirms that a shipment has reached its destination.

Voting Systems: Smart Contracts could be used to create secure and transparent voting systems, where votes are automatically tallied, and results are immediately available once the voting period ends, without any possibility of tampering.

Importance of Smart Contracts:

Trust and Security: Smart Contracts provide a high level of security and enforceability, reducing the risk of fraud or non-compliance.

Cost Reduction: By automating tasks that were traditionally handled by intermediaries (like lawyers, brokers, and banks), Smart Contracts can significantly reduce transaction costs.

Innovation: Smart Contracts enable new types of agreements and business models, particularly in decentralized and automated systems, fostering innovation across various sectors.

Remember:

Smart Contracts revolutionize traditional agreements by embedding the terms directly into code and automatically executing them when conditions are met, much like a vending machine that delivers a product once the correct payment is inserted. This automation enhances trust, security, and efficiency in transactions, paving the way for innovative business practices and reducing the need for intermediaries. Understanding Smart Contracts is key to grasping the potential of blockchain technology to transform a wide range of industries and interactions.

See also: Automated Machine Learning (AutoML) (pg. 37)

Structured Data

Imagine walking into a well-organized library where every book has a specific place based on its genre, author, and title. You can easily find a cookbook, a novel, or a science encyclopedia because everything is categorized and labeled, following a clear system. This library is a lot like "Structured Data" in the digital world—a way of organizing information so that it's easily accessible and understandable, both by humans and computers.

In Topic(s): Data Analytics (DA) (pg. 223) | Data Science (DS) (pg. 227) | Fundamental Data Concepts (pg. 237)

Figure 83: An amusing illustration of "Structured Data".

What is Structured Data?

Structured Data refers to any type of data that is organized in a predefined format, typically stored in tables like those you'd find in a spreadsheet or a database. Each table is like a bookshelf in our library analogy, where the columns are the categories (like author, title, genre) and each row is a specific book, with details filled in for each category.

Key Features of Structured Data:

Organization: Structured data is highly organized, much like the books in a library. It follows a specific schema or blueprint that dictates how the data is stored and arranged.

Ease of Access: Because of its organization, structured data can be easily searched and retrieved. It's like knowing exactly where to find a cookbook on Italian cuisine in our library.

Compatibility with Systems: Most traditional databases and data processing systems are designed to handle structured data, making it widely compatible and useful in various technological contexts.

Examples of Structured Data:

Customer Databases: Imagine a business that keeps a database of customer information. Each customer's name, address, phone number, and email would be stored in separate columns within a table, making it easy to manage and query.

Inventory Lists: A retail store might have an inventory list in a structured format, with columns for item ID, description, price, and quantity in stock, helping them keep track of their products efficiently.

Employee Records: A company's HR system might use structured data to store employee information, including ID numbers, names, positions, and departments.

Why Structured Data is Important:

Efficiency: Structured data allows for quick and efficient processing, analysis, and retrieval of information, saving time and resources.

Accuracy: The clear organization minimizes the chances of errors and inconsistencies in data handling.

Decision Making: With data that's easily accessible and analyzable, businesses and organizations can make informed decisions based on accurate, up-to-date information.

Challenges with Structured Data:

Rigidity: The predefined nature of structured data means it's not as flexible for storing data that doesn't fit neatly into tables, such as text, images, or unstructured notes.

Scalability: As the amount and variety of data grow, maintaining and scaling structured databases can become challenging, requiring careful planning and management.

Remember:

Structured Data is like the backbone of data organization, providing a clear and efficient way to store, retrieve, and analyze information. Its role is akin to that of a well-organized library, ensuring that every piece of information has its place and can be easily accessed when needed. Understanding and leveraging structured data is crucial in a data-driven world, enabling businesses, scientists, and individuals to make sense of and utilize their information effectively.

See also: Semi-Structured Data (pg. 162)

Supervised Learning

Imagine you're teaching a child to identify different types of fruits. You show them an apple and say, "This is an apple," then a banana with, "This is a banana," and so on. With each example, the child learns to associate the specific look of each fruit with its name. Over time, even when presented with a fruit they haven't seen before, they can make a good guess about what it might be by relating it to what they've already learned. This process of teaching by example and guiding the learning through direct feedback is akin to the concept of Supervised Learning in Artificial Intelligence (AI) and Machine Learning (ML).

In Topic(s): Artificial Intelligence (AI) (pg. 210) | Core Applications (pg. 218) | Data Science (DS) (pg. 227) | Ethical AI, Social Implications and Cultural Considerations (pg. 235) | Machine Learning (ML) (pg. 250) | Supervised Learning (pg. 266)

Figure 84: A humorous illustration of "Supervised Learning".

What is Supervised Learning?

Supervised Learning is a type of AI and ML where the computer is taught to do something using examples. Just like teaching the child about fruits, in supervised learning, an AI model is given a set of data where the 'answer' (like the fruit's name) is already known. This data set is often called 'labeled data.' The model uses these examples to learn how to identify or predict the answers for new, unseen data.

Key Elements of Supervised Learning:

Labeled Data: This is the set of data that's already tagged with the correct answers, similar to how each fruit shown to the child is named. It's the foundational information that the model learns from.

Training: This is the learning phase, where the model goes through the labeled data, trying to understand the patterns or features that correspond to each label, much like the child memorizes and understands what makes an apple an apple.

Prediction: After training, the model can start making predictions or identifications on new data it hasn't seen before, using the knowledge it gained during training.

Feedback and Improvement: Often, the model's predictions are checked, and any mistakes are used to further improve its learning, refining its ability to make more accurate predictions in the future.

Examples of Supervised Learning in Use:

Email Filtering: Email services use supervised learning to distinguish between 'spam' and 'non-spam' by learning from examples of both types that have been labeled by users.

Medical Diagnosis: AI systems can help diagnose diseases by learning from a database of patient records where the diagnosis is known, allowing them to identify patterns associated with specific conditions.

Credit Scoring: Financial institutions use supervised learning to predict creditworthiness by learning from historical customer data where the outcomes (like who defaulted on a loan) are known.

Facial Recognition: Security systems and social media platforms use supervised learning to recognize individuals in images by learning from a labeled dataset of faces.

Remember:

Supervised Learning is a powerful method in AI and ML that mimics the way humans often learn–through examples and guidance. By training on labeled data, AI models can learn to make predictions, identify patterns, and make decisions, applying this knowledge to new, unseen data. Understanding supervised learning allows us to appreciate how AI can be tailored to specific tasks, from everyday applications like email filtering to complex challenges like medical diagnoses, enhancing both the convenience and efficiency of various processes in our lives.

See also: Classification (pg. 41) | Semi-Supervised Learning (pg. 164) | Unsupervised Learning (pg. 196)

Target Variable

Imagine you're playing a game of darts. Your main aim is to hit the bullseye. In this game, the bullseye is your target–it's what you're aiming for. In the field of AI and machine learning, the concept of a "Target Variable" is similar. It's the specific thing you're trying to predict or understand through your model.

In Topic(s): Fundamental Data Concepts (pg. 237) | Supervised Learning (pg. 266)

Figure 85: An amusing illustration of "Target Variable".

What is a Target Variable?

A Target Variable, also known as a dependent variable, is what you're trying to predict or explain in a machine learning model. It's the main focus of your model's task. When you feed data into a machine learning algorithm, you're usually trying to find out something specific about this data, and the target variable is that specific thing.

Key Aspects of Target Variables:

Focus of Prediction: The target variable is what your model is trained to predict or estimate.

Dependent on Other Variables: It's called 'dependent' because its value depends on other variables in your data, known as independent variables or features.

Type of Tasks: In classification tasks, the target variable is categorical (like 'spam' or 'not spam'). In regression tasks, it's numerical (like house prices).

Outcome Measurement: The accuracy of a machine learning model is often determined by how well it can predict the target variable.

Examples of Target Variables in Use:

Weather Prediction: If you're building a model to predict the temperature, 'temperature' is your target variable.

Credit Approval: In a model predicting whether a loan should be approved, the target variable is the loan approval status (approved or not approved).

Sales Forecasting: For a model predicting next month's sales, the amount of sales (in dollars or units) is the target variable.

Remember:

The Target Variable in machine learning is the main element you're trying to predict or analyze. It's the 'bullseye' of your data analysis effort, guiding the focus and purpose of your model. Understanding the target variable is essential for developing effective machine learning models that accurately predict outcomes or glean insights from data.

See also: Supervised Learning (pg. 170)

Temporal Order Prediction

Imagine you're watching a series of short video clips from a day in the life of a farmer. The clips are out of order, showing various activities such as feeding the animals, harvesting crops, and having lunch. Your task is to arrange these clips in the order they likely occurred, using clues like the position of the sun, the farmer's tasks, and the sequence of daily routines. This challenge of piecing together the sequence based on the context and logical progression of events is akin to the concept of Temporal Order Prediction in Artificial Intelligence (AI) and Machine Learning (ML).

Figure 86: A playful illustration of "Temporal Order Prediction".

What is Temporal Order Prediction?

Temporal Order Prediction is a task in AI where a model learns to understand and predict the sequence or order of events over time. It involves analyzing data that occurs in a series, like frames in a video, words in a sentence, or steps in a process, and determining the correct chronological order. This ability helps AI systems grasp the concept of time and causality in data, allowing them to make sense of sequences and predict future events based on observed patterns.

Key Elements of Temporal Order Prediction:

Sequence Understanding: Just as you deduce the farmer's daily routine, AI models learn to recognize patterns and relationships in sequences, understanding how one event leads to another.

Contextual Clues: Models use contextual information, much like you might use the sun's position to guess the time of day in the farmer's clips, to understand the temporal relationship between events.

Predicting Progressions: The aim is not just to understand existing sequences but also to predict the next steps in a sequence, like forecasting what the farmer might do after harvesting crops.

Examples of Temporal Order Prediction in Use:

Video Analysis: In security footage analysis, AI can predict potential security breaches by understanding the usual sequence of activities and identifying deviations that might indicate suspicious behavior.

Predictive Text and Auto-Complete: When you type a message, AI predicts the next word based on the temporal order of words in a sentence, improving efficiency in communication.

Sports Coaching: AI can analyze sequences of an athlete's movements to predict and improve performance outcomes, suggesting corrections and enhancements.

Medical Diagnosis: By studying the progression of symptoms over time, AI can predict the development of diseases or conditions, aiding in early diagnosis and treatment planning.

Remember:

Temporal Order Prediction enables AI systems to understand and anticipate the flow of events over time, a crucial aspect of interpreting real-world data and making informed predictions. By learning the sequence and context of events, AI can assist in a wide range of applications, from enhancing security to supporting healthcare, offering insights that are not only reactive to the present but also predictive of the future. This concept showcases the growing ability of AI to process and interpret complex sequences, mirroring human cognitive skills in understanding time-based patterns and causality.

See also: Self-Supervised Learning (pg. 158)

TensorFlow

Imagine you have a set of advanced Lego blocks, each with a specific function. Some blocks can perform calculations, while others can hold data. Now, if you want to build a complex structure, you'd strategically assemble these blocks to create it. TensorFlow, in the realm of AI and ML, is somewhat like this set of specialized Lego blocks. It's a tool that allows developers to build and train complex machine learning models by assembling 'blocks' of code.

In Topic(s): AI Hardware and Accelerators (pg. 209)

Figure 87: A humorous illustration of "TensorFlow".

What is TensorFlow?

TensorFlow is an open-source software library created by Google for building and training machine learning models. It provides a range of tools and libraries that make it easier to develop AI applications. TensorFlow is especially known for its capabilities in handling tensors, which are the multi-dimensional arrays of data we use in machine learning.

Key Features of TensorFlow:

Flexible Architecture: TensorFlow allows users to create complex models with various levels of abstraction, making it suitable for both beginners and experts.

Handling of Tensors: As its name suggests, TensorFlow excels at processing tensors, which are crucial in machine learning for handling large datasets.

Automatic Differentiation: TensorFlow can automatically calculate derivatives, a key feature needed in optimization algorithms for machine learning models.

Scalability: TensorFlow is designed to scale from running on a single machine to large clusters of computers, making it suitable for a wide range of applications.

Visualizations: With tools like TensorBoard, TensorFlow provides powerful visualizations, making it easier to understand and debug models.

Examples of TensorFlow in Use:

Image Recognition: TensorFlow can be used to create models that identify objects or people in images, useful in applications like photo tagging or security systems.

Voice Recognition: It's also used in building models for voice recognition, enabling applications like virtual assistants to understand spoken commands.

Predictive Analytics: Companies use TensorFlow for predictive analytics, like forecasting sales or customer behavior based on historical data.

Healthcare Research: In healthcare, TensorFlow is used for tasks like analyzing medical images to assist in diagnosing diseases.

Remember:

TensorFlow is a versatile and powerful tool in the field of AI and ML, enabling the creation, training, and deployment of sophisticated machine learning models. Its ability to process large amounts of data and its user-friendly interface have made it a popular choice among developers and researchers. Understanding TensorFlow is key to appreciating how complex AI tasks are tackled and the wide array of applications it enables.

See also: PyTorch (pg. 142)

Text Data

Imagine walking into a vast library filled with every kind of written material you can think of: books, newspapers, magazines, personal diaries, letters, and even digital content like blogs, emails, and social media posts. Each piece of writing, whether printed on paper or displayed on a screen, is a treasure trove of information, stories, facts, opinions, and ideas. This entire collection of written words, in all its varied forms, represents what we call "Text Data" in the digital age, especially within the realms of Artificial Intelligence (AI) and Machine Learning (ML).

In Topic(s): Natural Language Processing (NLP) (pg. 254) | Natural Language Understanding (NLU) (pg. 256) | Text and Language Processing (pg. 270)

Figure 88: A cheery illustration of "Text Data".

What is Text Data?

Text Data refers to any information that is recorded in written form. It can range from structured documents, like a database of book titles and authors, to unstructured narratives, like the endless stream of posts on social media platforms. Text Data is the raw material that AI and ML technologies process, analyze, and interpret to uncover patterns, trends, sentiments, and insights that might not be immediately apparent to the human eye.

Key Features of Text Data:

Volume: Text Data is abundant and continuously growing, with millions of words generated every minute through emails, social media, news articles, and more.

Variety: It comes in many forms and styles, from the formal, structured language of scientific papers to the informal, colloquial expressions found in text messages and comments.

Veracity: The quality and reliability of Text Data can vary greatly, with some sources providing accurate, well-researched information, and others spreading rumors or misinformation.

Value: Despite the challenges, Text Data holds immense potential value, offering insights into human behavior, preferences, trends, and societal shifts.

Examples of Text Data in Use:

Customer Service: Businesses analyze customer inquiries, feedback, and reviews to understand common concerns, improve products or services, and enhance customer satisfaction.

Market Research: Companies and analysts sift through news articles, forum discussions, and social media to gauge public sentiment about products, services, or brands and to spot emerging trends.

Healthcare: Researchers study medical records, patient notes, and research articles to identify patterns in diseases, treatments, and patient outcomes, leading to better healthcare strategies.

Education: Text Data from course feedback, online forums, and educational materials is analyzed to improve teaching methods, curricula, and learning resources.

Remember:

Text Data is an all-encompassing term that captures the vast universe of written content, both offline and online. In the context of AI and ML, it is both a challenge and an opportunity, offering a rich vein of insights waiting to be mined. Understanding Text Data and its implications is essential for harnessing the power of language, enabling us to make informed decisions, predict future trends, and uncover the deeper meanings hidden within the words we create and share every day.

See also: Audio Data (pg. 33)

Text Generation

Imagine you're a storyteller crafting a new tale. You start with a few words or ideas and gradually build upon them, stringing together sentences to create a narrative. Now, suppose you have a magical pen that can write stories for you based on the themes and styles you provide. This magical pen is somewhat like a Text Generation model in the world of Artificial Intelligence (AI) and Machine Learning (ML).

In Topic(s): Core Applications (pg. 218) | Natural Language Processing (NLP) (pg. 254) | Text and Language Processing (pg. 270)

Figure 89: A playful illustration of "Text Generation".

What is Text Generation?

Text Generation is the process of using AI and ML techniques to automatically produce written text, such as sentences, paragraphs, or entire documents, based on input data or predefined patterns. These models learn to understand the structure and style of text and can generate new content that resembles human-written language.

Key Aspects of Text Generation:

Learning Language Patterns: Text Generation models are trained on large datasets of text to learn the underlying patterns and structures of language. They analyze how words, phrases, and sentences are typically arranged and use this knowledge to generate new text.

Conditional Generation: Some Text Generation models can generate text based on specific prompts or conditions provided by the user. For example, you could ask a model to write a poem about love, and it would generate text accordingly, drawing inspiration from the patterns it learned during training.

Quality vs. Creativity: Text Generation models vary in their ability to produce high-quality and creative content. Some models focus on generating text that is grammatically correct and coherent, while others prioritize generating novel and imaginative content, sometimes at the expense of accuracy.

Examples of Text Generation in Use:

Chatbots: Text Generation models power chatbots that engage in conversations with users. These chatbots can provide customer support, answer questions, or simulate human-like interactions in various applications.

Content Creation: Text Generation is used to automate content creation tasks, such as writing product descriptions, generating news articles, or creating marketing copy. This helps businesses produce large volumes of content quickly and efficiently.

Language Translation: Text Generation models are used in machine translation systems to convert text from one language to another. These models analyze the input text and generate a translated version that preserves the meaning and context as accurately as possible.

Creative Writing Assistance: Writers and authors use Text Generation tools to brainstorm ideas, overcome writer's block, or generate inspiration for their writing projects. These tools can suggest plotlines, character descriptions, or even generate entire passages of text based on user input.

Remember:

Text Generation is a fascinating application of AI and ML that enables the automatic production of written text. By learning from vast amounts of existing text data, Text Generation models can generate new content that resembles human-written language, opening up a wide range of possibilities in areas like communication, content creation, and creative writing. While these models still have limitations, they continue to improve in quality and capability, shaping the future of how we interact with and generate written text.

See also: Natural Language Generation (NLG) (pg. 124)

Text Summarization

Picture yourself after a long, bustling day, eager to catch up on the news, but the sheer volume of articles feels overwhelming. Now, imagine having a friend who's read all the news of the day and can give you a concise rundown of each story, highlighting the main points, so you're informed without having to read every word. This friend's knack for distilling information is akin to the process of Text Summarization in the realm of Artificial Intelligence (AI) and Machine Learning (ML).

In Topic(s): Core Applications (pg. 218) | Industry Applications (pg. 247) | Natural Language Processing (NLP) (pg. 254) | Natural Language Understanding (NLU) (pg. 256) | Text and Language Processing (pg. 270)

Figure 90: An amusing illustration of "Text Summarization".

What is Text Summarization?

Text Summarization is the AI-powered technique of condensing a large piece of text into a shorter version, capturing only the most essential points or the core essence of the original content. It's like boiling down a pot of broth until only the rich, concentrated flavors remain, ensuring you get all the taste without the bulk.

Core Principles of Text Summarization:

Extraction: This involves identifying key sentences or phrases from the text and pulling them out directly to form a summary, much like picking the ripest fruits from a tree to make a fruit salad.

Abstraction: A more complex approach where the AI rephrases or rewrites the main ideas in its own words, akin to painting a miniature version of a large landscape, capturing the essence without duplicating every detail.

Relevance and Coherence: The process ensures that the summary is not only concise but also maintains the logical flow and relevance of the original text, similar to telling a story where every sentence contributes to the overall narrative.

Context Preservation: Despite the reduction in length, the summary aims to preserve the context and intent of the original text, ensuring that the reader grasps the intended message or information.

Examples of Text Summarization in Action:

News Aggregation: Apps and websites that compile news stories often use text summarization to present brief versions of articles, allowing readers to skim through headlines and summaries to stay informed with minimal time investment.

Research: Academics and students use summarization tools to condense lengthy research papers or documents, enabling quick understanding of studies without reading through every page.

Business Reports: Executives and managers benefit from summarized versions of reports or meetings, capturing key points and decisions, facilitating efficient review and decision-making.

Email Management: Summarization can help in managing an overflowing inbox by providing briefs of long emails, ensuring important information is not missed in the deluge of communication.

Remember:

Text Summarization acts as a bridge between the information overload we face and our limited time to consume it, offering a distilled version of written content that retains the core message and essential details. In the fast-paced digital age, understanding and utilizing text summarization can significantly enhance our ability to stay informed and make informed decisions, making it a valuable tool in the arsenal of AI and ML technologies.

See also: Natural Language Generation (NLG) (pg. 124)

Train vs. Test

Imagine you're a chef developing a new recipe. Before presenting it to your guests, you need to practice and refine it to ensure it tastes just right. Now, suppose you divide your cooking process into two parts: the first part where you experiment and perfect the recipe (training), and the second part where you actually cook the dish for your guests (testing). This division of tasks parallels the concept of Train vs. Test in Machine Learning (ML).

In Topic(s): Data Science (DS) (pg. 227) | Machine Learning (ML) (pg. 250) | Supervised Learning (pg. 266)

Figure 91: A whimsical illustration of "Train vs. Test".

What is Train vs. Test?

In the realm of Machine Learning (ML), Train vs. Test refers to the division of data into two separate sets for the purpose of training and evaluating a machine learning model.

Key Aspects of Train vs. Test:

Training Data: The training set, often denoted as X_Train and y_Train, consists of a portion of the available data that is used to train or teach the machine learning model. This data contains input features (X_Train) and corresponding labels or outcomes (y_Train) that the model learns from.

Testing Data: The testing set, denoted as X_Test and y_Test, is another portion of the data that is kept separate from the training set. This set is used to evaluate the performance of the trained model on new, unseen examples. It helps assess how well the model generalizes to data it hasn't been explicitly trained on.

Preventing Overfitting: The division of data into training and testing sets helps prevent overfitting, a common issue in machine learning where the model learns the training data too well, including noise and irrelevant patterns. By evaluating the model's performance on unseen test data, we can ensure it has learned to make predictions or classifications accurately, not just memorized the training examples.

Examples of Train vs. Test in Use:

Email Spam Detection: Suppose you're building a model to classify emails as spam or not spam. You would divide your dataset of emails into two parts - one for training the model on examples of both spam and non-spam emails (training set), and another for evaluating how well the trained model identifies spam in new, unseen emails (testing set).

Handwritten Digit Recognition: For a model trained to recognize handwritten digits, you would split your dataset of digit images into a training set for teaching the model to identify patterns in handwritten digits, and a testing set for assessing its accuracy in recognizing new, unseen digit images.

Medical Diagnosis: In healthcare, you might develop a machine learning model to diagnose diseases based on patient data. The training set would include patient records with diagnoses, while the testing set would contain new patient cases for evaluating the model's diagnostic accuracy on unseen data.

Remember:

Train vs. Test is a fundamental concept in Machine Learning that involves dividing data into separate sets for training and evaluation purposes. By training the model on one portion of the data and testing it on another, we can ensure that the model learns to make accurate predictions or classifications on new, unseen examples. This division helps in assessing the model's ability to generalize to real-world data and prevents issues like overfitting, ultimately leading to more reliable and effective machine learning models.

See also: Cross-Validation (pg. 57)

Transformer Architecture

Think of a large, complex office building with many rooms and departments, each handling different tasks but all working together for the overall functioning of the office. In AI and machine learning, the "Transformer Architecture" is somewhat like this building. It's a framework made up of different components, each performing a specific function, and together they process and understand language in a sophisticated way.

In Topic(s): Artificial Intelligence (AI) (pg. 210) | Artificial Neural Networks (ANN) (pg. 214) | Cutting-edge Technologies (pg. 221) | Deep Learning (DL) (pg. 231) | Emerging Technologies (pg. 233) | Future Directions, Trends and Challenges (pg. 243) | Natural Language Processing (NLP) (pg. 254) | Natural Language Understanding (NLU) (pg. 256) | Sound and Audio Processing (pg. 264) | Text and Language Processing (pg. 270)

Figure 92: A charming illustration of "Transformer Architecture".

What is Transformer Architecture?

Transformer Architecture is a design or blueprint used in AI, particularly for tasks involving natural language processing (NLP). It's a model that's uniquely structured to handle sequential data, like text, in a way that's different from earlier models. Transformers can process entire sequences of data (like sentences or paragraphs) all at once, rather than one piece at a time.

Key Components of Transformer Architecture:

Attention Mechanism: The heart of the Transformer is the 'attention mechanism.' It allows the model to focus on different parts of the input data (like words in a sentence) and understand how they relate to each other.

Encoder and Decoder: The Transformer architecture typically has two main parts - the encoder and the decoder. The encoder processes the input data (like a sentence in English), while the decoder generates the output (like the translated sentence in French).

Parallel Processing: Unlike previous sequential models, Transformers process all parts of the data simultaneously. This parallel processing makes them faster and more efficient.

No Recurrence or Convolution: Transformers do not use recurrent layers (found in older models like RNNs) or convolutional layers (used in image processing), relying entirely on the attention mechanism to process data.

Examples of Transformer Architecture in Use:

Language Translation Services: Translating text from one language to another while maintaining context and meaning across entire sentences.

Content Generation: Writing coherent and contextually relevant articles or generating creative content based on certain prompts.

Speech Recognition: Converting spoken language into text, understanding the context and nuances of speech.

Question-Answering Systems: Systems that can understand a user's question and provide relevant and accurate answers.

Remember:

Transformer Architecture represents a groundbreaking approach in the field of NLP within AI. Its ability to process language data in parallel and understand the context and relationships within text has led to significant advancements in tasks like translation, content generation, and more. Understanding this architecture is essential for appreciating the complexities and capabilities of modern AI language processing systems.

See also: Deep Learning (DL) (pg. 69)

Tri-training

Imagine you're learning to cook a complex dish, and you have not one but three experienced chefs at your disposal. Each chef offers you advice and guidance based on their expertise, but they also consult with each other to ensure the best techniques and recipes are shared. As you progress, they compare notes on your performance, and if at least two chefs agree on a particular piece of advice or correction, they present it to you as a consensus to follow. This collaborative, reinforcing approach to learning and decision-making mirrors the essence of Tri-Training in the realm of Artificial Intelligence (AI) and Machine Learning (ML).

In Topic(s): Semi-supervised Learning (pg. 262)

Figure 93: A humorous illustration of "Tri-training".

What is Tri-Training?

Tri-Training is a technique in machine learning where three different models or learners are trained simultaneously on the same task. Initially, they learn from a small set of labeled data (where the correct outcomes are known). As they progress, they start making predictions on unlabeled data (where outcomes aren't known). If at least two of the models agree on a prediction for a piece of unlabeled data, that data, along with the agreed-upon label, is added to the training set. This process allows the models to 'learn' from each other, improving their accuracy and robustness over time through this collaborative effort.

Key Features of Tri-Training:

Collaborative Learning: Just as the chefs share their knowledge with you, the three models in tri-training share insights, learning from each other's predictions to improve their understanding of the task.

Consensus Decision-Making: The models only accept new training data when at least two of them agree on the outcome, similar to how the chefs' consensus on a cooking technique assures its reliability.

Expanding the Training Set: By adding new, pseudo-labeled data (unlabeled data that the models have confidently labeled) to the training set, the models continuously enrich their learning material, akin to how your cooking skills would improve as the chefs introduce more recipes and techniques.

Examples of Tri-Training in Use:

Spam Detection in Emails: Tri-training can help email systems identify and filter spam more effectively. As the models become more adept at recognizing spam, they can apply these insights to less clear-cut cases, refining the filtering process.

Sentiment Analysis in Social Media: In analyzing user comments to gauge public sentiment on various topics, tri-training allows models to become more nuanced in understanding context and subtleties in language, improving the accuracy of sentiment analysis.

Medical Image Classification: Tri-training can enhance the ability of AI systems to classify medical images, such as X-rays or MRI scans, by continuously refining their criteria for what constitutes different medical conditions based on model consensus.

Customer Support Automation: In automating responses to customer inquiries, tri-training can help ensure that the generated responses are accurate and contextually appropriate, improving over time as the models learn from a broader set of inquiries and responses.

Remember:

Tri-Training represents a collaborative and self-reinforcing approach to machine learning, where multiple models enhance their performance by learning from each other's successes. By requiring a consensus before accepting new data for training, this method ensures a higher level of reliability and accuracy in the models' predictions. Understanding tri-training illuminates how collaboration and shared learning principles can be applied in AI to tackle complex problems more effectively, much like how multiple experts can come together to enhance the learning experience in various fields.

See also: Semi-Supervised Learning (pg. 164)

Underfitting

Imagine you're trying to learn how to make a variety of dishes from a cookbook. If you only practice making a simple salad and then try to prepare a gourmet three-course meal, you'll likely fall short. This is because you haven't learned enough from your practice to handle more complex tasks. In the realm of Artificial Intelligence (AI) and Machine Learning (ML), this situation is akin to what we call "Underfitting."

Figure 94: A whimsical illustration of "Underfitting".

What is Underfitting?

Underfitting occurs when a machine learning model is too simple to capture the underlying patterns in the data it's trained on. Just like trying to tackle a complex meal with only basic cooking skills, an underfitted model can't make accurate predictions or decisions because it hasn't learned enough from its training data.

Key Aspects of Underfitting:

Simplicity: The model is too simple and doesn't have enough parameters or complexity to understand the data fully.

Poor Performance: Because the model is too basic, it performs poorly on both the training data (the data it learned from) and new, unseen data.

Lack of Learning: The model hasn't captured the essential patterns or relationships in the training data, leading to inaccurate or oversimplified predictions.

Examples of Underfitting:

Weather Prediction: If a model is trained to predict the weather using only temperature data, ignoring factors like humidity, wind speed, and atmospheric pressure, it's likely to underfit. This means it won't accurately predict the weather because it's not considering all relevant variables.

Stock Market Analysis: An underfitted model might use only past stock prices to predict future prices, neglecting other influential factors like economic indicators, market sentiment, and company news. As a result, its predictions would likely be inaccurate.

Medical Diagnosis: If a diagnostic tool is developed based on a very limited number of symptoms or cases, it might fail to diagnose conditions correctly when presented with real-world patients, missing out on the complex interplay of symptoms and conditions.

Avoiding Underfitting:

Complexity: Increasing the model's complexity can help, provided it's done thoughtfully to avoid the opposite problem of overfitting, where the model is too complex.

More Data: Providing the model with more training data can give it more opportunities to learn and understand the underlying patterns.

Feature Engineering: Adding more relevant features or variables for the model to consider can improve its ability to make accurate predictions.

Remember:

Underfitting in AI and ML is like trying to solve a complex problem with an overly simplistic approach. It occurs when a model can't capture the essential patterns in the training data, leading to poor performance. Understanding and addressing underfitting is crucial in developing effective AI and ML models, ensuring they are sophisticated enough to learn from their training and make accurate predictions or decisions in real-world applications.

See also: Overfitting (pg. 130)

Unlabeled Data

Imagine you have a box full of various types of fruits mixed together. If these fruits aren't tagged or named, you have a collection where you know there are fruits, but you don't know which is which–this is similar to "Unlabeled Data" in the world of AI and machine learning.

In Topic(s): Data Analytics (DA) (pg. 223) | Data Science (DS) (pg. 227) | Ethical AI, Social Implications and Cultural Considerations (pg. 235) | Fundamental Data Concepts (pg. 237) | Machine Learning (ML) (pg. 250) | Semi-supervised Learning (pg. 262) | Unsupervised Learning (pg. 272)

Figure 95: A charming illustration of "Unlabeled Data".

What is Unlabeled Data?

Unlabeled Data refers to data that has not been tagged with labels, descriptions, or indicators of what it represents. In other words, while the data contains information, there's no direct annotation or identification of what each piece of data signifies or corresponds to.

Key Aspects of Unlabeled Data:

No Indicators: Unlike labeled data, where each data point has a corresponding label (like 'cat' or 'dog' for images), unlabeled data has no such markers.

Raw Data: Unlabeled data is often considered 'raw' as it hasn't been processed or categorized.

Use in Machine Learning: While more challenging, unlabeled data can be used in unsupervised learning, where the model tries to make sense of the data by detecting patterns, clusters, or relationships.

Abundance: Unlabeled data is more abundant and easier to collect than labeled data, as it doesn't require the time-consuming process of tagging each data point.

Examples of Unlabeled Data in Use:

Social Media Analysis: Collecting posts from social media platforms without any categorization and then using algorithms to identify trends or topics.

Customer Behavior Analysis: Gathering data on customer interactions with a website without specific markers and analyzing it to understand browsing patterns or preferences.

Market Research: Collecting large amounts of consumer data, like shopping habits, without specific labels, and then analyzing to find hidden patterns or trends.

Image Collections: A set of images gathered without any descriptions or tags. The AI system might process these to group them into different categories based on visual similarities.

Remember:

Unlabeled Data is a fundamental concept in AI and machine learning, especially in scenarios where the objective is to explore and find hidden patterns without pre-defined categories or labels. It represents a more natural, albeit complex, form of data that AI systems encounter and work with. Understanding unlabeled data is key to appreciating the challenges and approaches in training machine learning models, particularly in unsupervised learning scenarios.

See also: Labeled Data (pg. 112)

Unstructured Data

Imagine walking into an artist's studio filled with canvases, some with vivid paintings and others with just a few brushstrokes. Alongside, there are sculptures, sketches, and an assortment of art supplies. Each piece tells a story or conveys an emotion, but there's no specific order or system to how they're arranged or what they represent. This eclectic and free-form collection is akin to "Unstructured Data" in the digital world.

In Topic(s): Data Analytics (DA) (pg. 223) | Data Science (DS) (pg. 227) | Fundamental Data Concepts (pg. 237) | Unsupervised Learning (pg. 272)

Figure 96: A cheery illustration of "Unstructured Data".

What is Unstructured Data?

Unstructured Data refers to information that doesn't fit neatly into traditional row-and-column databases. It's like the diverse array of art in the studio, encompassing a wide range of formats and mediums. In the realm of Artificial Intelligence (AI) and Machine Learning (ML), unstructured data can include text, images, audio, and video - rich in information but lacking a clear, predefined structure.

Characteristics of Unstructured Data:

Diversity: Just as an artist's studio might contain everything from oil paintings to clay sculptures, unstructured data encompasses a broad spectrum of formats, such as emails, social media posts, videos, and more.

Volume: There's an abundance of unstructured data, much like the plethora of art pieces in the studio. It makes up a significant portion of the data generated daily, from tweets and blog posts to surveillance footage and podcasts.

Complexity: Understanding and interpreting unstructured data can be challenging, similar to deciphering the meaning behind an abstract painting. It requires sophisticated tools and techniques to extract meaningful insights.

Richness: Despite its lack of structure, unstructured data is rich in information and potential insights, offering a deep, nuanced understanding of topics, much like a detailed mural offers more to the story upon closer inspection.

Examples of Unstructured Data in Use:

Social Media Analysis: Companies sift through social media posts (text, images, videos) to gauge public sentiment about their brand, products, or services, extracting valuable insights from the diverse content.

Medical Diagnostics: Healthcare professionals use unstructured data, such as patient notes, medical imaging, and lab results, to diagnose conditions and develop treatment plans.

Customer Service: Businesses analyze customer emails, call center transcripts, and online reviews to improve service, identify common issues, and enhance customer satisfaction.

Research and Development: Researchers rely on unstructured data, including academic papers, patents, and technical reports, to fuel innovation, discover trends, and develop new technologies.

Remember:

Unstructured Data, with its vast diversity and richness, is like the raw material of creativity in the digital landscape. It holds a wealth of untapped knowledge and insights, akin to an artist's studio brimming with potential masterpieces. Understanding and harnessing this data through AI and ML technologies enable us to paint a more complete picture of the world around us, driving innovation and enhancing our understanding across various fields.

See also: Semi-Structured Data (pg. 162) | Structured Data (pg. 168)

Unsupervised Learning

Imagine you're given a box full of various toys without any instructions. Your task is to organize them into groups. How would you do it? You might start sorting them by color, size, or type of toy. This process of categorizing objects without any predefined categories or guidance is similar to "Unsupervised Learning" in AI and machine learning.

In Topic(s): Artificial Intelligence (AI) (pg. 210) | Core Applications (pg. 218) | Data Analytics (DA) (pg. 223) | Data Science (DS) (pg. 227) | Ethical AI, Social Implications and Cultural Considerations (pg. 235) | Machine Learning (ML) (pg. 250)

Figure 97: A charming illustration of "Unsupervised Learning".

What is Unsupervised Learning?

Unsupervised Learning is a type of machine learning where the algorithm is given data without any explicit instructions on what to do with it. There are no labels or categories provided, so the algorithm tries to make sense of the data by finding patterns, structures, or relationships within the data itself.

Key Aspects of Unsupervised Learning:

No Labels or Guidance: The data used in unsupervised learning doesn't come with labels or answers. The algorithm has to figure out the patterns and structures on its own.

Discovery of Hidden Patterns: The goal is often to discover hidden patterns or groupings in the data, like clustering similar data points together.

Data Exploration: Unsupervised learning is useful for exploring and understanding the underlying structure of data, especially when you're not sure what you're looking for.

Common Techniques: Techniques in unsupervised learning include clustering (grouping similar items), association (identifying rules that describe large portions of data), and dimensionality reduction (reducing the number of variables under consideration).

Examples of Unsupervised Learning in Use:

Market Segmentation: Businesses use unsupervised learning to segment customers into groups based on purchasing behavior or preferences, without pre-defined categories.

Social Network Analysis: Analyzing social networks to find communities or groups of people who have similar interests or connections.

Organizing Large Photo Collections: Grouping together photos based on similarities like locations, objects, or people, without any prior tagging.

Anomaly Detection: Identifying unusual patterns or anomalies in data, such as fraudulent credit card transactions.

Remember:

Unsupervised Learning is a method in AI and machine learning where the focus is on exploring and finding patterns in data without pre-set labels or instructions. It's particularly useful for gaining insights into data where the relationships or structures are not known in advance. Understanding unsupervised learning is key to appreciating how AI can help us make sense of complex, unstructured data in various fields.

See also: Semi-Supervised Learning (pg. 164) | Supervised Learning (pg. 170)

Value Function

Imagine you're planning a road trip through a scenic landscape with various routes to choose from. Each path offers a unique combination of beautiful vistas, charming towns, and historical landmarks. Your goal is to maximize the overall enjoyment of your journey, considering factors like the beauty of the scenery, the convenience of the route, and the attractions along the way. To make your decision, you mentally assign a 'value' to each potential route based on these factors, helping you choose the one that promises the most rewarding experience. This process of evaluating and choosing the best option based on expected enjoyment is similar to how a "Value Function" works in Artificial Intelligence (AI) and Machine Learning (ML), particularly in decision-making systems and games.

In Topic(s): Fundamental Data Concepts (pg. 237) | Fundamental Mathematics and Statistics (pg. 241) | Reinforcement Learning (pg. 259)

Figure 98: A quirky illustration of "Value Function".

What is a Value Function?

A Value Function in AI is a mathematical tool that helps an AI system evaluate the potential 'worth' or 'goodness' of different states or decisions within a given task or environment. It's like your mental calculation of which road trip route would offer the most enjoyment. In AI, this function calculates scores based on how beneficial different actions or paths are toward achieving a goal, guiding the system to make choices that maximize this value.

Key Aspects of Value Functions:

Evaluating Choices: Just as you evaluate different routes for your trip, a value function assesses various possible actions or states the AI could take, predicting the long-term benefit of each.

Guiding Decisions: The value function helps the AI decide which action to take at each step, much like choosing your next turn on the road trip based on expected enjoyment.

Long-Term Outlook: It considers not just the immediate rewards but also the future benefits, similar to choosing a slightly longer scenic route that promises more enjoyment over the entire journey.

Examples of Value Functions in Use:

Board Games like Chess or Go: The AI evaluates potential moves by assigning a value to each possible board state, guiding it to make moves that increase its chances of winning.

Navigation Systems: Just as you plan your road trip, navigation AI uses value functions to calculate the best routes, considering factors like distance, traffic, and scenic value.

Investment Strategies: Financial AI systems use value functions to evaluate different investment options, guiding decisions that maximize potential returns over time.

Personalized Recommendations: AI in streaming services or e-commerce sites uses value functions to predict the enjoyment or satisfaction you'd get from movies, shows, or products, guiding personalized recommendations.

Remember:

The Value Function is a foundational concept in AI that helps systems make informed, strategic decisions by evaluating the potential long-term benefits of different actions or states. Much like planning the best route for a road trip, value functions enable AI to navigate complex environments and tasks, aiming to maximize success, enjoyment, or reward. This concept underscores the ability of AI to not just react to immediate situations but to strategically plan for optimal outcomes over time, enhancing its effectiveness in a wide range of applications.

See also: Reinforcement Learning (RL) (pg. 150)

Video Data

Imagine you're directing a play where each actor's movement, expression, and interaction tells a part of the story. Now, imagine if you could teach a computer to understand and interpret these movements and expressions, just like a keen audience member, to make its own predictions about the storyline or even suggest how a scene could be improved. This is akin to the role of video data in the realms of Artificial Intelligence (AI) and Machine Learning (ML).

In Topic(s): Computer Vision (CV) (pg. 216) | Image Processing (pg. 245) | Supervised Learning (pg. 266) | Video Processing (pg. 274)

Figure 99: A charming illustration of "Video Data".

What is Video Data?

In AI and ML, video data is like a treasure trove of dynamic information. It's not just a series of images but a continuous flow of visual narratives that AI can analyze to understand movements, identify objects, recognize faces, and even predict future actions. Each frame in a video can provide context to the next, creating a rich dataset from which AI and ML algorithms can learn and make decisions.

Key Components of Video Data:

Frames as Data Points: Each video is made up of frames (still images shown in rapid succession to create the illusion of motion). AI sees each frame as a data point, analyzing the details to understand the video's content.

Temporal Information: Unlike static images, videos provide temporal (time-based) information. AI algorithms use this to understand how objects and people move and change over time.

Contextual Understanding: Videos offer context that helps AI understand the relationship between objects and actions within a scene, much like understanding the interplay between actors on stage.

Multidimensional Analysis: AI and ML can analyze video data across multiple dimensions (space and time), extracting insights about the environment, detecting anomalies, or recognizing patterns of behavior.

Examples of Video Data:

Surveillance and Security: AI systems analyze surveillance footage in real-time to detect unusual activities, identify unauthorized individuals, or track objects across different frames.

Autonomous Vehicles: Self-driving cars use video data to navigate roads, recognizing traffic signals, pedestrians, other vehicles, and road conditions, making split-second decisions based on continuous visual input.

Healthcare: AI models analyze video data from surgeries or patient interactions to assist in training, diagnostics, and patient monitoring, recognizing patterns or anomalies that may require attention.

Sports Analysis: Coaches and athletes use AI to analyze video footage of games and practices, understanding plays, player movements, and strategies to improve performance.

Content Creation and Editing: In the entertainment industry, AI algorithms analyze video data to automate editing, enhance visual effects, or even generate new content based on existing footage.

Remember:

Video data in AI and ML is like giving a computer the ability to watch, understand, and learn from the unfolding scenes of life captured on camera. It transforms passive viewing into active analysis, enabling machines to interpret complex visual information, make predictions, and even take actions based on what they "see." As AI and ML technologies advance, the potential applications of video data continue to expand, opening new possibilities for innovation and improvement across various fields.

See also: Action Recognition (pg. 17) | Audio Data (pg. 33)

Video Summarization

Imagine you've just returned from a breathtaking vacation and you've captured hours of video footage: serene sunsets, bustling marketplaces, and quiet, introspective moments. You want to share the essence of your journey with friends and family, but the thought of them sitting through hours of footage is daunting. So, you decide to create a highlight reel that captures the most memorable moments, giving viewers the flavor of your experience without the need for a marathon viewing session. This process of distilling your extensive footage into a concise, engaging summary is akin to "Video Summarization" in the realm of Artificial Intelligence (AI) and Machine Learning (ML).

In Topic(s): Computer Vision (CV) (pg. 216) | Core Applications (pg. 218) | Image Processing (pg. 245) | Industry Applications (pg. 247) | Video Processing (pg. 274)

Figure 100: An amusing illustration of "Video Summarization".

What is Video Summarization?

Video Summarization is the process of automatically creating a short clip or a set of key frames from a longer video, capturing the most important or interesting parts. It's like sifting through a novel to find and present the most pivotal scenes that define the story, giving someone a glimpse of the narrative without reading every page.

Key Elements of Video Summarization:

Content Selection: Just as you might choose the most breathtaking sunsets or the most colorful market scenes from your vacation footage, video summarization involves selecting segments or frames that best represent the overall content.

Brevity and Coherence: The summary should be concise, fitting into a much shorter timeframe than the original, but also coherent, ensuring that the transitions between selected segments are smooth and that the summary tells a cohesive story.

Highlighting Key Moments: Similar to how your highlight reel might focus on moments of laughter, awe, or excitement, video summarization aims to include the most impactful, informative, or emotional parts of the video.

Customization: Just as your vacation highlight reel might differ based on whether it's for family, friends, or a travel blog, video summarization can be tailored to the specific interests or needs of the audience.

Examples of Video Summarization in Use:

Event Recaps: From weddings to conferences, video summarization can distill hours of footage into short recaps that capture the event's essence, making it easy for attendees or those who couldn't attend to experience the highlights.

Educational Content: Lengthy educational videos or lectures can be summarized to provide quick overviews of key concepts, aiding in revision or catching up on missed classes.

Sports Highlights: Summarizing a sports match into key plays, goals, or points, allowing fans to catch up on the action without watching the entire game.

Surveillance Efficiency: In security, video summarization can help in quickly reviewing hours of surveillance footage, highlighting moments of activity or interest amidst long periods of inactivity.

Remember:

Video Summarization transforms the way we consume and interact with video content, offering a time-saving solution that condenses lengthy footage into digestible, engaging summaries. Whether it's reliving the highlights of a personal adventure or catching up on missed events, video summarization uses AI and ML to ensure that the essence and narrative of the original content are preserved and presented in a fraction of the time.

See also: Video Data (pg. 200)

Virtual Assistant

Think about having a personal assistant who's always at your service, but instead of a human, it's a digital helper living in your smartphone, computer, or a smart home device. You can ask it questions, tell it to do tasks, and it responds. This digital helper is what we call a "Virtual Assistant."

In Topic(s): Core Applications (pg. 218) | Industry Applications (pg. 247)

Figure 101: A playful illustration of "Virtual Assistant".

What is a Virtual Assistant?

A Virtual Assistant is a software program designed to assist users through voice commands, text inputs, or both. It uses AI technologies, especially natural language processing, to understand and respond to user requests. Virtual assistants can perform a variety of tasks, provide information, and even control other smart devices.

Key Aspects of Virtual Assistants:

Voice Interaction: Most virtual assistants are voice-activated, meaning they can listen to and understand spoken commands or questions.

Artificial Intelligence: They use AI to comprehend and interpret user requests and then provide relevant responses or actions.

Connectivity: Virtual assistants often connect to the internet to access information, control other devices, or perform tasks like playing music or setting alarms.

Personalization: They can learn from interactions to provide personalized responses or suggestions based on user preferences or past behavior.

Examples of Virtual Assistants in Use:

Smartphones: Siri on iPhones and Google Assistant on Android phones help users make calls, send messages, check the weather, and get directions.

Smart Homes: Devices like Amazon Echo and Google Nest can control lighting, thermostats, and security systems via voice commands.

Online Customer Service: Some websites use virtual assistants to answer common customer questions, guide them through purchases, or provide support.

Personal Organization: Virtual assistants can manage calendars, set reminders, or even help with to-do lists.

Remember:

Virtual Assistants are a practical application of AI, offering convenient and efficient ways to interact with technology and manage everyday tasks. They represent how AI can be seamlessly integrated into daily life, providing assistance that's just a voice command or text away. Understanding virtual assistants helps in appreciating the advancements in AI that make life easier and more connected.

See also: Conversational Agent (pg. 49)

Terms Grouped by Topic

AI Governance

These terms inherently involve considerations of policy, ethics, regulation, and oversight, making them pertinent to discussions around AI Governance.

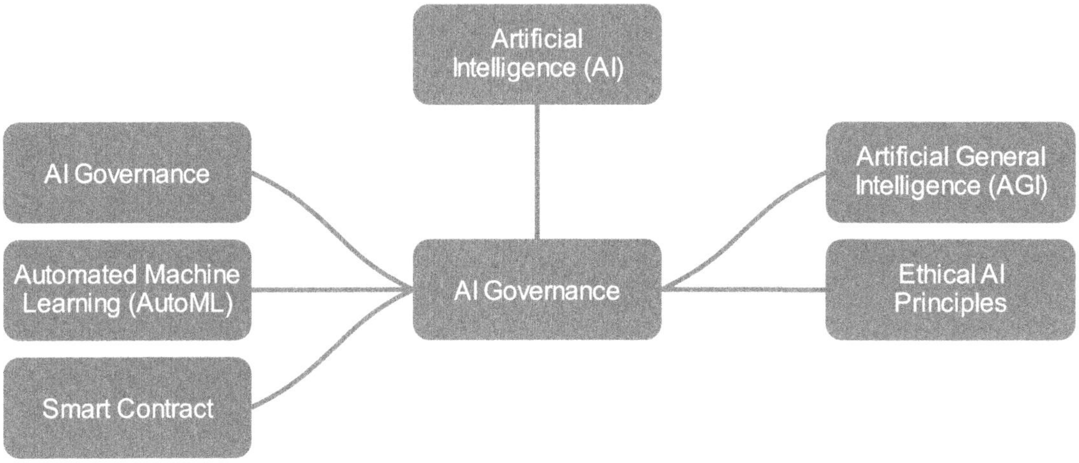

Figure 102: A simple mind map of "AI Governance".

AI Governance (pg. 23) - The framework and processes through which the development, deployment, and operation of AI systems are regulated and controlled to ensure ethical, legal, and societal compliance.

Artificial General Intelligence (AGI) (pg. 4) - While not directly a governance term, discussions around AGI often involve significant governance considerations due to its potential impact on society.

Automated Machine Learning (AutoML) (pg. 37) - This involves the use of AI to automate the process of applying machine learning to real-world problems, which raises questions of governance in terms of transparency, control, and bias.

Ethical AI Principles (pg. 77) - Refers to the guidelines designed to ensure that AI technologies are developed and used in a manner that is ethical, responsible, and for the benefit of society.

Smart Contract (pg. 166) - While primarily a blockchain term, smart contracts intersect with AI in areas like automated enforcement of agreements, which requires careful governance to ensure fairness and accountability.

AI Hardware and Accelerators

In the context of AI hardware and accelerators, discussions often revolve around GPUs, TPUs, and other specialized hardware designed to speed up AI computations. These terms listed here are closely related to the operation and performance optimization of tools and platforms.

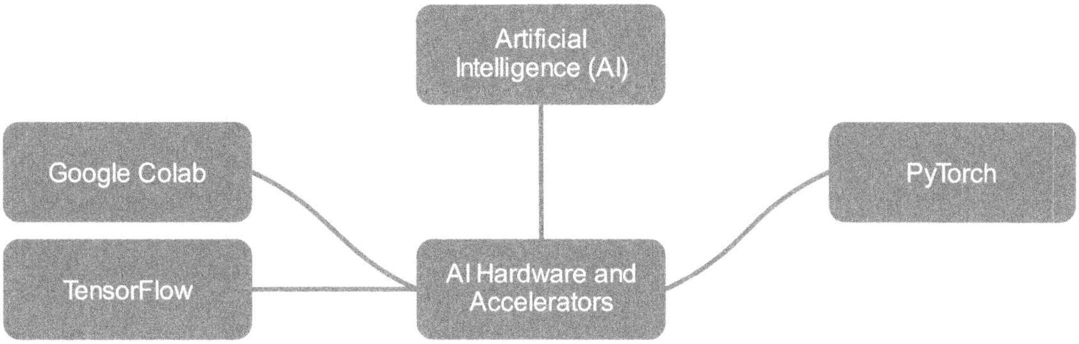

Figure 103: A simple mind map of "AI Hardware and Accelerators".

Google Colab (pg. 96) - Cloud-based services that provide access to powerful computing resources, including GPUs and TPUs, for running machine learning and deep learning models. While Google Colab is a cloud service platform and not hardware per se, it's a gateway for many to access AI accelerators.

PyTorch (pg. 142) - Software framework that are widely used for developing machine learning models. It is optimized to run on various types of hardware, including GPUs (Graphics Processing Units) and TPUs (Tensor Processing Units), which are crucial for accelerating AI computations. Though TensorFlow and PyTorch themselves are not hardware, they are intrinsically linked to AI hardware acceleration through their efficient utilization of such resources.

TensorFlow (pg. 176) - Software framework that are widely used for developing machine learning models. It is optimized to run on various types of hardware, including GPUs (Graphics Processing Units) and TPUs (Tensor Processing Units), which are crucial for accelerating AI computations. Though TensorFlow and PyTorch themselves are not hardware, they are intrinsically linked to AI hardware acceleration through their efficient utilization of such resources.

Artificial Intelligence (AI)

These terms represent the foundational concepts, methodologies, and application areas that are central to the field of AI, encompassing the theoretical underpinnings, the development of algorithms, and the implementation of systems capable of intelligent behavior.

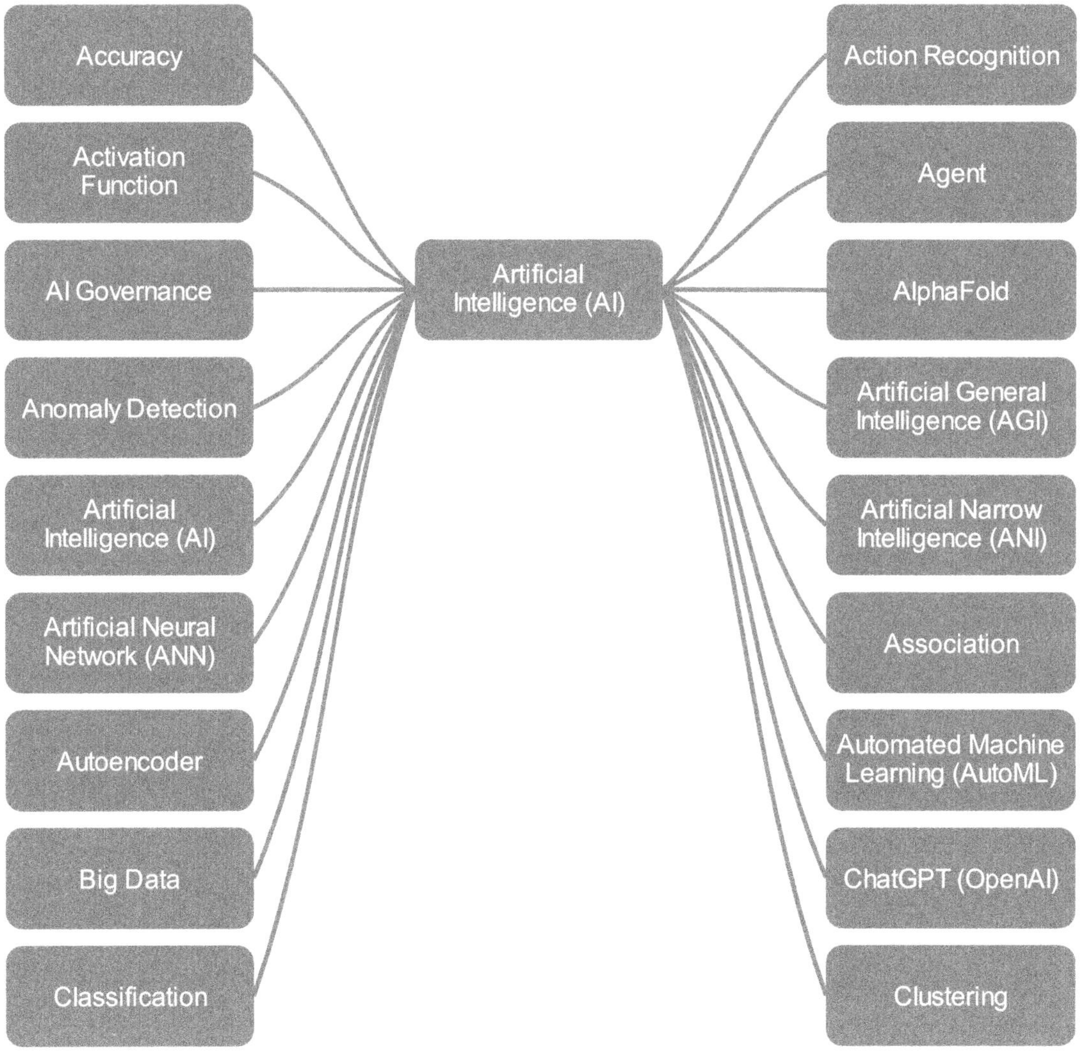

Figure 104: A simple mind map of "Artificial Intelligence (AI)".

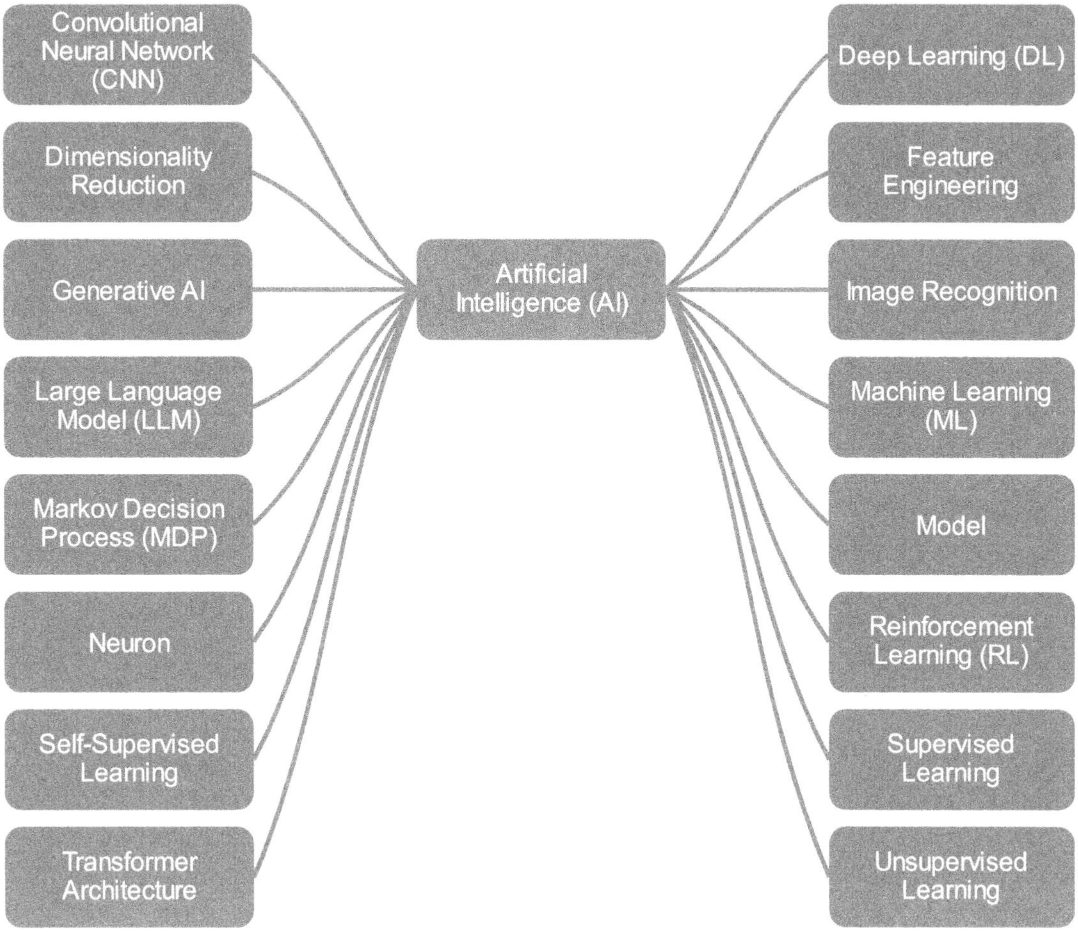

Figure 105: A simple mind map of "Artificial Intelligence (AI)" continued.

Accuracy (pg. 15) - A fundamental measure in AI for evaluating the correctness of a model's predictions.

Action Recognition (pg. 17) - A task in AI focused on identifying actions in sequences, such as videos, which is a core part of understanding and interpreting dynamic data.

Activation Function (pg. 19) - A key component in neural networks that determines the output of a node, given a set of inputs.

Agent (pg. 21) - In AI, an agent is an entity that perceives its environment and takes actions to achieve certain goals, a foundational concept in many AI systems.

AI Governance (pg. 23) -

AlphaFold (pg. 25) - An AI program developed by DeepMind that predicts protein folding structures.

Anomaly Detection (pg. 27) - The use of AI to identify patterns in data that do not conform to expected behavior.

Artificial General Intelligence (AGI) (pg. 4) - A theoretical form of AI that has the ability to understand, learn, and apply knowledge in ways that are indistinguishable from human intelligence.

Artificial Intelligence (AI) (pg. 2) - The overarching field that encompasses all the methodologies, technologies, and applications aimed at creating machines capable of performing tasks that would require intelligence if done by humans.

Artificial Narrow Intelligence (ANI) (pg. 6) - AI systems that are designed and trained for a specific task, representing the current state of most AI technologies.

Artificial Neural Network (ANN) (pg. 29) - Inspired by the biological neural networks, these computational models are fundamental to deep learning and many AI applications.

Association (pg. 31) - A concept in AI related to finding and establishing connections between data points or features, fundamental in rule-based systems and association rule learning.

Autoencoder (pg. 35) - A type of artificial neural network used for unsupervised learning of efficient codings, fundamental for understanding deep learning architectures.

Automated Machine Learning (AutoML) (pg. 37) - A core advancement in AI that automates the process of applying machine learning, making AI more accessible.

Big Data (pg. 39) - Refers to extremely large datasets that traditional data processing software cannot manage, a foundational concept in understanding the scale of data AI technologies can work with.

ChatGPT (OpenAI) (pg. 8) - An example of a large language model that represents a significant advancement in natural language processing, a core area in AI.

Classification (pg. 41) - A fundamental machine learning task where models are trained to categorize input data, a core technique in many AI applications.

Clustering (pg. 43) - An unsupervised learning technique where models group sets of data points, fundamental for data analysis and pattern recognition in AI.

Convolutional Neural Network (CNN) (pg. 51) - A specialized kind of neural network for processing data with a grid-like topology, crucial for computer vision tasks, a core application area in AI.

Deep Learning (DL) (pg. 69) - A subset of machine learning involving neural networks with many layers, central to the significant advances in AI capabilities.

Dimensionality Reduction (pg. 71) - The process of reducing the number of input variables in a dataset, crucial for simplifying AI models and reducing computational complexity.

Feature Engineering (pg. 88) - The process of selecting, modifying, or creating new input variables to improve model performance, a core practice in the development of AI models.

Generative AI (pg. 10) - AI systems capable of generating new content, offering a core methodology for creative AI applications.

Image Recognition (pg. 102) - The ability of AI to identify objects, places, people, writing, and actions in images, a fundamental task in image processing.

Large Language Model (LLM) (pg. 114) - These models, trained on vast amounts of text data, are at the core of modern natural language processing and generation tasks.

Machine Learning (ML) (pg. 12) - A core subset of AI, focusing on the development of algorithms that allow computers to learn from and make predictions or decisions based on data.

Markov Decision Process (MDP) (pg. 118) - A mathematical framework for modeling decision making, foundational in reinforcement learning, a key area in AI.

Model (pg. 122) - In AI, a model is the representation of what has been learned by a machine learning algorithm, central to all AI applications.

Neuron (pg. 126) - The basic computational unit of an artificial neural network, inspired by biological neurons, and foundational to understanding how neural networks function.

Reinforcement Learning (RL) (pg. 150) - A type of machine learning where an agent learns to make decisions by taking actions in an environment to achieve some notion of reward, a core methodology in AI.

Self-Supervised Learning (pg. 158) - An innovative learning paradigm where models learn to predict part of the input from other parts, reducing the dependency on labeled data.

Supervised Learning (pg. 170) - A fundamental machine learning paradigm where models learn from labeled training data, crucial for a wide range of AI applications.

Transformer Architecture (pg. 186) - A model architecture that has revolutionized natural language processing, a core area in AI.

Unsupervised Learning (pg. 196) - Learning patterns from unlabeled data, a core machine learning paradigm that underpins many exploratory data analysis methods in AI.

Artificial Neural Networks (ANN)

These terms encapsulate the fundamental concepts, structures, and variations within the field of artificial neural networks, highlighting the key components and types of ANNs that are instrumental in modern AI and machine learning.

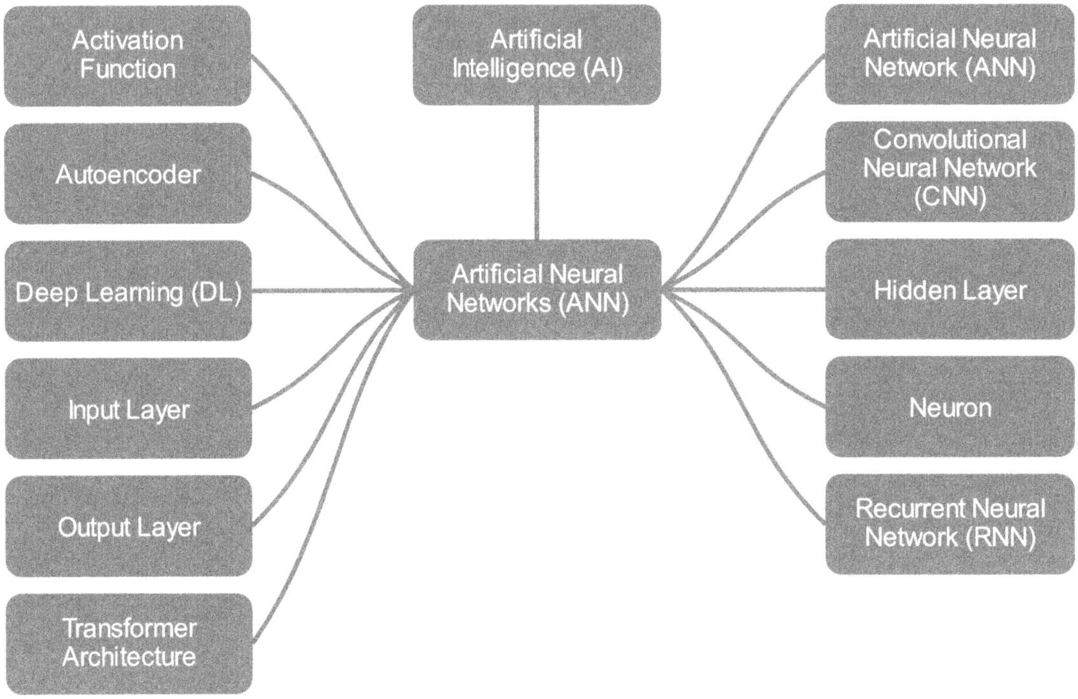

Figure 106: A simple mind map of "Artificial Neural Networks (ANN)".

Activation Function (pg. 19) - A function in a neural network node that determines the output of that node given an input or set of inputs.

Artificial Neural Network (ANN) (pg. 29) - A computational model inspired by the structure and function of biological neural networks, used in machine learning.

Autoencoder (pg. 35) - A type of neural network used for unsupervised learning tasks, such as dimensionality reduction or feature learning, by learning to encode input into a (typically) lower-dimensional space and then decode it back to the original form.

Convolutional Neural Network (CNN) (pg. 51) - A class of deep neural networks, most commonly applied to analyzing visual imagery, characterized by their use of convolutional layers.

Deep Learning (DL) (pg. 69) - A subset of machine learning involving neural networks with multiple layers that learn representations of data with multiple levels of abstraction.

Hidden Layer (pg. 100) - Layers of nodes between the input layer and output layer in a neural network that are not directly exposed to the input.

Input Layer (pg. 104) - The first layer in a neural network that receives the input signal to be processed by subsequent layers of neurons.

Neuron (pg. 126) - A node in an artificial neural network that simulates the neurons in a biological brain, processing and transmitting information.

Output Layer (pg. 128) - The final layer in a neural network where the ultimate output is derived from the processed inputs.

Recurrent Neural Network (RNN) (pg. 146) - A type of neural network where connections between nodes form a directed graph along a temporal sequence, which allows it to exhibit temporal dynamic behavior and use its internal state (memory) to process sequences of inputs.

Transformer Architecture (pg. 186) - A neural network architecture that relies on self-attention mechanisms and is particularly effective for tasks involving sequential data, such as natural language processing.

Computer Vision (CV)

These terms represent key concepts, tasks, and technologies within the field of computer vision, highlighting the focus on enabling machines to interpret and understand the visual world.

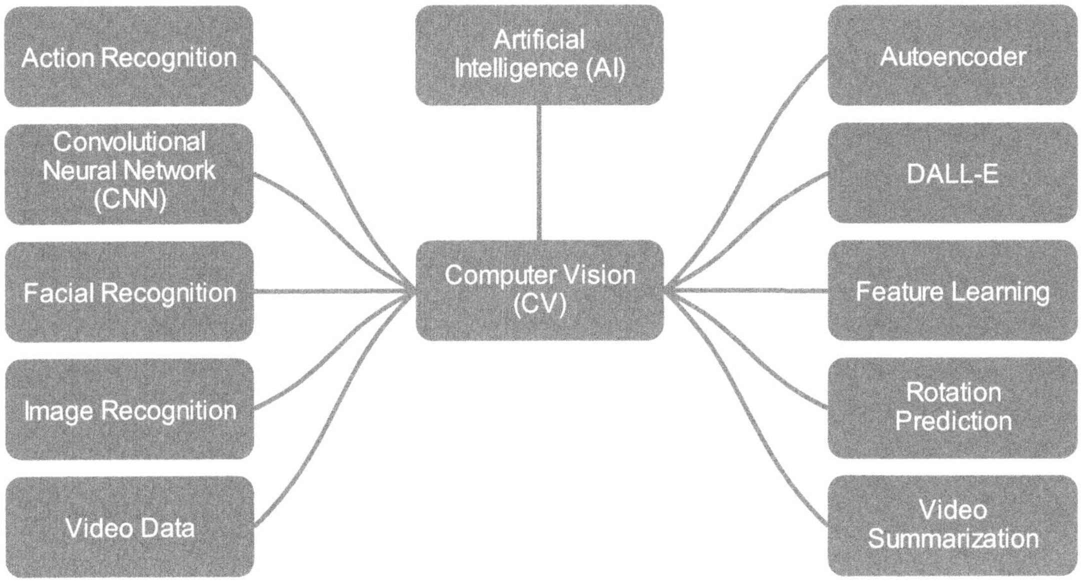

Figure 107: A simple mind map of "Computer Vision (CV)".

Action Recognition (pg. 17) - The process of identifying and categorizing actions in videos or sequences of images, a fundamental task in computer vision.

Autoencoder (pg. 35) - Although used in various contexts, in computer vision, autoencoders are used for tasks such as dimensionality reduction of images, denoising, and feature learning.

Convolutional Neural Network (CNN) (pg. 51) - A specialized kind of neural network that is particularly effective for processing data with a grid-like topology, such as images, making it a cornerstone of modern computer vision.

DALL-E (pg. 59) - An AI model developed by OpenAI that generates images from textual descriptions, showcasing the intersection of natural language processing and computer vision.

Facial Recognition (pg. 86) - The use of computer vision technology to identify or verify individuals from digital images or video frames.

Feature Learning (pg. 90) - In computer vision, this involves algorithms learning to automatically identify and use the relevant features in images for tasks like classification or recognition.

Image Recognition (pg. 102) - The ability of AI to identify objects, places, people, writing, and actions in images.

Rotation Prediction (pg. 154) - A self-supervised learning task used in computer vision where a model is trained to predict the rotation applied to an input image, aiding in learning general features about the visual world.

Video Data (pg. 200) - Refers to the use and analysis of video data within artificial intelligence and machine learning, particularly within the domain of computer vision for tasks such as action recognition, motion analysis, and video summarization.

Video Summarization (pg. 202) - The process of creating a short summary that captures the essential elements of a video, a task that involves understanding and interpreting visual content, making it part of computer vision.

Core Applications

These terms encompass a wide range of AI's practical applications, illustrating how AI technologies are being utilized to solve real-world problems, enhance user experiences, and drive innovation across various sectors.

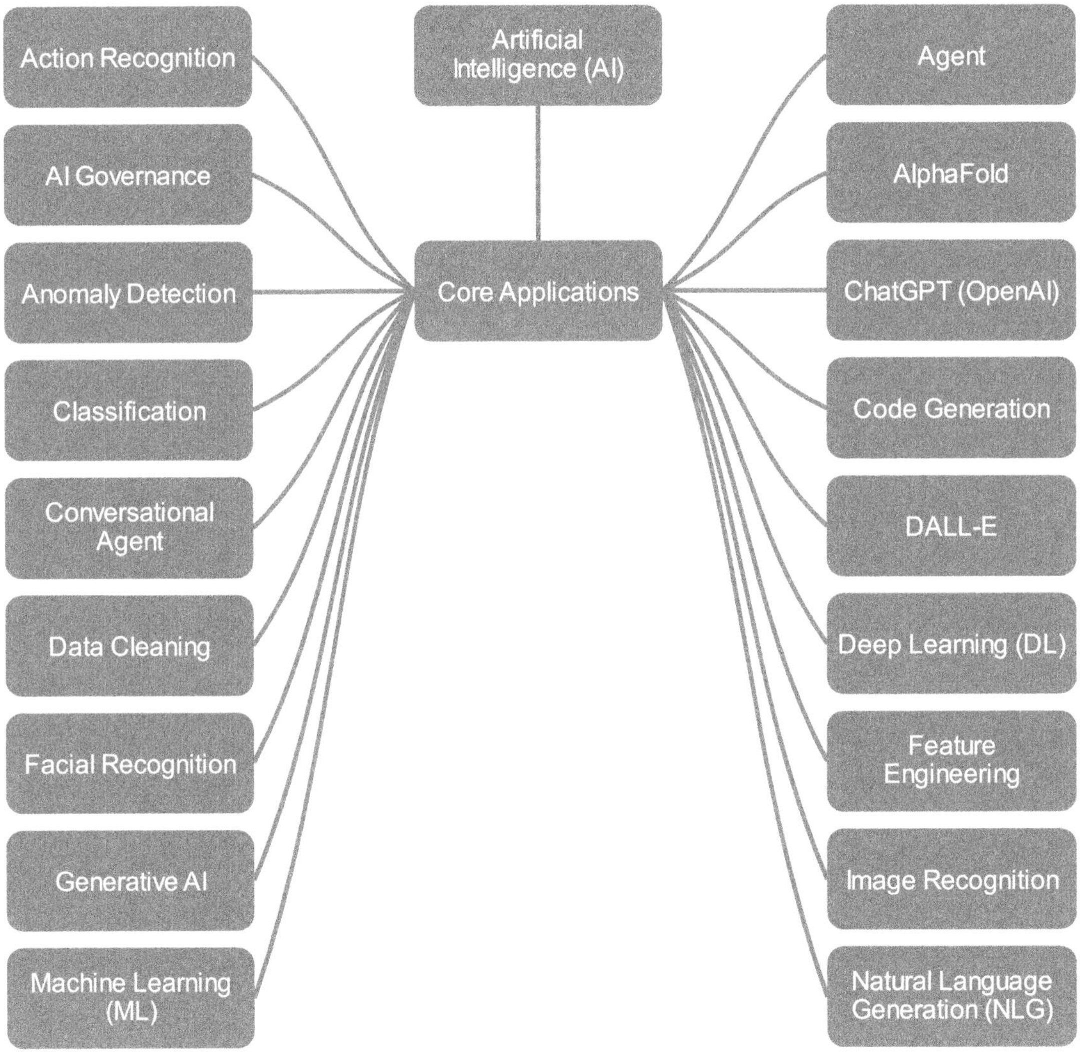

Figure 108: A simple mind map of "Core Applications".

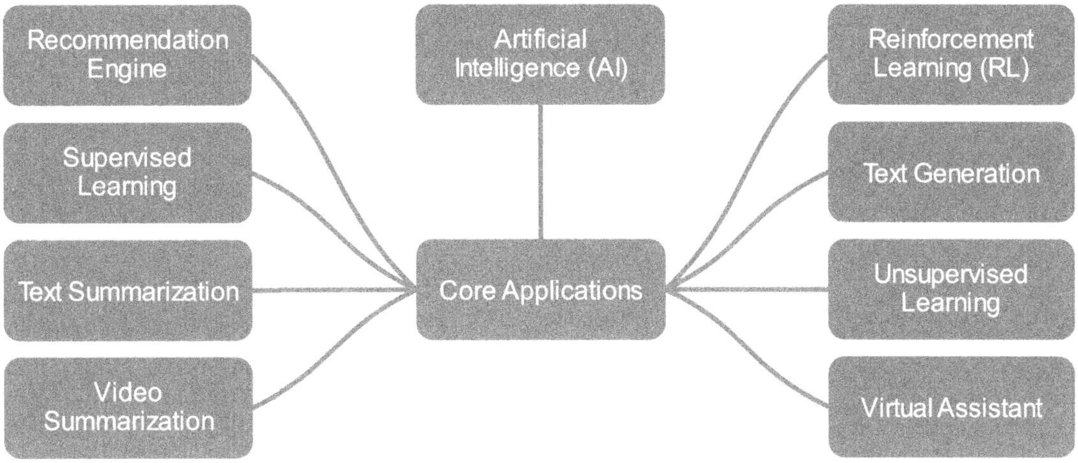

Figure 109: A simple mind map of "Core Applications" continued.

Action Recognition (pg. 17) - A core application in both security and entertainment, identifying specific actions within video data.

Agent (pg. 21) - In AI, an agent is a system that perceives its environment and takes actions to achieve specific goals.

AI Governance (pg. 23) -

AlphaFold (pg. 25) - A groundbreaking application in the field of biology, using AI for predicting the 3D structures of proteins.

Anomaly Detection (pg. 27) - Widely used in fraud detection, system health monitoring, and outlier detection in data analysis.

ChatGPT (OpenAI) (pg. 8) - An application of AI in natural language processing, providing conversational agents capable of understanding and generating human-like text.

Classification (pg. 41) - The process of predicting the category or class of given data points.

Code Generation (pg. 45) - An application of AI where models generate programming code based on specifications or prompts, aiding in software development.

Conversational Agent (pg. 49) - AI applications that simulate human conversation, used in virtual assistants, customer service bots, and more.

DALL-E (pg. 59) - An AI application that generates images from textual descriptions, showcasing the creative potential of AI in art and design.

Data Cleaning (pg. 61) - The process of detecting and correcting (or removing) corrupt or inaccurate records from a dataset.

Deep Learning (DL) (pg. 69) - A subset of machine learning involving neural networks with many layers, enabling the learning of complex patterns.

Facial Recognition (pg. 86) - Used in security, personal identification, and even in marketing, to recognize individuals from images or video.

Feature Engineering (pg. 88) - The process of selecting, modifying, or creating new features from raw data to improve the performance of ML models.

Generative AI (pg. 10) - Applications that involve generating new content or data, such as images, text, or music, that mimic the distribution of a given dataset.

Image Recognition (pg. 102) - A foundational application in computer vision, used in various industries from healthcare to automotive for identifying objects in images.

Machine Learning (ML) (pg. 12) - The scientific study of algorithms and statistical models that computer systems use to perform specific tasks without using explicit instructions.

Natural Language Generation (NLG) (pg. 124) - The use of AI to produce written or spoken narrative from a dataset, used in report generation, content creation, and more.

Recommendation Engine (pg. 144) - A core application in e-commerce, streaming services, and content platforms, suggesting products, movies, or music to users based on their preferences and behavior.

Reinforcement Learning (RL) (pg. 150) - While a technique, its applications are core to developments in robotics, autonomous vehicles, and game playing.

Supervised Learning (pg. 170) - A type of machine learning where the model is trained on a labeled dataset, which includes both the input data and the correct outputs.

Text Generation (pg. 180) - The application of AI in creating coherent and contextually relevant text based on a given prompt, used in content creation, chatbots, and more.

Text Summarization (pg. 182) - An application where AI distills the most important information from a source text to create a concise summary, useful in information retrieval, news aggregation, and research.

Unsupervised Learning (pg. 196) - A type of machine learning where the model is trained using information that is neither classified nor labeled.

Video Summarization (pg. 202) - Used in editing, surveillance, and content creation, this application condenses videos into shorter versions that retain essential information.

Virtual Assistant (pg. 204) - AI-powered applications that understand spoken or written commands and perform tasks for the user, such as Siri, Alexa, and Google Assistant.

Cutting-edge Technologies

These terms highlight the forefront of AI and ML research, where significant investments, discoveries, and innovations are driving the field forward.

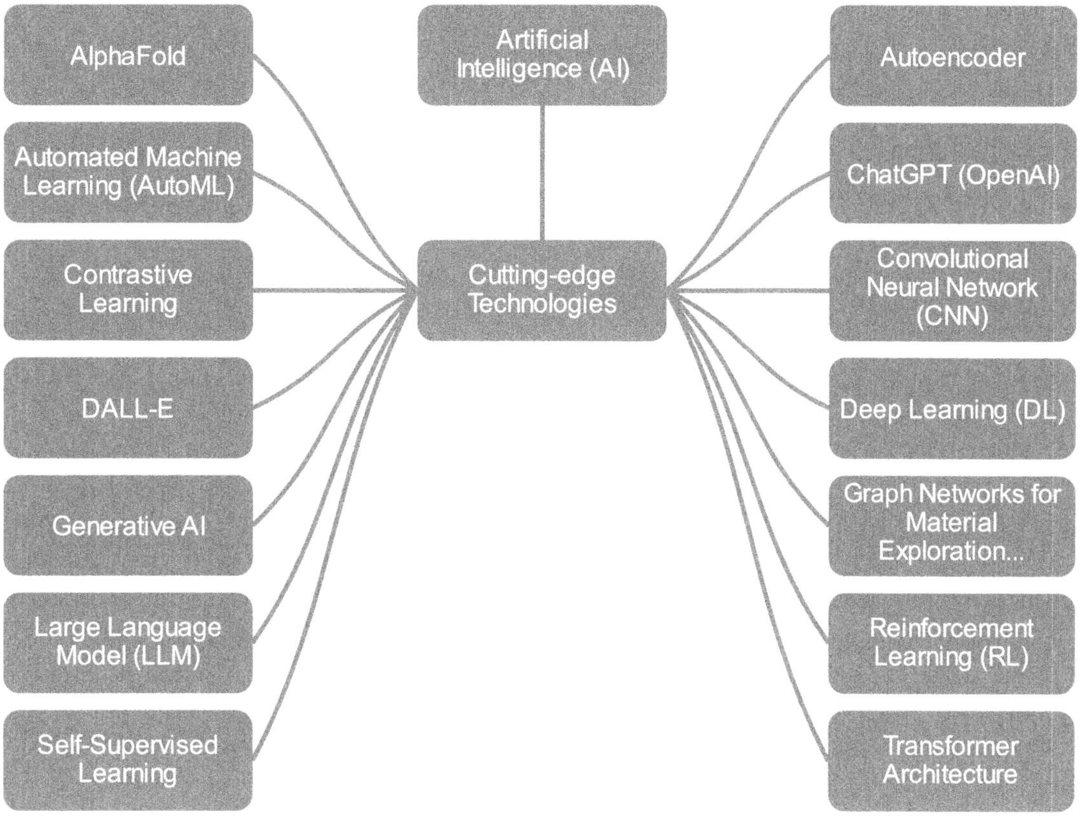

Figure 110: A simple mind map of "Cutting-edge Technologies".

AlphaFold (pg. 25) - Represents a breakthrough in the field of biology and bioinformatics, using AI to predict the 3D structures of proteins accurately.

Autoencoder (pg. 35) - A type of artificial neural network used to learn efficient codings of unlabeled data.

Automated Machine Learning (AutoML) (pg. 37) - A modern approach to automating the end-to-end process of applying machine learning to real-world problems.

ChatGPT (OpenAI) (pg. 8) - A state-of-the-art language model known for its ability to generate human-like text, indicative of the latest advancements in natural language processing.

Contrastive Learning (pg. 47) - A state-of-the-art language model known for its ability to generate human-like text, indicative of the latest advancements in natural language processing.

Convolutional Neural Network (CNN) (pg. 51) - While not new, CNNs remain at the forefront of developments in computer vision and related fields.

DALL-E (pg. 59) - An AI model by OpenAI capable of generating complex images from textual descriptions, showcasing the cutting-edge intersection of natural language understanding and generative models.

Deep Learning (DL) (pg. 69) - Represents a core set of cutting-edge techniques in AI, enabling advancements in fields like computer vision, natural language processing, and beyond.

Generative AI (pg. 10) - Refers to AI models that can generate new content, whether it be text, images, music, etc., that resemble the training data, embodying the forefront of creative AI applications.

Graph Networks for Material Exploration (GNoME) (pg. 98) - Analyzes the complex structures and properties of materials at an atomic or molecular level, predicting new materials with desired properties or identifying new uses for existing materials.

Large Language Model (LLM) (pg. 114) - Large-scale models that have significantly pushed the boundaries of what's possible in natural language understanding and generation.

Reinforcement Learning (RL) (pg. 150) - While an established method, its application in complex environments and tasks like AlphaGo and autonomous vehicles keeps it at the cutting-edge of AI research and applications.

Self-Supervised Learning (pg. 158) - An innovative learning paradigm where models learn to predict part of the input from other parts, reducing the dependency on labeled data.

Transformer Architecture (pg. 186) - The backbone of many current state-of-the-art language models, transformers have revolutionized natural language processing and beyond.

Data Analytics (DA)

These terms encapsulate the fundamental techniques, processes, and challenges in the field of data analytics, highlighting how data is prepared, processed, analyzed, and visualized to derive meaningful insights and inform decision-making.

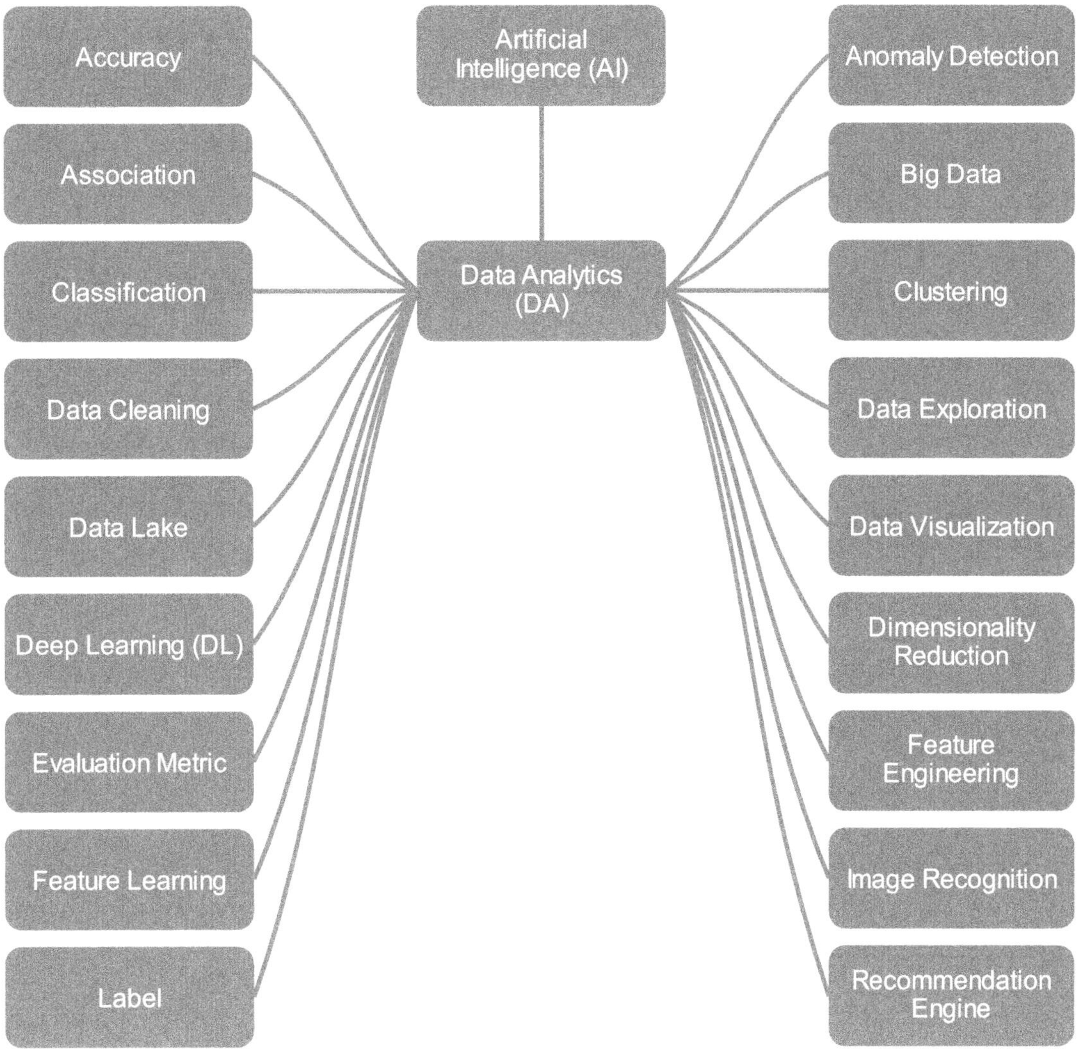

Figure 111: A simple mind map of "Data Analytics (DA)".

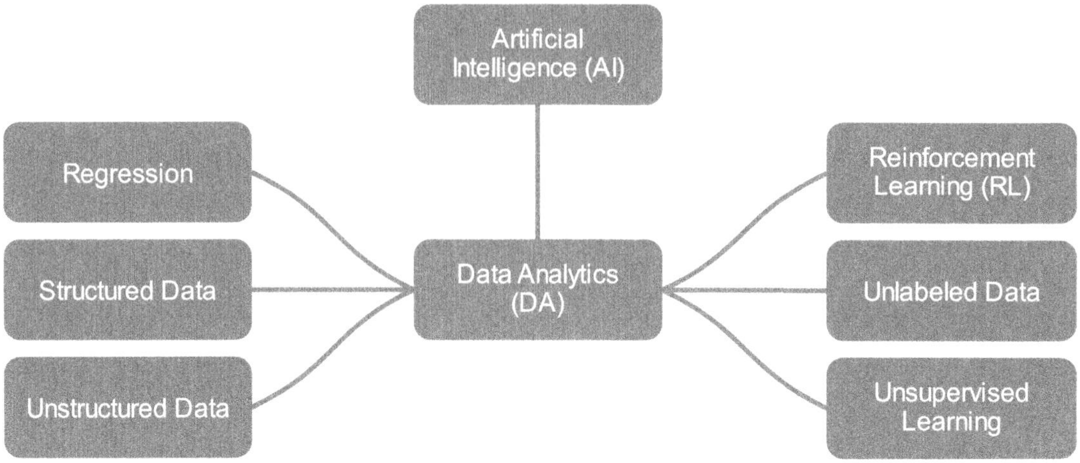

Figure 112: A simple mind map of "Data Analytics (DA)" continued.

Accuracy (pg. 15) - A measure of correctness in data analytics, reflecting the degree to which the results of an analysis match the true values or expected outcomes.

Anomaly Detection (pg. 27) - The identification of unusual patterns or outliers in data that do not conform to expected behavior, crucial in many data analytics applications like fraud detection.

Association (pg. 31) - A technique in data analytics used to discover patterns or relationships between variables in large datasets, often used in market basket analysis.

Big Data (pg. 39) - Represents large, complex datasets that traditional data processing applications are inadequate to deal with, and is foundational to modern data analytics challenges and solutions.

Classification (pg. 41) - A data analytics task that involves categorizing data into predefined groups or classes, making it a fundamental method in machine learning for data analysis.

Clustering (pg. 43) - An unsupervised learning technique used in data analytics to group a set of objects in such a way that objects in the same group are more similar to each other than to those in other groups.

Data Cleaning (pg. 61) - The process of detecting and correcting (or removing) corrupt or inaccurate records from a dataset, a critical initial step in the data analytics process.

Data Exploration (pg. 63) - The initial step in data analysis, where users explore a large set of data to find initial patterns, characteristics, and points of interest without having a specific goal in mind.

Data Lake (pg. 65) - A storage repository that holds a vast amount of raw data in its native format until it is needed, an important concept in managing the diverse and massive datasets used in data analytics.

Data Visualization (pg. 67) - The graphical representation of information and data, a key technique in data analytics for communicating findings and insights in an accessible and intuitive manner.

Deep Learning (DL) (pg. 69) - The use of deep neural networks to analyze and infer from complex data structures.

Dimensionality Reduction (pg. 71) - The process of reducing the number of random variables under consideration, by obtaining a set of principal variables, crucial for simplifying data analytics models without significant loss of information.

Evaluation Metric (pg. 80) - Measures used to assess the performance of a data analytics model or algorithm, helping analysts understand the effectiveness of their analytical models.

Feature Engineering (pg. 88) - The process of using domain knowledge to extract features from raw data, a crucial step in improving the performance of data analytics algorithms.

Feature Learning (pg. 90) - An aspect of some machine learning techniques that allows a system to automatically discover the representations needed for feature detection or classification from raw data.

Image Recognition (pg. 102) - The ability of software to identify objects, people, places, and actions in images.

Label (pg. 108) - In supervised learning, a label is the answer or outcome that the model is designed to predict, based on the input data.

Recommendation Engine (pg. 144) - Systems that suggest products, services, information to users based on analysis of data.

Regression (pg. 148) - A data analytics technique that estimates the relationships among variables, often used for prediction and forecasting.

Reinforcement Learning (RL) (pg. 150) - An area of machine learning concerned with how software agents ought to take actions in an environment to maximize some notion of cumulative reward.

Structured Data (pg. 168) - Data that is organized in a predefined manner, typically in databases, making it easily searchable and understandable by data analytics algorithms.

Unlabeled Data (pg. 192) - Data that does not have explicit labels or annotations, often used in unsupervised learning tasks within data analytics to find hidden patterns or intrinsic structures.

Unstructured Data (pg. 194) - Data that is not organized in a predefined way, common in text, images, and videos, which poses unique challenges and opportunities in data analytics.

Unsupervised Learning (pg. 196) - Learning patterns from untagged data, without any given outcomes or answers.

Data Science (DS)

These terms cover a wide range of concepts, processes, and techniques fundamental to the field of data science, from data preparation and exploration to the application of machine learning models for extracting insights and making predictions.

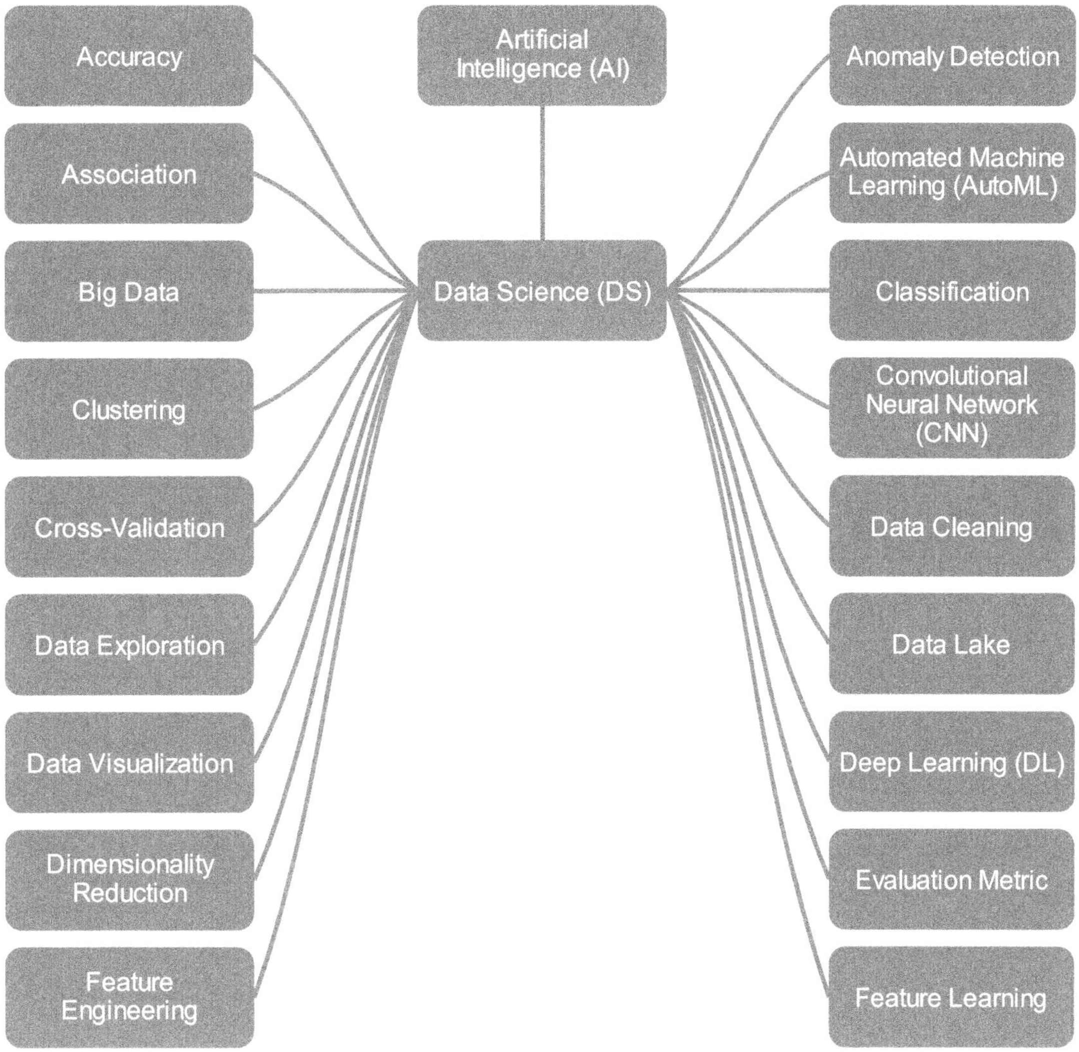

Figure 113: A simple mind map of "Data Science (DS)".

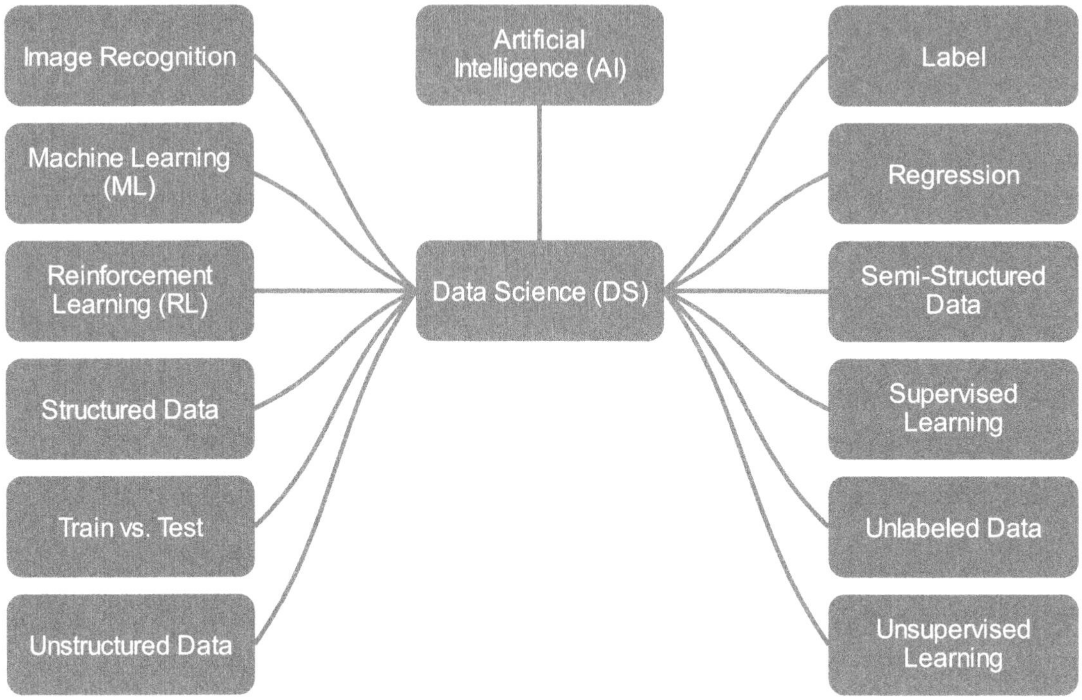

Figure 114: A simple mind map of "Data Science (DS)" continued.

Accuracy (pg. 15) - A fundamental metric in data science used to measure the correctness of a model's predictions.

Anomaly Detection (pg. 27) - The identification of unusual patterns that do not conform to expected behavior, widely used in data science for fraud detection, network security, and anomaly detection in time series data.

Association (pg. 31) - A method in data mining to discover the probability of the co-occurrence of items in a collection.

Automated Machine Learning (AutoML) (pg. 37) - The process of automating the tasks of applying machine learning to real-world problems.

Big Data (pg. 39) - Refers to extremely large datasets that cannot be analyzed with traditional data processing techniques, a key area of focus in data science.

Classification (pg. 41) - A data science technique where models are trained to categorize inputs into predefined classes or groups.

Clustering (pg. 43) - An unsupervised learning technique used in data science to group similar data points together based on their characteristics.

Convolutional Neural Network (CNN) (pg. 51) - A deep learning algorithm which can take in an input image, assign importance to various aspects/objects in the image and be able to differentiate one from the other.

Cross-Validation (pg. 57) - A model validation technique in data science used to assess how the results of a statistical analysis will generalize to an independent dataset.

Data Cleaning (pg. 61) - The process of preparing data for analysis by removing or correcting data that is incorrect, incomplete, irrelevant, duplicated, or improperly formatted.

Data Exploration (pg. 63) - The initial phase in data analysis where data scientists use statistical summaries and visualization techniques to understand the characteristics and relationships within the data.

Data Lake (pg. 65) - A storage repository that holds a vast amount of raw data in its native format until needed, often used in data science for big data storage and analysis.

Data Visualization (pg. 67) - The graphical representation of data, an essential part of data science for communicating findings and insights effectively.

Deep Learning (DL) (pg. 69) - A class of machine learning algorithms that use several layers of neural networks to extract progressively higher level features from the raw input.

Dimensionality Reduction (pg. 71) - A process used in data science to reduce the number of input variables in a dataset, simplifying models without losing significant information.

Evaluation Metric (pg. 80) - Criteria used in data science to assess the performance of a model or algorithm, such as accuracy, precision, recall, and F1 score.

Feature Engineering (pg. 88) - The process of selecting, modifying, or creating new features from raw data, a critical step in improving the performance of data science models.

Feature Learning (pg. 90) - Techniques that allow a system to automatically discover the representations needed from raw data for detection or classification.

Image Recognition (pg. 102) - The process of identifying and detecting an object or a feature in a digital image or video.

Label (pg. 108) - In supervised learning, a label is the target variable that a model is trained to predict, based on the input features.

Machine Learning (ML) (pg. 12) - A core component of data science, focusing on developing algorithms that allow computers to learn from and make predictions or decisions based on data.

Regression (pg. 148) - A statistical method used in data science for modeling and analyzing the relationships between dependent and independent variables.

Reinforcement Learning (RL) (pg. 150) - A type of machine learning technique that enables an algorithm to learn through trial and error using feedback from its own actions and experiences.

Semi-Structured Data (pg. 162) - Data that does not reside in a relational database but has some organizational properties that make it easier to analyze, common in data science.

Structured Data (pg. 168) - Data that adheres to a pre-defined data model and is easy to analyze. Structured data includes numbers, dates, and strings.

Supervised Learning (pg. 170) - A type of machine learning where the model is trained on a labeled dataset, which includes both the input data and the correct output.

Train vs. Test (pg. 184) - In data science, this refers to the practice of dividing a dataset into a training set used to train a model, and a test set used to evaluate its performance.

Unlabeled Data (pg. 192) - Data that lacks explicit labels, making it suitable for unsupervised learning tasks in data science, such as clustering or dimensionality reduction.

Unstructured Data (pg. 194) - Data that does not have a pre-defined data model, often text-heavy and requiring special processing to derive value from it, a common challenge in data science.

Unsupervised Learning (pg. 196) - A type of machine learning where the model is trained on data without explicit answers, used in data science for clustering, association, and dimensionality reduction tasks.

Deep Learning (DL)

These terms cover the essential concepts and architectures that are foundational to deep learning, highlighting the structures and methodologies used to build models capable of learning from data in ways that mimic the depth and complexity of human learning processes.

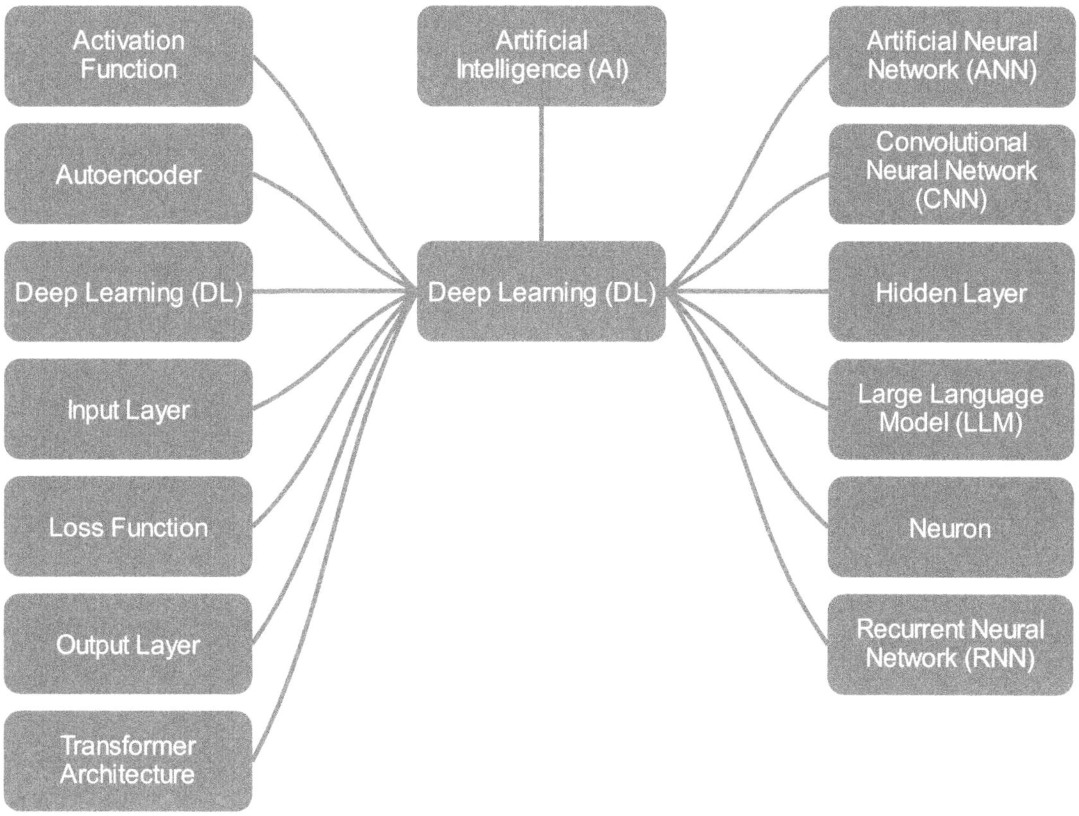

Figure 115: A simple mind map of "Deep Learning (DL)".

Activation Function (pg. 19) - Functions that decide whether a neuron should be activated or not, influencing the neuron's output based on its input.

Artificial Neural Network (ANN) (pg. 29) - The foundational structure for deep learning, composed of layers of interconnected nodes or "neurons" that process data.

Autoencoder (pg. 35) - A type of neural network used for unsupervised tasks like dimensionality reduction or feature learning, where the network is trained to encode input data as representations and then decode these representations back to the original input format.

Convolutional Neural Network (CNN) (pg. 51) - A class of deep neural networks, most commonly applied to analyzing visual imagery, using convolutional layers to process data in a grid-like topology.

Deep Learning (DL) (pg. 69) - A subset of machine learning involving neural networks with many layers (deep networks) that learn representations of data through a hierarchy of increasing complexity or abstraction.

Hidden Layer (pg. 100) - Layers within a neural network that are neither input nor output layers. In deep learning, networks often contain multiple hidden layers, contributing to the "depth" of the network.

Input Layer (pg. 104) - The first layer in a neural network that receives the input signal to be processed by subsequent layers.

Large Language Model (LLM) (pg. 114) - A type of deep learning model that processes and generates natural language, trained on vast amounts of text data. Examples include models like GPT (Generative Pretrained Transformer).

Loss Function (pg. 116) - A function that measures the difference between the actual output of the model and the expected output, guiding the training of deep learning models by minimizing this loss.

Neuron (pg. 126) - A basic unit of computation in neural networks, modeled after biological neurons, which processes inputs and generates an output signal.

Output Layer (pg. 128) - The layer in a neural network that produces the final output of the model, providing the end result of the computation.

Recurrent Neural Network (RNN) (pg. 146) - A type of neural network where connections between units form a directed cycle, allowing it to use internal memory to process sequences of inputs, useful in time-series data or natural language.

Transformer Architecture (pg. 186) - A model architecture designed for handling sequential data, without requiring the sequence to be processed in order. It relies heavily on self-attention mechanisms and is widely used in state-of-the-art natural language processing tasks.

Emerging Technologies

These terms represent some of the most dynamic and rapidly evolving areas within artificial intelligence and machine learning, signifying the frontier of research and application in the field.

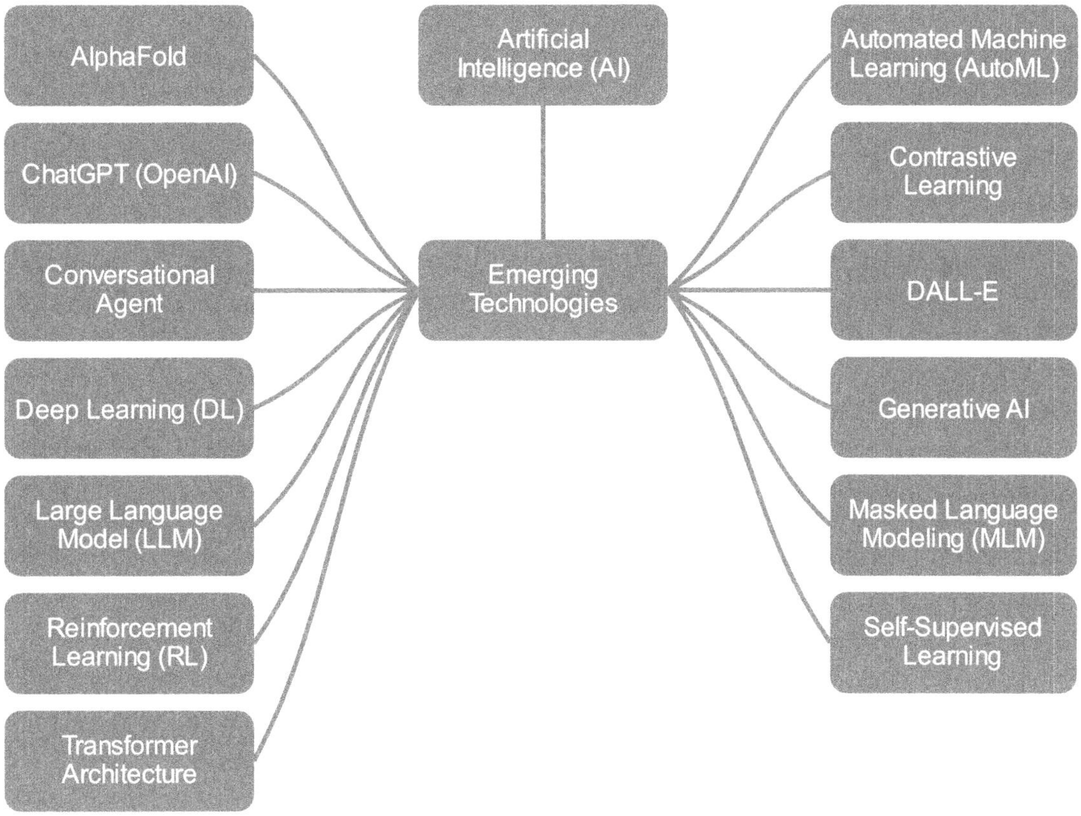

Figure 116: A simple mind map of "Emerging Technologies".

AlphaFold (pg. 25) - A state-of-the-art AI system developed by DeepMind for predicting the 3D structures of proteins, representing a significant breakthrough in the field of biology.

Automated Machine Learning (AutoML) (pg. 37) - The process of automating the end-to-end process of applying machine learning to real-world problems, making ML more accessible to non-experts.

ChatGPT (OpenAI) (pg. 8) - A variant of the GPT (Generative Pretrained Transformer) models by OpenAI, designed for generating human-like text, indicative of rapid advancements in natural language processing.

Contrastive Learning (pg. 47) - A relatively recent approach in unsupervised learning that learns representations by contrasting positive examples with negative examples, enhancing the ability of models to learn more robust features.

Conversational Agent (pg. 49) - AI systems designed to communicate with humans in a natural, conversational manner.

DALL-E (pg. 59) - An AI program by OpenAI that generates images from textual descriptions, showcasing the intersection of natural language understanding and creative image generation.

Deep Learning (DL) (pg. 69) - Although not new, deep learning continues to be at the forefront of AI advancements, driving innovations across various fields including computer vision, NLP, and more.

Generative AI (pg. 10) - Refers to AI models that can generate new data that resembles the training data, such as new images, music, or text, and includes technologies like GANs (Generative Adversarial Networks).

Large Language Model (LLM) (pg. 114) - These models, such as GPT-3, represent the cutting edge in natural language processing, capable of tasks ranging from writing essays to coding, based on vast amounts of training data.

Masked Language Modeling (MLM) (pg. 120) - A training strategy used in models like BERT, where some words in a sentence are masked and the model is trained to predict them, pushing the boundaries of context understanding in NLP.

Reinforcement Learning (RL) (pg. 150) - A dynamic and promising area of ML where models learn to make decisions by trying to maximize some notion of cumulative reward, increasingly used in complex decision-making and gaming.

Self-Supervised Learning (pg. 158) - An emerging learning paradigm where the algorithm learns to predict part of the input from other parts, reducing the need for labeled data and expanding AI's applicability.

Transformer Architecture (pg. 186) - The foundation of many state-of-the-art language models, including GPT and BERT, transformers have revolutionized natural language processing and are being explored in other domains.

Ethical AI, Social Implications and Cultural Considerations

These terms underscore the importance of integrating ethical considerations, societal impacts, and cultural sensitivities into the development, deployment, and governance of AI technologies, ensuring they serve the common good and respect human dignity and rights.

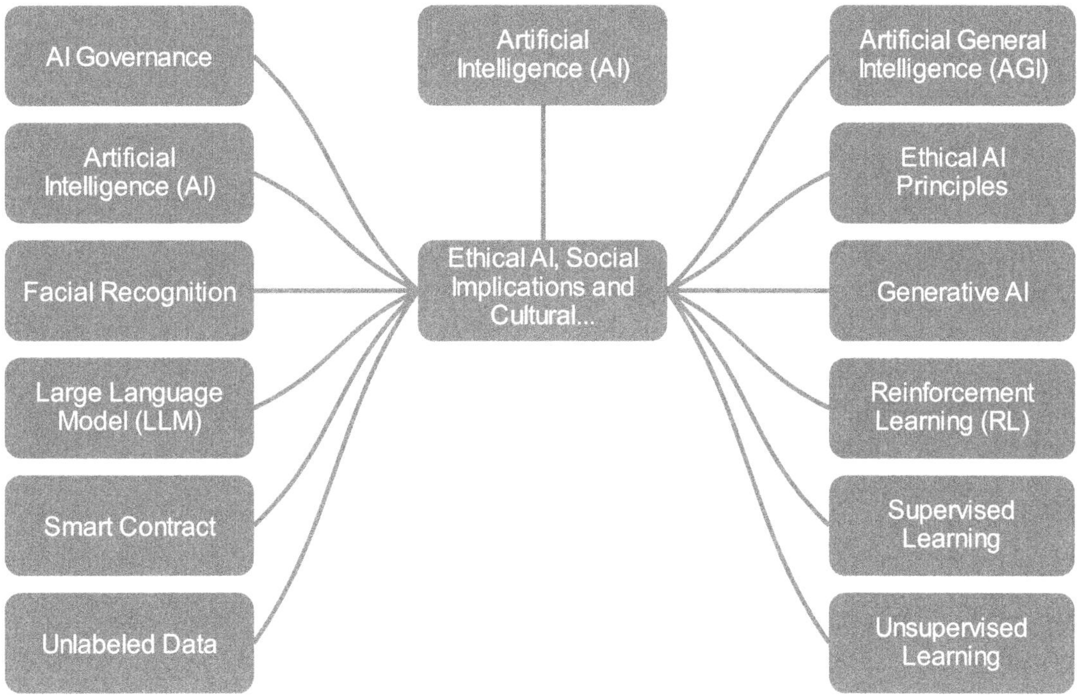

Figure 117: A simple mind map of "Ethical AI, Social Implications and Cultural Considerations".

AI Governance (pg. 23) -

Artificial General Intelligence (AGI) (pg. 4) - The concept of machines with the ability to understand, learn, and apply intelligence to solve any problem, similar to human intelligence, raising significant ethical and social implications regarding autonomy, control, and the future role of humans.

Artificial Intelligence (AI) (pg. 2) - The broader field itself necessitates consideration of ethical and social implications, including issues of bias, privacy, job displacement, and the broader impact on society and cultural norms.

Ethical AI Principles (pg. 77) - Guidelines and frameworks designed to ensure the development and use of AI technologies align with ethical standards, promoting fairness, accountability, transparency, and respect for human rights.

Facial Recognition (pg. 86) - A technology with profound ethical and social implications, particularly concerning privacy, surveillance, consent, and the potential for discriminatory practices.

Generative AI (pg. 10) - This encompasses technologies that generate new content, such as deepfakes or synthetic media, which raise concerns about misinformation, authenticity, and the ethical use of generated content.

Large Language Model (LLM) (pg. 114) - Such models, like ChatGPT (OpenAI), bring forward questions of ethical content generation, the propagation of biases, the potential for misuse in generating misleading information, and the cultural context of generated content.

Reinforcement Learning (RL) (pg. 150) - This method, especially when applied in social contexts or autonomous systems, raises ethical considerations around decision-making criteria, reward systems, and unintended consequences of learned behaviors.

Smart Contract (pg. 166) - While primarily a blockchain concept, when integrated with AI, it raises ethical considerations regarding autonomous decision-making, legal implications, and transparency.

Supervised Learning (pg. 170) - The reliance on labeled data introduces the potential for perpetuating existing biases and inequalities present in the data, necessitating ethical considerations in data selection and model evaluation.

Unlabeled Data (pg. 192) - The use of unlabeled data, especially in contexts involving personal information, raises concerns around privacy, consent, and the ethical use of data.

Unsupervised Learning (pg. 196) - This approach can uncover hidden patterns in data, which, while powerful, raises ethical questions about surveillance, privacy, and the potential discovery and use of sensitive or personal information without explicit consent.

Fundamental Data Concepts

These terms encapsulate the core data concepts essential for understanding, processing, and leveraging data within the fields of artificial intelligence and machine learning, forming the basis for a wide range of applications and innovations.

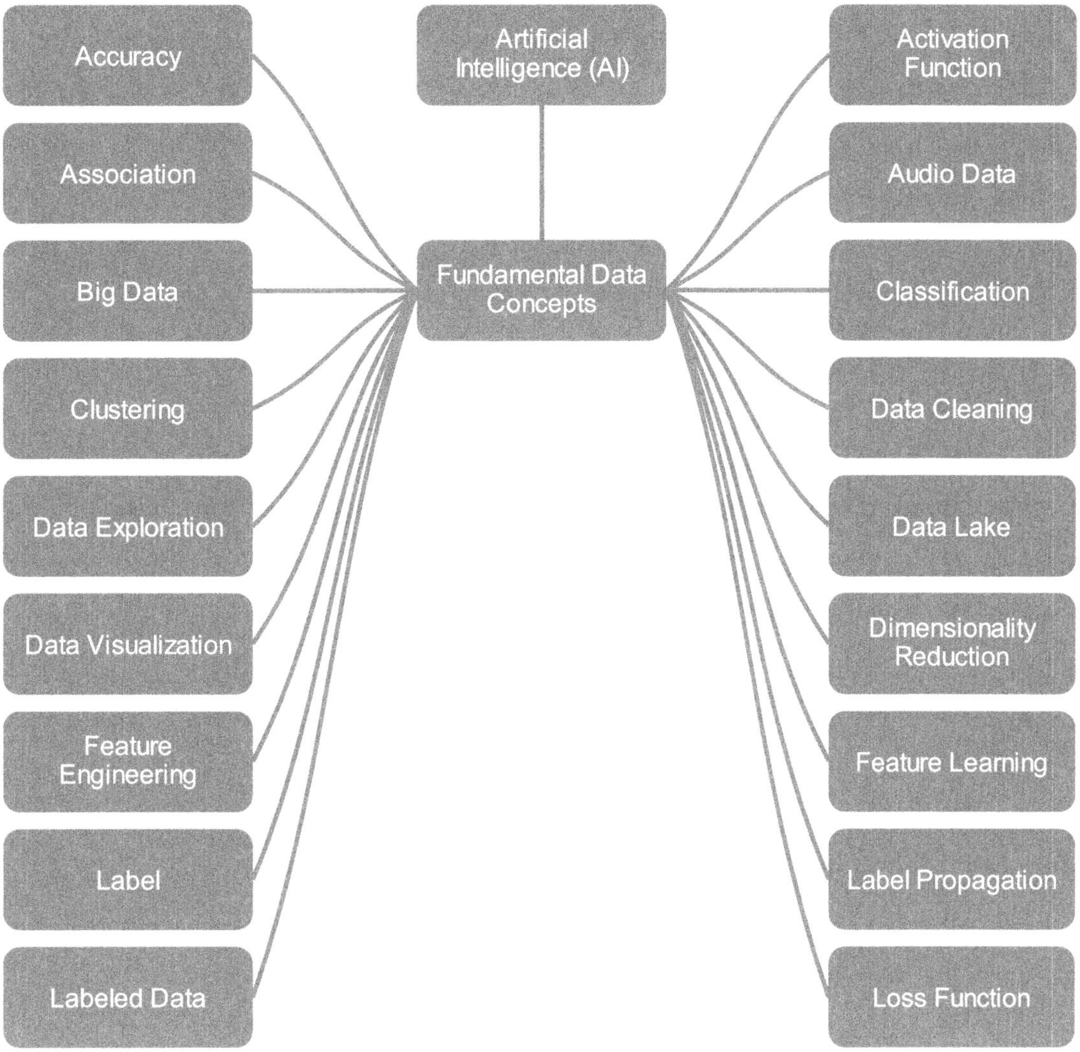

Figure 118: A simple mind map of "Fundamental Data Concepts".

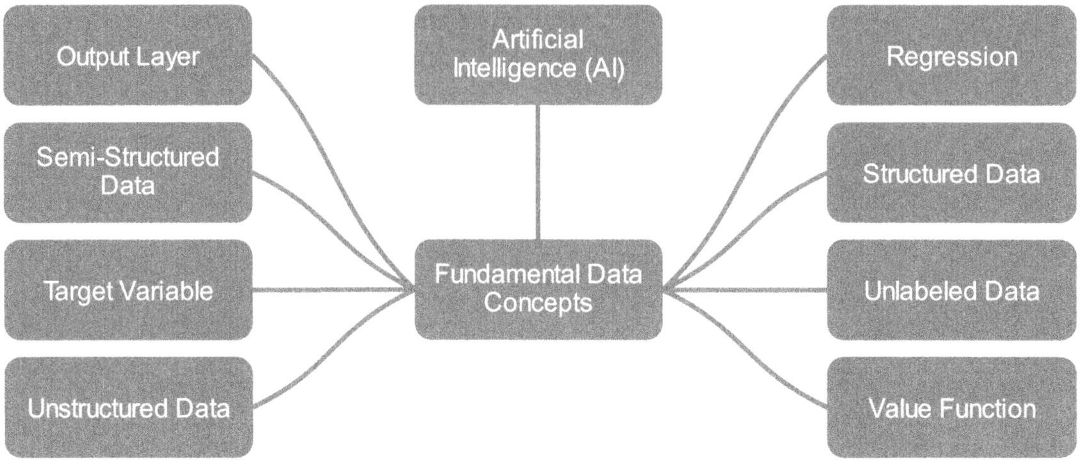

Figure 119: A simple mind map of "Fundamental Data Concepts" continued.

Accuracy (pg. 15) - A measure of how correct or precise an outcome is compared to the true value, fundamental in evaluating the performance of AI models.

Activation Function (pg. 19) - A function in a neural network that helps determine the output of a neuron.

Association (pg. 31) - A concept in data analysis that involves finding relationships between variables in datasets, crucial for understanding correlations and causations in data.

Audio Data (pg. 33) - Represents sound information, a fundamental type of data in AI for tasks like speech recognition, music analysis, and environmental sound understanding.

Big Data (pg. 39) - Refers to extremely large datasets that traditional data processing software cannot manage, a foundational concept in understanding the scale of data AI technologies can work with.

Classification (pg. 41) - A fundamental data concept where objects are categorized into predefined groups, a basic task in supervised learning within AI.

Clustering (pg. 43) - An unsupervised learning technique where data is grouped into clusters based on similarity, fundamental for discovering patterns and structures in data without prior labeling.

Data Cleaning (pg. 61) - The process of fixing or removing incorrect, corrupted, duplicate, or incomplete data within a dataset, crucial for ensuring the quality and reliability of data in AI models.

Data Exploration (pg. 63) - Involves analyzing datasets to find initial patterns, characteristics, and points of interest without having a specific goal in mind, a foundational step in data analysis.

Data Lake (pg. 65) - A storage system that holds a large amount of raw data in its native format until needed, fundamental for managing diverse and unstructured data in AI and ML projects.

Data Visualization (pg. 67) - The graphical representation of data, essential for understanding complex datasets and communicating findings effectively in AI and ML.

Dimensionality Reduction (pg. 71) - The process of reducing the number of input variables in a dataset, crucial for simplifying AI models and reducing computational complexity.

Feature Engineering (pg. 88) - The process of using domain knowledge to extract features from raw data.

Feature Learning (pg. 90) - The technique of learning features directly from data, used in machine learning for improving model accuracies.

Label (pg. 108) - In supervised learning, the part of the dataset that denotes the outcome for each instance.

Label Propagation (pg. 110) - A semi-supervised technique where labels are propagated from labeled data to unlabeled data within a dataset, fundamental for leveraging both labeled and unlabeled data in learning.

Labeled Data (pg. 112) - Data that has been tagged with one or more labels, identifying certain properties or categories, essential for supervised learning in AI.

Loss Function (pg. 116) - A method to evaluate how well a specific algorithm models the given data. If predictions deviate from actual results, loss functions provide a measure of this deviation, fundamental in training AI models.

Output Layer (pg. 128) - The final layer in a neural network that produces the model's predictions.

Regression (pg. 148) - A type of supervised learning that aims to predict a continuous value.

Semi-Structured Data (pg. 162) - A type of data that does not conform to a formal structure of data models but contains tags or other markers to separate semantic elements and enforce hierarchies of records and fields, important in dealing with diverse data sources.

Structured Data (pg. 168) - Data that adheres to a pre-defined data model and is easy to analyze, typically stored in relational databases, fundamental for traditional data processing and analysis.

Target Variable (pg. 172) - The variable that a model is trained to predict, a fundamental concept in supervised learning within AI and ML.

Unlabeled Data (pg. 192) - Data that does not have explicit labels, making it suitable for unsupervised learning tasks, fundamental for exploring data patterns without preconceived notions.

Unstructured Data (pg. 194) - Data that does not have a pre-defined data model or is not organized in a predefined manner, such as texts, images, and videos, presenting unique challenges and opportunities in AI and ML.

Value Function (pg. 198) - In the context of reinforcement learning, it represents the total amount of reward an agent can expect to accumulate over the future, guiding decision-making processes.

Fundamental Mathematics and Statistics

These terms highlight the core mathematical and statistical concepts that underpin the theory and practice of artificial intelligence and machine learning, providing the foundation for developing algorithms and understanding their behavior.

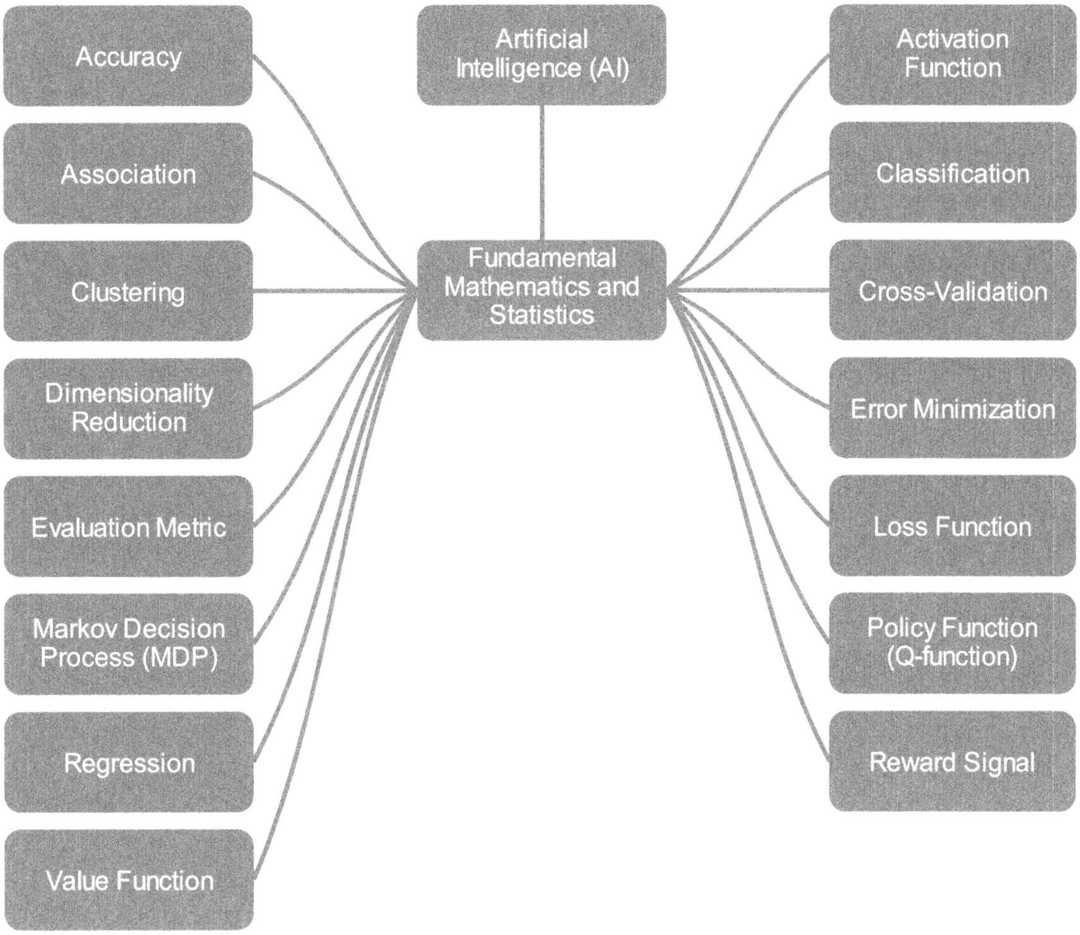

Figure 120: A simple mind map of "Fundamental Mathematics and Statistics".

Accuracy (pg. 15) - A statistical measure of how well a binary classification test correctly identifies or excludes a condition, fundamental in evaluating model performance.

Activation Function (pg. 19) - A mathematical equation that determines the output of a neural network node given an input or set of inputs, crucial for introducing non-linearity into the model.

Association (pg. 31) - Refers to rules or patterns that describe how variables within a dataset relate to each other, based on principles of correlation and causation in statistics.

Classification (pg. 41) - A problem where the output variable is a category, such as "spam" or "not spam", involving statistical methods for assigning inputs into categories.

Clustering (pg. 43) - A statistical method used to group a set of objects in such a way that objects in the same group (called a cluster) are more similar to each other than to those in other groups.

Cross-Validation (pg. 57) - A statistical method used to estimate the skill of machine learning models. It divides the data into subsets, trains the model on some subsets and validates it on others.

Dimensionality Reduction (pg. 71) - A process of reducing the number of random variables under consideration, by obtaining a set of principal variables. Techniques like PCA (Principal Component Analysis) are foundational statistical methods used here.

Error Minimization (pg. 75) - Involves mathematical optimization techniques to adjust the parameters of a model to minimize the difference between the predicted and actual values.

Evaluation Metric (pg. 80) - Statistical measures used to assess the performance of a model or algorithm, including precision, recall, F1 score, and others.

Loss Function (pg. 116) - A mathematical function that quantifies the difference between the expected outcomes and the outcomes predicted by the model, guiding the optimization process in machine learning.

Markov Decision Process (MDP) (pg. 118) - A mathematical framework for modeling decision making in situations where outcomes are partly random and partly under the control of a decision-maker.

Policy Function (Q-function) (pg. 132) - In reinforcement learning, a function that represents the expected return of taking an action in a given state, following a certain policy, grounded in the mathematics of decision processes.

Regression (pg. 148) - A statistical method for estimating the relationships among variables. It's fundamental in predicting a continuous-valued attribute associated with an object.

Reward Signal (pg. 152) - In reinforcement learning, a scalar feedback signal that indicates how well an action taken by an agent is at achieving the goal, central to the statistical concept of reward maximization.

Value Function (pg. 198) - In the context of reinforcement learning, a function that estimates how good a particular state is for an agent to be in, based on expected future rewards, embodying principles of predictive modeling and expectation in statistics.

Future Directions, Trends and Challenges

These terms highlight the dynamic nature of AI and ML, pointing to areas where significant advancements and breakthroughs are anticipated, along with the challenges and ethical considerations that accompany these technological evolutions.

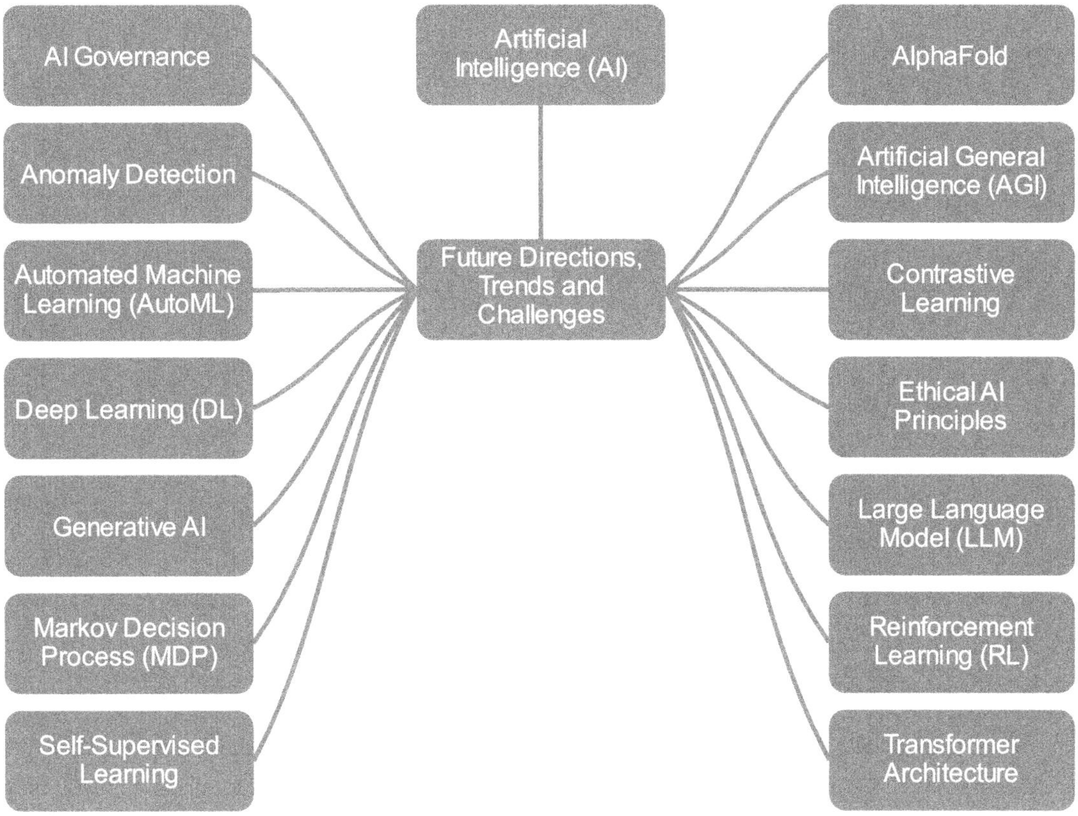

Figure 121: A simple mind map of "Future Directions, Trends and Challenges".

AI Governance (pg. 23) -

AlphaFold (pg. 25) - Representing a significant breakthrough in the prediction of protein structures, AlphaFold symbolizes the future direction of AI in revolutionizing fields like biology and drug discovery.

Anomaly Detection (pg. 27) - The identification of items, events, or observations which do not conform to an expected pattern.

Artificial General Intelligence (AGI) (pg. 4) - The pursuit of AGI, where machines would possess the ability to understand, learn, and apply intelligence across a broad range of tasks, remains a profound future challenge and direction for AI research.

Automated Machine Learning (AutoML) (pg. 37) - As a trend that democratizes and accelerates the AI development process, AutoML represents a future where more people can participate in creating AI solutions without deep technical expertise.

Contrastive Learning (pg. 47) - An emerging trend in unsupervised learning that might redefine how machines learn from data, minimizing the reliance on large labeled datasets.

Deep Learning (DL) (pg. 69) - While already transformative, the future of deep learning involves overcoming current limitations, such as data inefficiency and lack of interpretability, and finding new architectures beyond the current paradigms.

Ethical AI Principles (pg. 77) - As AI becomes more integrated into society, the future will increasingly demand robust frameworks and guidelines to ensure the ethical use of AI, addressing issues like bias, privacy, and accountability.

Generative AI (pg. 10) - With technologies like GANs (Generative Adversarial Networks) and models like DALL-E, generative AI is poised to redefine creative fields, content generation, and more, while also presenting challenges related to authenticity and misuse.

Large Language Model (LLM) (pg. 114) - The development and deployment of large language models present both opportunities for advancements in natural language understanding and generation, and challenges related to computational resources, biases, and ethical concerns.

Markov Decision Process (MDP) (pg. 118) - Fundamental to reinforcement learning, future advancements in solving complex Markov decision processes could unlock new levels of autonomy in AI systems, from robotics to decision support systems.

Reinforcement Learning (RL) (pg. 150) - As a paradigm that mimics the way humans learn from interaction with the environment, the future of reinforcement learning involves tackling more complex, real-world problems, but also addressing issues like safety and robustness in learned policies.

Self-Supervised Learning (pg. 158) - A trend that addresses the challenge of learning from unlabeled data, self-supervised learning represents a significant direction for making AI more adaptable and efficient in understanding the world.

Transformer Architecture (pg. 186) - The basis for many recent advancements in NLP, future research might extend the transformative impact of this architecture to other domains like computer vision, and address challenges related to computational efficiency and model interpretability.

Image Processing

These terms represent key concepts, tasks, and technologies within the field of image processing, highlighting the focus on enabling machines to interpret and understand visual information from the world around us.

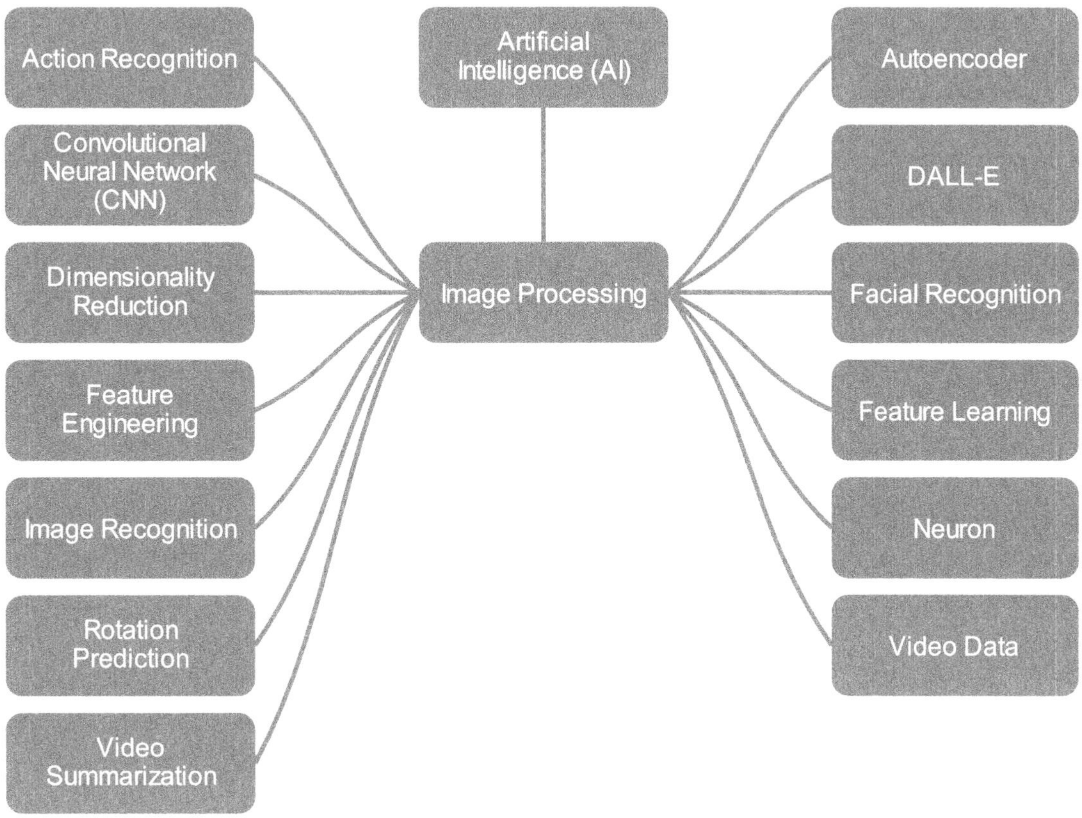

Figure 122: A simple mind map of "Image Processing".

Action Recognition (pg. 17) - A task in image processing and computer vision that involves analyzing video sequences to identify specific actions or behaviors.

Autoencoder (pg. 35) - A type of artificial neural network used in image processing for tasks such as dimensionality reduction, feature learning, and image reconstruction.

Convolutional Neural Network (CNN) (pg. 51) - A specialized kind of neural network for processing data with a grid-like topology, such as images, making it a cornerstone of modern image processing techniques.

DALL-E (pg. 59) - An AI model developed by OpenAI that generates images from textual descriptions, showcasing the intersection of natural language processing and image generation.

Dimensionality Reduction (pg. 71) - A technique in image processing that involves reducing the number of input variables or features in images, used to simplify models and reduce computational complexity.

Facial Recognition (pg. 86) - The use of image processing to identify or verify individuals from digital images or video frames based on facial features.

Feature Engineering (pg. 88) - The process of selecting, modifying, or creating new features from raw data, crucial in image processing for improving the performance of machine learning models.

Feature Learning (pg. 90) - An aspect of image processing where models learn to automatically identify and use the relevant features in images for tasks like classification or recognition.

Image Recognition (pg. 102) - The ability of AI to identify objects, places, people, writing, and actions in images, a fundamental task in image processing.

Neuron (pg. 126) - While a basic unit in artificial neural networks, in the context of image processing, neurons in layers of a CNN can specialize in detecting specific features in images, like edges or textures.

Rotation Prediction (pg. 154) - A task often used in self-supervised learning within image processing where a model is trained to predict the rotation applied to an input image, aiding in learning feature representations.

Video Data (pg. 200) - Refers to the processing and analysis of video data to understand its content and context within AI and ML frameworks.

Video Summarization (pg. 202) - The process of creating a condensed version of a video that still conveys the most important information.

Industry Applications

These terms reflect the diverse and transformative applications of AI and ML technologies across different sectors, showcasing their ability to solve industry-specific challenges, enhance efficiency, and create new opportunities.

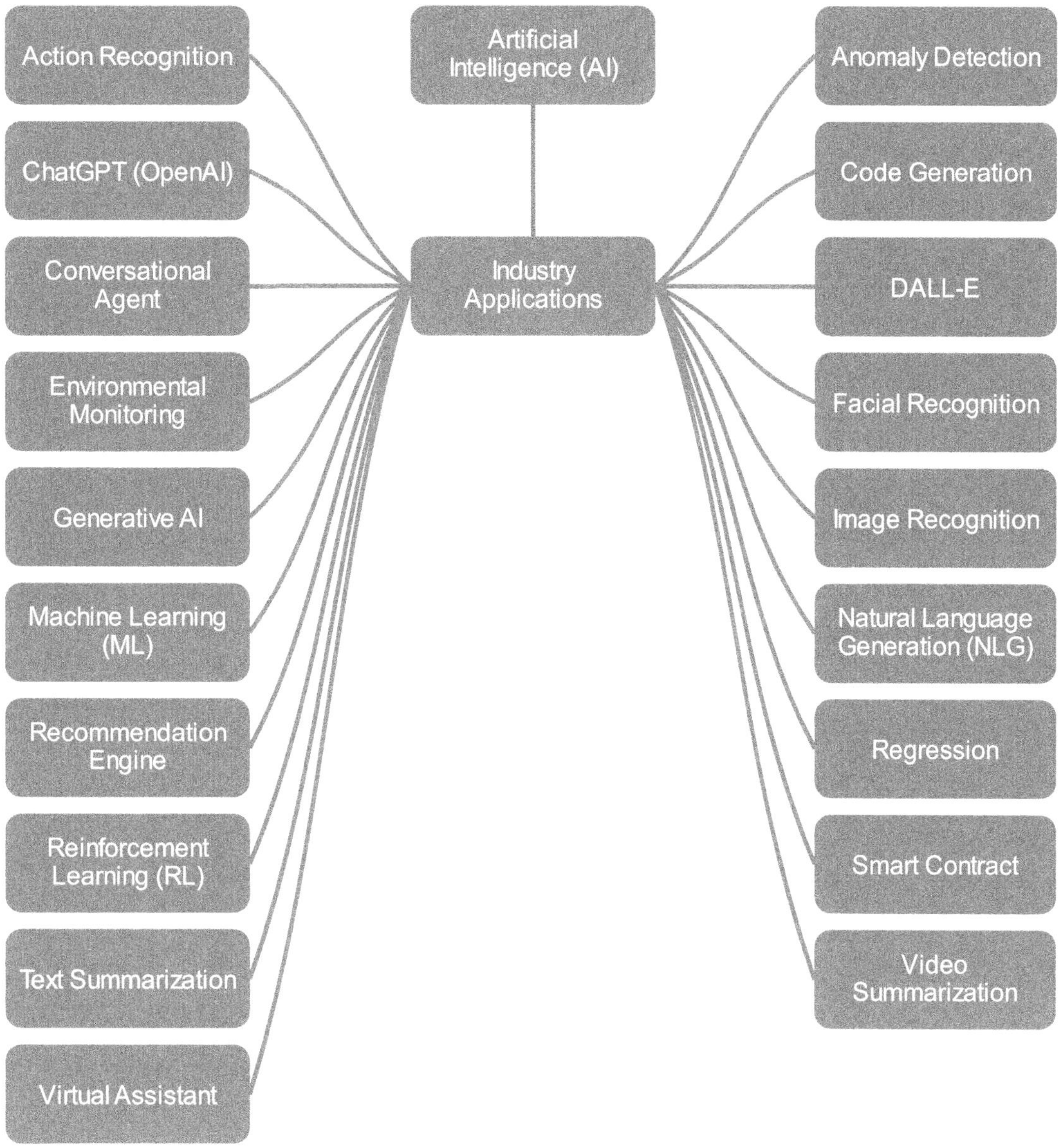

Figure 123: A simple mind map of "Industry Applications".

Action Recognition (pg. 17) - Used in security, surveillance, sports analytics, and entertainment industries to identify specific actions or behaviors in video content.

Anomaly Detection (pg. 27) - Widely applied in finance for fraud detection, manufacturing for defect detection, and IT for network security and system health monitoring.

ChatGPT (OpenAI) (pg. 8) - Employed in customer service for automated responses, content creation industries for generating articles or scripts, and education for tutoring and learning support.

Code Generation (pg. 45) - Utilized in the software development industry to automate coding tasks, enhance productivity, and reduce human error.

Conversational Agent (pg. 49) - Used in customer service and support across various sectors including retail, banking, and healthcare to provide automated, real-time user assistance.

DALL-E (pg. 59) - Applied in creative industries like advertising, graphic design, and content creation to generate unique visual content from textual descriptions.

Environmental Monitoring (pg. 73) - The use of technology and AI to monitor natural environments and ecosystems for changes or threats.

Facial Recognition (pg. 86) - Employed in security and surveillance, smartphone authentication, and personalized customer service experiences in retail and hospitality.

Generative AI (pg. 10) - Used in entertainment for music and video creation, fashion for design ideation, and gaming for content generation.

Image Recognition (pg. 102) - Applied in healthcare for medical imaging and diagnosis, automotive for driver assistance systems, and retail for product identification and cataloging.

Machine Learning (ML) (pg. 12) - Broadly applied across sectors like finance for predictive analysis and algorithmic trading, healthcare for patient diagnosis and treatment recommendations, and manufacturing for predictive maintenance.

Natural Language Generation (NLG) (pg. 124) - Utilized in media and journalism for automated report generation, marketing for content creation, and customer service for automated responses.

Recommendation Engine (pg. 144) - Widely used in e-commerce for personalized shopping experiences, streaming services for content suggestions, and social media for personalized feeds.

Regression (pg. 148) - Employed in real estate for price prediction, finance for risk assessment, and marketing for sales forecasting.

Reinforcement Learning (RL) (pg. 150) - Applied in robotics for autonomous behavior, gaming for AI player strategies, and logistics for optimization problems.

Smart Contract (pg. 166) - Used in the finance industry for automated, self-executing contractual agreements, supply chain for transparent and automated transactions, and digital rights management.

Text Summarization (pg. 182) - Utilized in legal and research fields for summarizing documents, news aggregation platforms for creating concise news snippets, and businesses for generating executive reports from large datasets.

Video Summarization (pg. 202) - Applied in surveillance for quick event recaps, media for creating highlights of long videos, and personal media management for summarizing personal video collections.

Virtual Assistant (pg. 204) - Employed across various industries including technology, healthcare, and automotive for providing user assistance, information retrieval, and task automation.

Machine Learning (ML)

These terms encapsulate the core concepts, methodologies, and challenges within the field of machine learning, from the basics of model training and evaluation to the complexities of different learning paradigms.

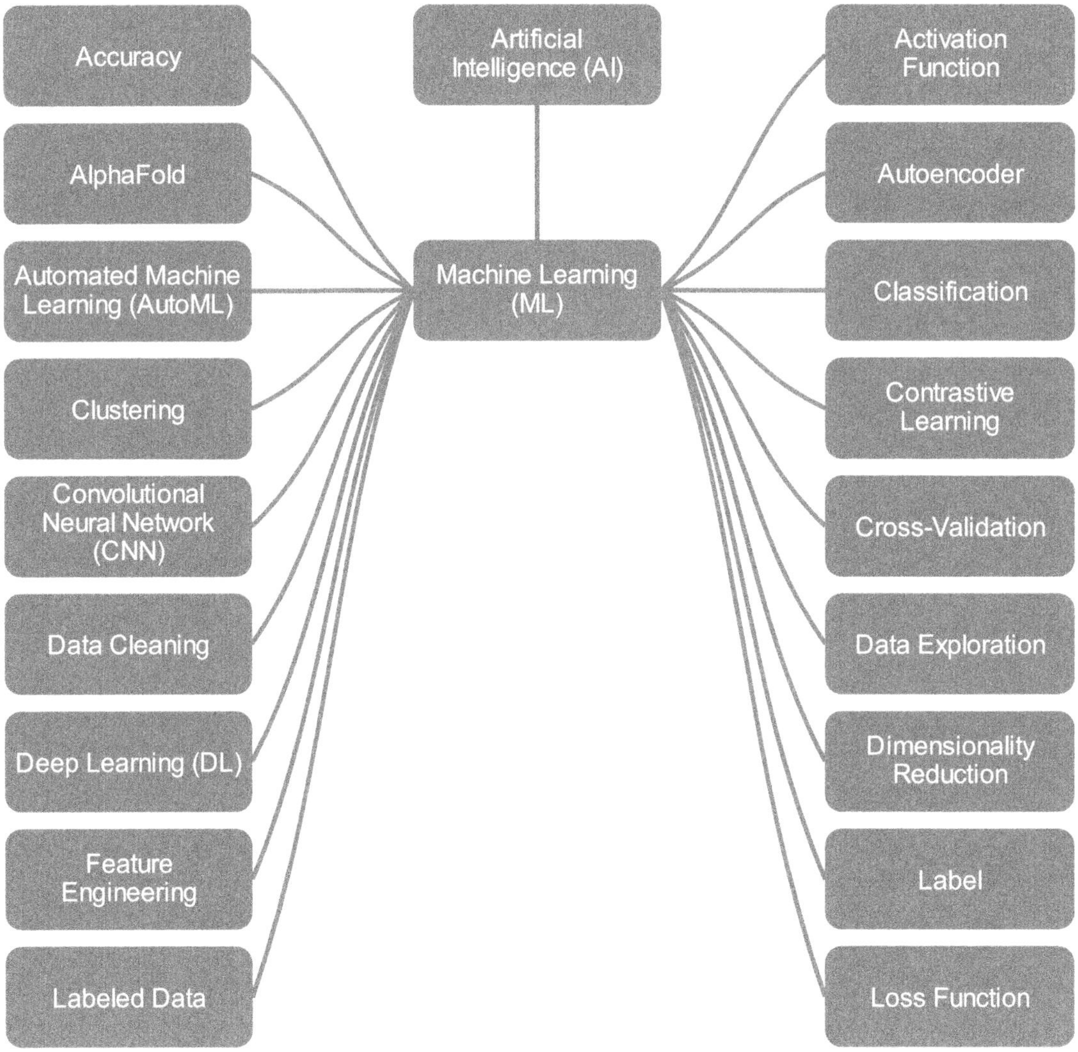

Figure 124: A simple mind map of "Machine Learning (ML)".

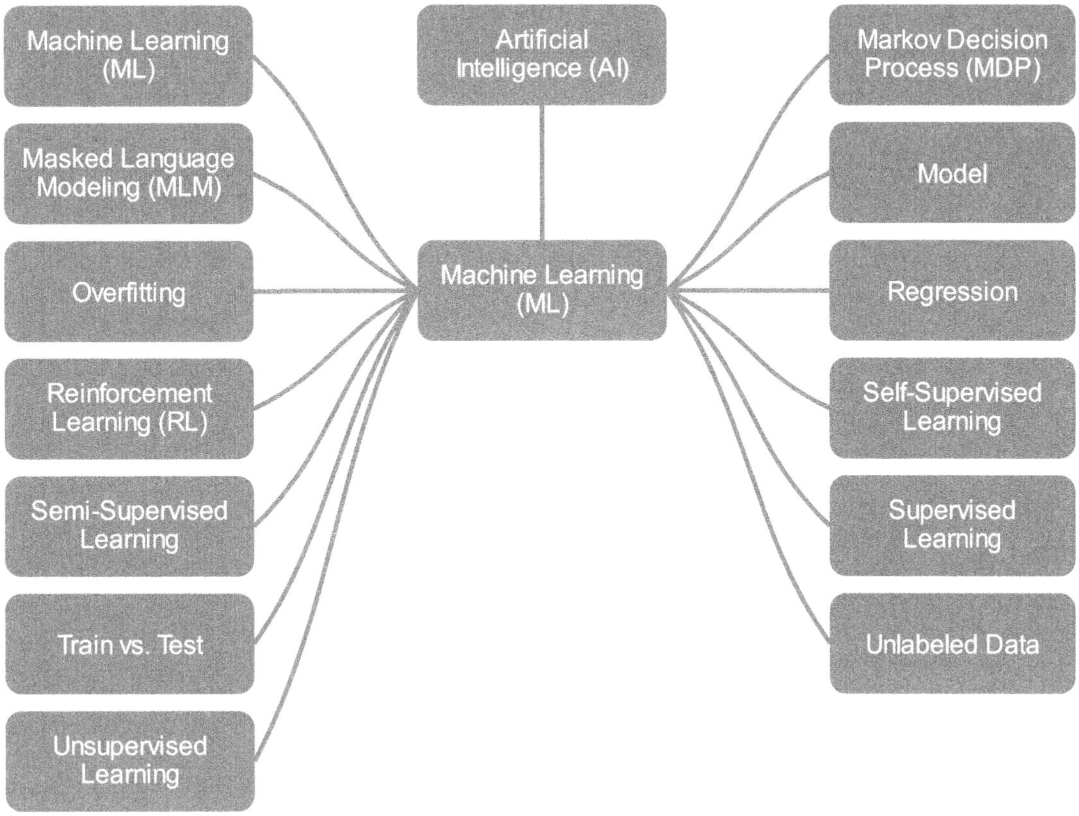

Figure 125: A simple mind map of "Machine Learning (ML)" continued.

Accuracy (pg. 15) - A metric used to evaluate the performance of a machine learning model, indicating the percentage of correct predictions made by the model.

Activation Function (pg. 19) - A function in a neural network that determines the output of a node given an input or set of inputs, crucial for adding non-linearity to the model's learning process.

AlphaFold (pg. 25) - DeepMind's AI for predicting the 3D structures of proteins.

Autoencoder (pg. 35) - A type of neural network used in unsupervised learning tasks, such as feature learning and dimensionality reduction, by learning to encode input data as representations and then decode these representations back to the original format.

Automated Machine Learning (AutoML) (pg. 37) - The process of automating the process of applying machine learning to real-world problems

Classification (pg. 41) - A type of supervised machine learning task where the model is trained to categorize input data into predefined labels or classes.

Clustering (pg. 43) - An unsupervised learning technique where the algorithm groups a set of objects in such a way that objects in the same group are more similar to each other than to those in other groups.

Contrastive Learning (pg. 47) - A technique used in unsupervised learning that aims to learn representations by contrasting positive pairs against negative pairs.

Convolutional Neural Network (CNN) (pg. 51) - A deep learning algorithm particularly effective for image and video recognition, spatial hierarchies of features.

Cross-Validation (pg. 57) - A technique in machine learning to assess the generalizability of a model, involving partitioning the data into subsets, training the model on one subset, and validating it on another.

Data Cleaning (pg. 61) - The process of fixing or removing incorrect, corrupted, incorrectly formatted, duplicate, or incomplete data within a dataset.

Data Exploration (pg. 63) - The initial phase in data analysis, where users explore a large set of data and develop initial insights, patterns, and trends.

Deep Learning (DL) (pg. 69) - A subset of machine learning involving neural networks with multiple layers that learn representations of data with multiple levels of abstraction.

Dimensionality Reduction (pg. 71) - The process of reducing the number of random variables under consideration, by obtaining a set of principal variables.

Feature Engineering (pg. 88) - The process of selecting, modifying, or creating new input variables to improve the performance of machine learning models.

Label (pg. 108) - In supervised learning, a label is the answer or outcome that the model is trained to predict, based on the input data.

Labeled Data (pg. 112) - Data that has been tagged with one or more labels, identifying certain properties or categories, essential for supervised learning.

Loss Function (pg. 116) - A function that measures the difference between the actual output of the model and the expected output, used to guide the optimization of the model parameters.

Machine Learning (ML) (pg. 12) - The field of study that gives computers the ability to learn from data without being explicitly programmed, focusing on the development of algorithms that can learn from and make predictions on data.

Markov Decision Process (MDP) (pg. 118) - A mathematical framework for modeling decision-making in situations where outcomes are partly random and partly under the control of a decision-maker, used in reinforcement learning.

Masked Language Modeling (MLM) (pg. 120) - A fill-in-the-blank task, where a model uses the context to predict the masked words in a sentence.

Model (pg. 122) - In machine learning, a model is the representation learned from data; a mathematical structure that makes predictions based on input data.

Overfitting (pg. 130) - A modeling error that occurs when a machine learning model learns the detail and noise in the training data to the extent that it negatively impacts the model's performance on new data.

Regression (pg. 148) - A type of predictive modeling technique in machine learning that involves predicting a continuous outcome variable based on one or more predictor variables.

Reinforcement Learning (RL) (pg. 150) - A type of machine learning where an agent learns to make decisions by performing actions and receiving feedback in the form of rewards or penalties.

Self-Supervised Learning (pg. 158) - A form of unsupervised learning where the data itself provides supervision.

Semi-Supervised Learning (pg. 164) - A machine learning approach that involves a small amount of labeled data and a large amount of unlabeled data during training.

Supervised Learning (pg. 170) - A machine learning task where the model is trained on a labeled dataset, which includes both the input data and the correct output, and the model learns to predict the output from the input data.

Train vs. Test (pg. 184) - The practice in machine learning of dividing a dataset into a training set used to train the model, and a test set used to evaluate its performance.

Unlabeled Data (pg. 192) - Data that does not have explicit labels, making it suitable for unsupervised learning tasks in machine learning, such as clustering or dimensionality reduction.

Unsupervised Learning (pg. 196) - A type of machine learning where models learn patterns from unlabeled data without any explicit instructions on what to predict.

Natural Language Processing (NLP)

These terms highlight essential concepts and technologies within NLP, illustrating how AI models process, understand, and generate human language, enabling a wide range of applications that require interaction with textual data.

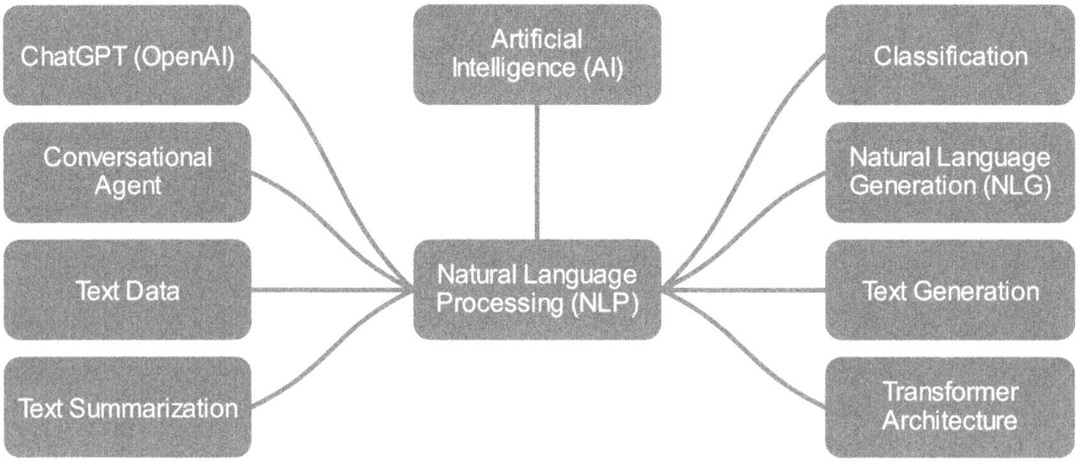

Figure 126: A simple mind map of "Natural Language Processing (NLP)".

ChatGPT (OpenAI) (pg. 8) - A variant of the Generative Pretrained Transformer models by OpenAI, designed specifically for generating human-like text, showcasing advancements in natural language understanding and generation.

Classification (pg. 41) - In NLP, classification tasks involve categorizing text into predefined categories or classes, such as sentiment analysis, spam detection, and topic categorization.

Conversational Agent (pg. 49) - AI systems that simulate human conversation, heavily reliant on NLP techniques to understand and generate natural language responses.

Natural Language Generation (NLG) (pg. 124) - The process of using AI to generate coherent and contextually relevant text based on a given input, used in applications like automated report writing, content creation, and chatbots.

Text Data (pg. 178) - Unstructured data in the form of text, which NLP aims to understand, interpret, and manipulate, encompassing everything from documents and emails to social media posts and web content.

Text Generation (pg. 180) - The creation of text content by AI models, an important aspect of NLP that enables applications such as content creation, language translation, and chatbots.

Text Summarization (pg. 182) - The process of creating a condensed version of a text document that captures the main points, an NLP task used in applications like news aggregation, research, and information retrieval.

Transformer Architecture (pg. 186) - A model architecture that has significantly advanced NLP through self-attention mechanisms, allowing models to weigh the importance of different words within a sentence, crucial for understanding context and meaning in language tasks.

Natural Language Understanding (NLU)

These terms underscore the core technologies and methodologies that enable machines to understand, interpret, and derive meaning from human language, a critical aspect of AI that powers a wide range of applications from chatbots to content analysis systems.

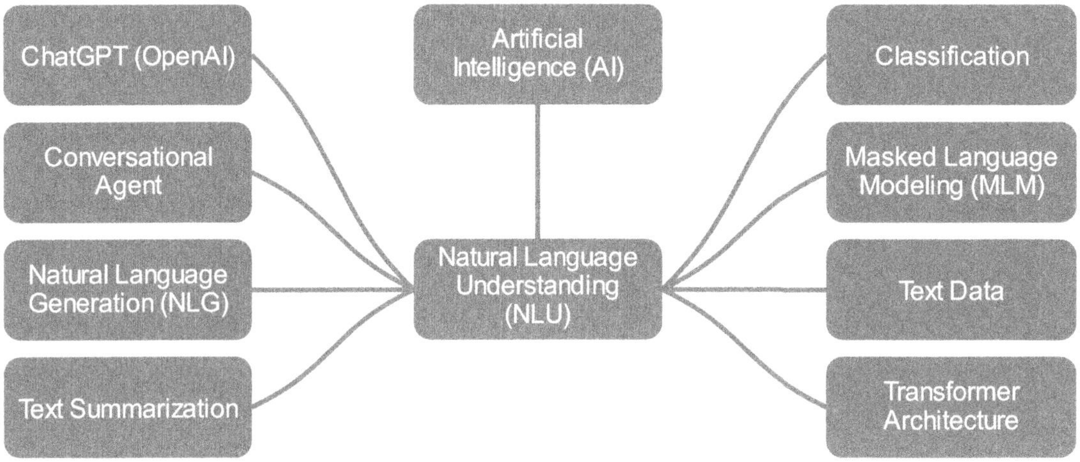

Figure 127: A simple mind map of "Natural Language Understanding (NLU)".

ChatGPT (OpenAI) (pg. 8) - A large language model developed by OpenAI that exemplifies advancements in NLU, capable of understanding context and generating human-like responses.

Classification (pg. 41) - In NLU, classification tasks involve understanding the intent or category of text, such as determining the sentiment of a review or the topic of a document.

Conversational Agent (pg. 49) - Systems that engage in dialogue with humans, requiring deep NLU capabilities to comprehend queries, discern intent, and generate appropriate responses.

Masked Language Modeling (MLM) (pg. 120) - A training technique used in models like BERT where some words in a sentence are masked, and the model learns to predict them, improving its understanding of language context and relationships.

Natural Language Generation (NLG) (pg. 124) - Although primarily focused on generating text, NLG relies on NLU to ensure the generated content is relevant and contextually appropriate, reflecting an understanding of the input and desired output.

Text Data (pg. 178) - The raw material for NLU, encompassing a wide variety of textual content that NLU technologies aim to interpret and derive meaning from.

Text Summarization (pg. 182) - Involves condensing large volumes of text while retaining key information, requiring deep understanding of the text to identify and extract the main points.

Transformer Architecture (pg. 186) - The foundation for many of the latest NLU models, transformers process text in a way that captures the nuances of language, including context and semantics, significantly advancing NLU capabilities.

Privacy and Security

These terms highlight key areas where privacy and security intersect with AI and ML, encompassing both the challenges and solutions in safeguarding data and ensuring ethical use of AI technologies.

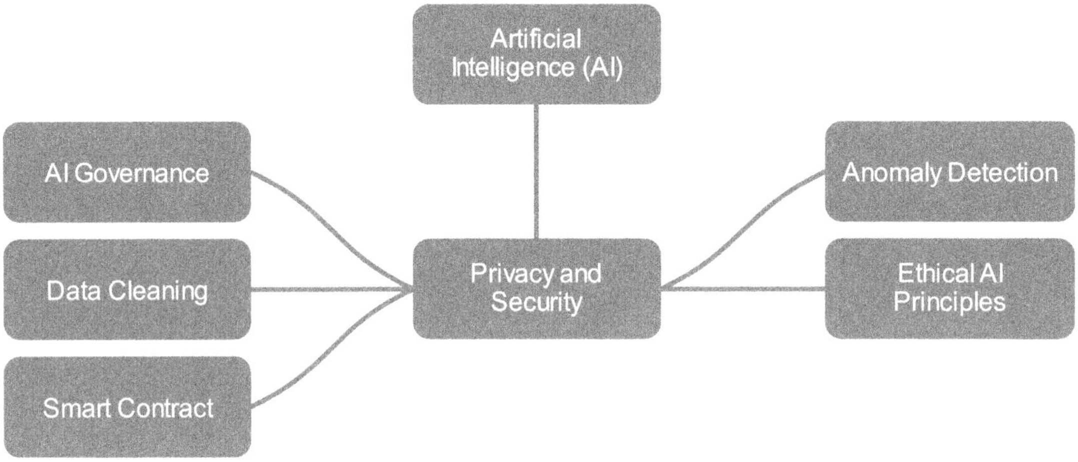

Figure 128: A simple mind map of "Privacy and Security".

AI Governance (pg. 23) -

Anomaly Detection (pg. 27) - A technique used in cybersecurity to identify unusual patterns that do not conform to expected behavior, often indicative of security breaches or malicious activities.

Data Cleaning (pg. 61) - While primarily a method for improving data quality, data cleaning can also involve the removal of sensitive information from datasets to protect privacy before analysis.

Ethical AI Principles (pg. 77) - These often include guidelines and standards for protecting user privacy and ensuring the security of AI systems against misuse and malicious attacks.

Smart Contract (pg. 166) - Blockchain-based contracts that execute automatically when conditions are met, which can include privacy and security protocols to ensure data integrity and confidentiality in transactions.

Reinforcement Learning

These terms collectively describe the key components and concepts of reinforcement learning, illustrating how agents learn to make decisions through trial and error, guided by the feedback received from their interactions with the environment.

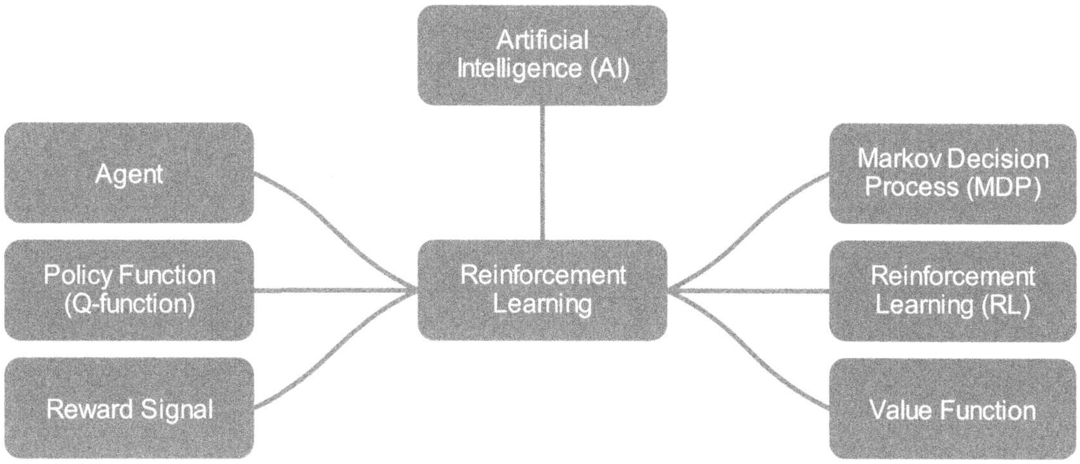

Figure 129: A simple mind map of "Reinforcement Learning".

Agent (pg. 21) - In the context of reinforcement learning, an agent is an entity that makes decisions by interacting with an environment to achieve certain goals or maximize a reward signal.

Markov Decision Process (MDP) (pg. 118) - A mathematical framework for modeling decision-making in situations where outcomes are partly random and partly under the control of a decision-maker, fundamental in formalizing reinforcement learning problems.

Policy Function (Q-function) (pg. 132) - Represents the strategy that the agent employs to determine the next action based on the current state, with Q-function specifically referring to the action-value function that estimates the value of taking an action in a given state.

Reinforcement Learning (RL) (pg. 150) - A type of machine learning where an agent learns to make decisions by performing actions and receiving feedback in the form of rewards or penalties, focusing on learning optimal policies for decision-making.

Reward Signal (pg. 152) - The feedback that an agent receives from the environment to evaluate the actions it has taken, guiding the learning process by indicating the desirability of an outcome.

Value Function (pg. 198) - A function that estimates the expected return (cumulative discounted reward) of being in a state, under a particular policy, guiding the agent's decision-making process in reinforcement learning.

Robotics

These terms highlight key areas of overlap between AI/ML and robotics, illustrating how concepts from AI and ML are applied to give robots the ability to perceive, reason, and act in the physical world.

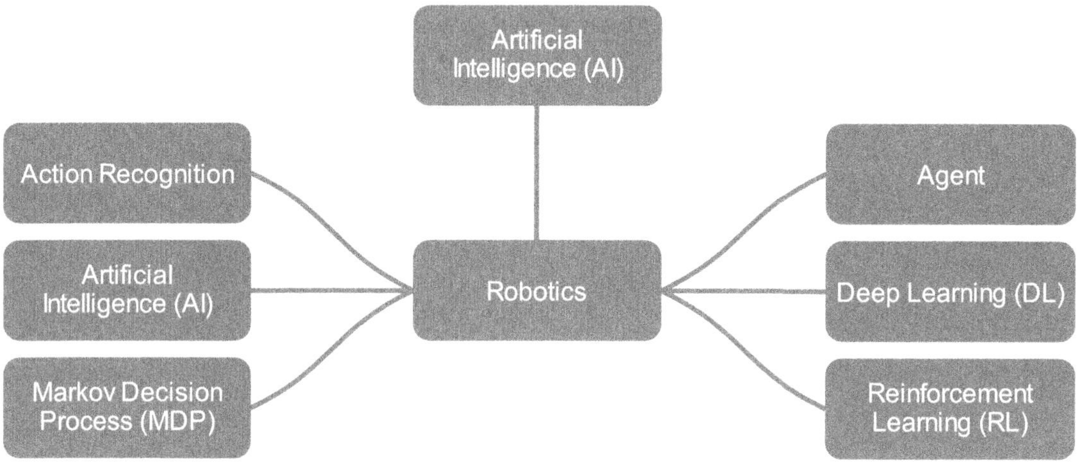

Figure 130: A simple mind map of "Robotics".

Action Recognition (pg. 17) - In robotics, this involves the ability of robots to understand and interpret human actions or the actions of other robots, which can be crucial for collaborative tasks and human-robot interaction.

Agent (pg. 21) - In the context of robotics, an agent can refer to a robot itself, which perceives its environment through sensors and acts upon it through actuators, based on the decision-making processes embedded in its control systems.

Artificial Intelligence (AI) (pg. 2) - AI is foundational to modern robotics, enabling robots to perform tasks autonomously, make decisions, and adapt to their environments through learning and optimization.

Deep Learning (DL) (pg. 69) - This subset of machine learning is used in robotics for tasks such as vision recognition, decision-making, and language understanding, allowing robots to process complex inputs and learn from them.

Markov Decision Process (MDP) (pg. 118) - A mathematical framework for modeling decision-making, which is used in robotics for planning and control, especially in uncertain or dynamic environments.

Reinforcement Learning (RL) (pg. 150) - A learning paradigm used in robotics for developing control policies that allow robots to learn optimal actions through trial and error, interacting with their environment to achieve specific goals.

Self-supervised Learning

These terms encapsulate key methodologies and concepts within self-supervised learning, highlighting how AI models can leverage inherent structures or patterns in data to learn meaningful representations or perform tasks without the need for explicit labels, bridging the gap between supervised and unsupervised learning paradigms.

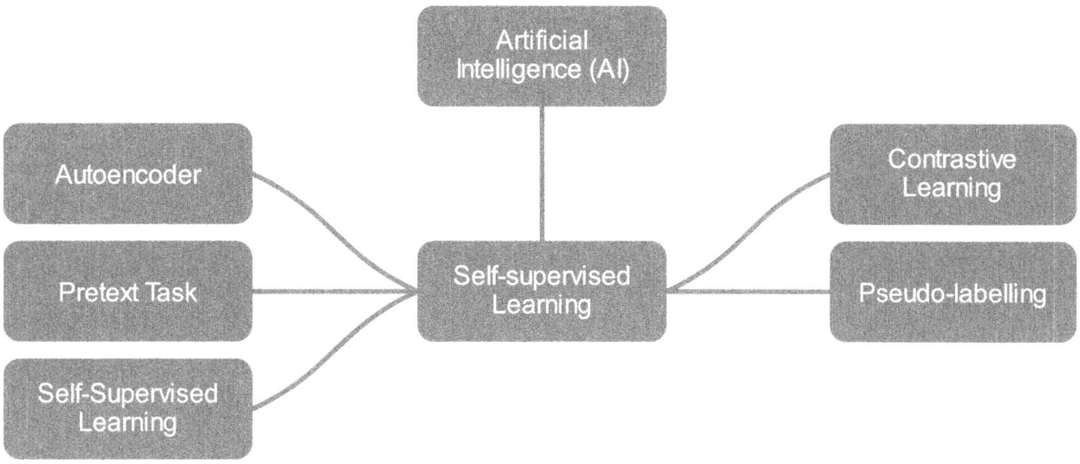

Figure 131: A simple mind map of "Self-supervised Learning".

Autoencoder (pg. 35) - A type of neural network used to learn efficient representations (encoding) of unlabeled data, typically for the purpose of dimensionality reduction or feature learning, by attempting to output a reconstruction of its input.

Contrastive Learning (pg. 47) - A technique used in self-supervised learning that teaches the model to understand which data points are similar or different, enhancing the model's ability to learn meaningful representations of data without explicit labels.

Pretext Task (pg. 136) - A task designed to generate artificial labels from unlabeled data, which is used in self-supervised learning to train models in a way that enables them to learn useful features or representations that can be leveraged for downstream tasks.

Pseudo-labelling (pg. 138) - A technique where a model's own predictions on unlabeled data are used as labels for training, commonly used in semi-supervised learning, which shares similarities with self-supervised learning in its use of unlabeled data for training models.

Self-Supervised Learning (pg. 158) - A learning paradigm where the model learns to predict any part of its input from any other part of its input, using the input data as its own supervision.

Semi-supervised Learning

These terms encapsulate the core methods and concepts of semi-supervised learning, illustrating how it bridges the gap between supervised learning (with ample labeled data) and unsupervised learning (with no labeled data), exploiting the abundance of unlabeled data to enhance model performance.

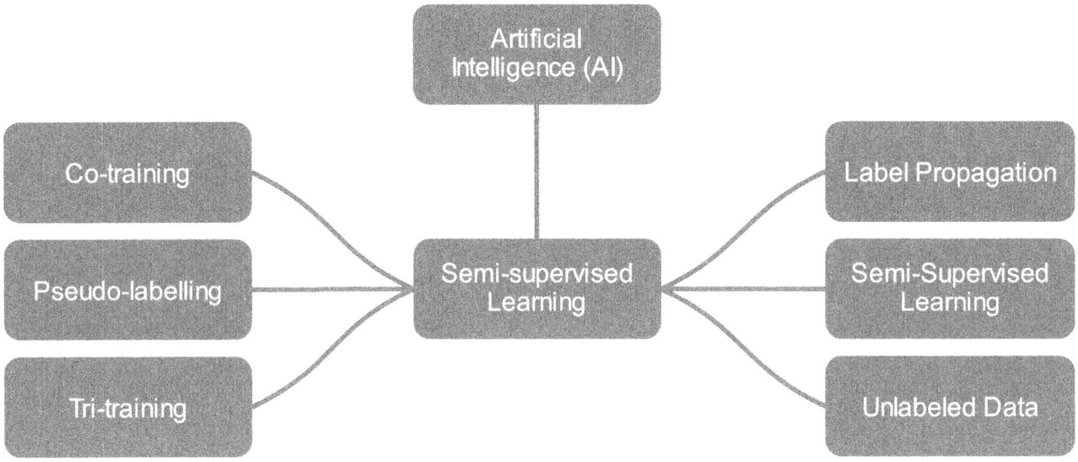

Figure 132: A simple mind map of "Semi-supervised Learning".

Co-training (pg. 55) - A semi-supervised learning technique where two classifiers are trained separately on different views of the data and then predict unlabeled examples for the other to train on.

Label Propagation (pg. 110) - A technique in semi-supervised learning where labels from a small subset of labeled data are propagated to a larger set of unlabeled data based on similarity or proximity, helping to classify or categorize unlabeled instances.

Pseudo-labelling (pg. 138) - A method in semi-supervised learning where a model trained on a small amount of labeled data predicts labels for unlabeled data, and these predicted labels are used as if they were true labels to retrain the model, enhancing its learning from the combination of labeled and unlabeled data.

Semi-Supervised Learning (pg. 164) - A learning paradigm that involves training models on a combination of a small amount of labeled data and a large amount of unlabeled data, leveraging the structure and distribution of the unlabeled data to improve learning accuracy and efficiency.

Tri-training (pg. 188) - Similar to co-training but involves three classifiers that help label unlabeled data for each other, improving as they learn more from the newly labeled data.

Unlabeled Data (pg. 192) - Data that has input features but no corresponding target values, crucial in semi-supervised learning for leveraging large amounts of available data.

Sound and Audio Processing

These terms underscore the application of AI and ML techniques in processing, analyzing, and generating audio data, highlighting how the field intersects with various aspects of sound engineering, speech technology, and musicology.

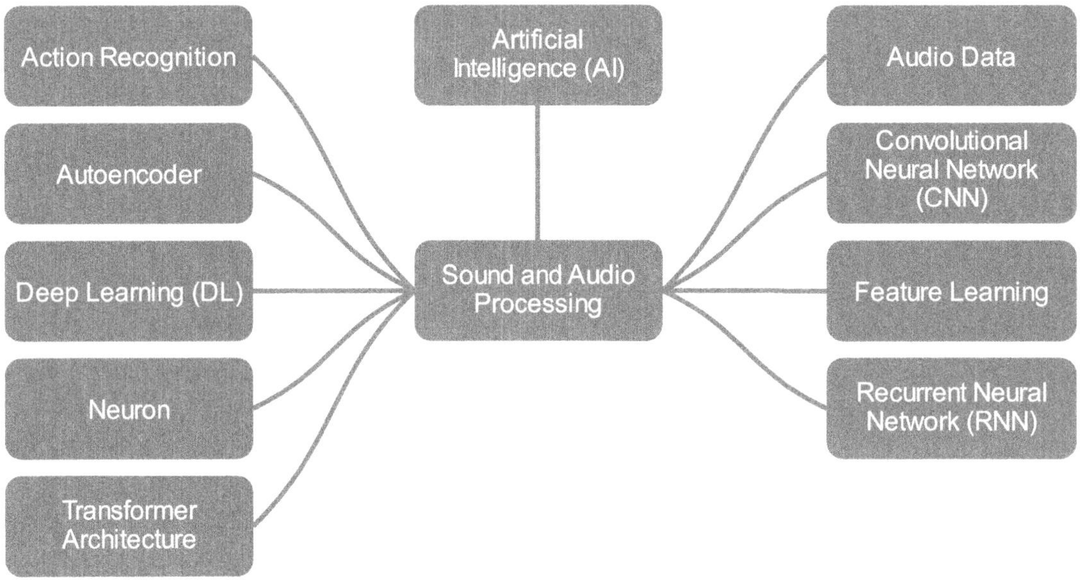

Figure 133: A simple mind map of "Sound and Audio Processing".

Action Recognition (pg. 17) - While often associated with visual data, action recognition can also apply to audio data in contexts where sounds or spoken words correspond to specific actions or commands, important in applications like voice-controlled systems.

Audio Data (pg. 33) - Represents sound information, which is fundamental in sound and audio processing tasks such as speech recognition, music analysis, and environmental sound classification.

Autoencoder (pg. 35) - In the context of audio processing, autoencoders can be used for tasks such as feature extraction, noise reduction, and even generation of new audio samples by learning efficient representations of audio data.

Convolutional Neural Network (CNN) (pg. 51) - Although more commonly associated with image processing, CNNs can also be applied to audio data when it is represented in a time-frequency domain, such as spectrograms, for tasks like audio classification and speech recognition.

Deep Learning (DL) (pg. 69) - Deep learning techniques are increasingly used in advanced audio processing tasks, including speech recognition, music generation, and audio synthesis, leveraging the ability of deep neural networks to model complex patterns in audio data.

Feature Learning (pg. 90) - In audio processing, feature learning involves algorithms automatically discovering the representations needed for audio recognition or classification tasks, which can include identifying unique characteristics in music, speech, or environmental sounds.

Neuron (pg. 126) - In the context of neural networks used for audio processing, each neuron processes input signals (which could be audio signals) and contributes to the network's ability to perform tasks like audio classification, speech recognition, or sound generation.

Recurrent Neural Network (RNN) (pg. 146) - RNNs are particularly suited to processing sequential data, making them useful in audio processing tasks that involve time series data, such as speech recognition or music composition, where the temporal dynamics of audio signals are important.

Transformer Architecture (pg. 186) - Originally developed for natural language processing, transformer models have also been adapted for audio processing tasks, particularly in areas like speech recognition and music generation, leveraging their ability to handle sequential data without the need for recurrence.

Supervised Learning

These terms represent key concepts and methodologies that underpin supervised learning, one of the primary categories of machine learning, where the focus is on learning a function that maps input data to known output labels.

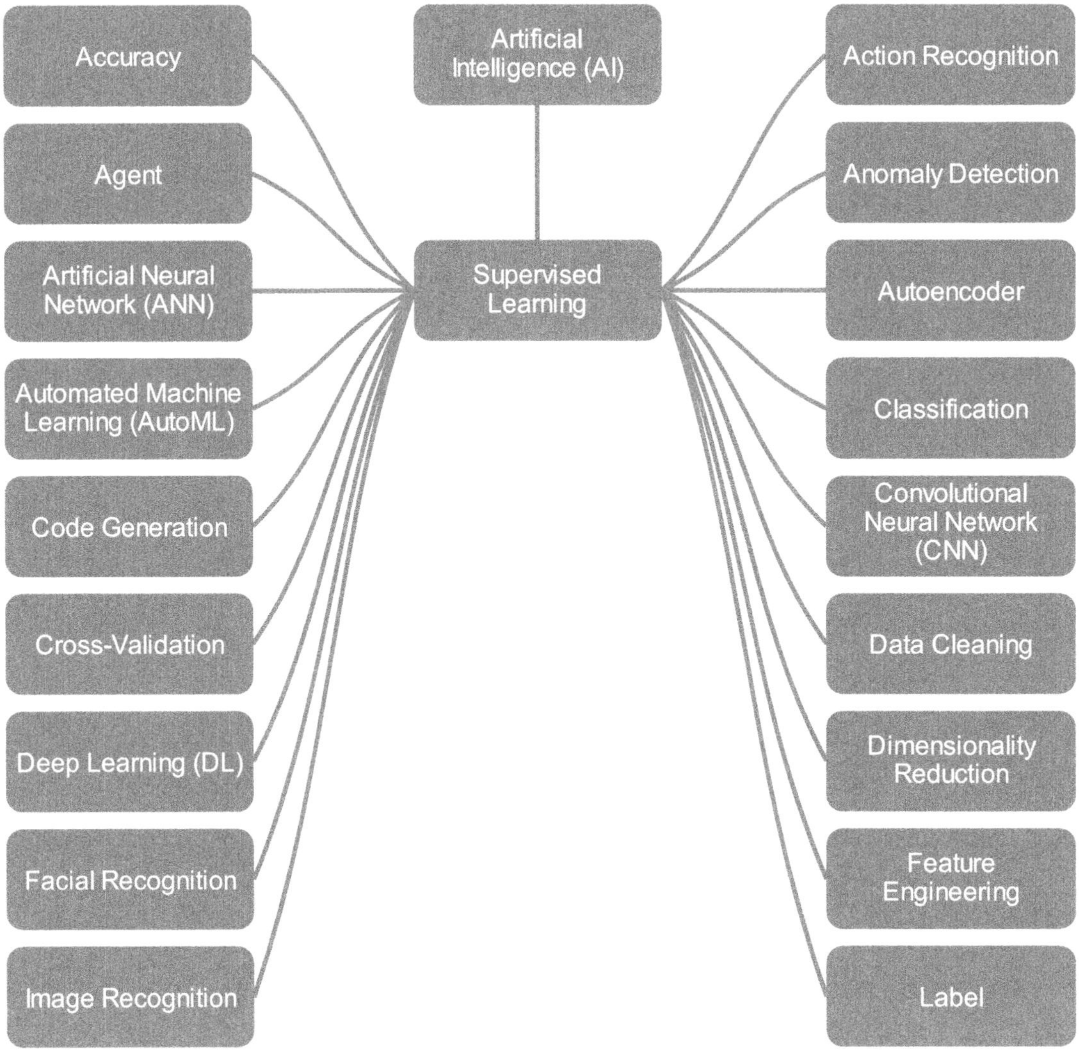

Figure 134: A simple mind map of "Supervised Learning".

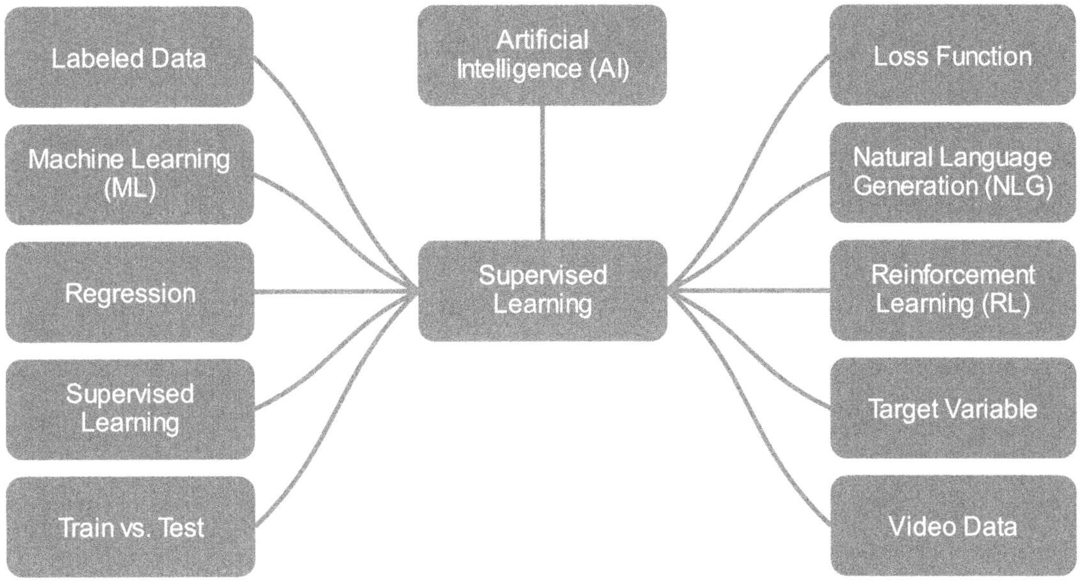

Figure 135: A simple mind map of "Supervised Learning" continued.

Accuracy (pg. 15) - A measure of how correct a supervised learning model's predictions are, commonly used as an evaluation metric.

Action Recognition (pg. 17) - The task of identifying a sequence of actions being performed in a video.

Agent (pg. 21) - In the context of supervised learning, it could refer to a system or model that is trained to perform specific tasks, making decisions based on data and the associated outcomes.

Anomaly Detection (pg. 27) - The identification of unusual data points, which differ significantly from the majority of the data.

Artificial Neural Network (ANN) (pg. 29) - A computing system made up of a number of simple, highly interconnected processing elements, which process information by their dynamic state response to external inputs.

Autoencoder (pg. 35) - In supervised contexts, it can be used for tasks like feature learning and dimensionality reduction, where the output targets are the inputs themselves.

Automated Machine Learning (AutoML) (pg. 37) - Automating the process of applying machine learning to real-world problems with minimal human intervention.

Classification (pg. 41) - A type of supervised learning task where the goal is to predict discrete labels, categorizing input data into two or more classes.

Code Generation (pg. 45) - The process of automatically writing code based on the requirements or data provided, which can be considered a form of supervised learning if the model is trained on code datasets.

Convolutional Neural Network (CNN) (pg. 51) - Used in supervised learning for tasks such as image and video recognition, classification, and segmentation.

Cross-Validation (pg. 57) - A technique used in supervised learning to assess the generalizability of a model by partitioning the data into subsets, training the model on one subset, and validating it on another.

Data Cleaning (pg. 61) - The practice of preparing data for analysis by removing or modifying data that is incorrect, incomplete, irrelevant, duplicated, or improperly formatted.

Deep Learning (DL) (pg. 69) - A subset of machine learning in artificial intelligence with networks capable of learning unsupervised from data that is unstructured or unlabeled.

Dimensionality Reduction (pg. 71) - The transformation of high-dimensional data into a meaningful representation of reduced dimensionality.

Facial Recognition (pg. 86) - A technology capable of identifying or verifying a person from a digital image or a video frame.

Feature Engineering (pg. 88) - The process of using domain knowledge to extract features from raw data that make machine learning algorithms work.

Image Recognition (pg. 102) - The ability of AI systems to identify objects, places, and actions in images.

Label (pg. 108) - In supervised learning, a label is the known output or result for a given input data point, used for training the model.

Labeled Data (pg. 112) - Data that includes both input features and the corresponding target outputs (labels), essential for training supervised learning models.

Loss Function (pg. 116) - A function that measures the discrepancy between the actual and predicted outputs in supervised learning, guiding the optimization process during model training.

Machine Learning (ML) (pg. 12) - The scientific study of algorithms and statistical models that computer systems use to effectively perform a specific task without using explicit instructions.

Natural Language Generation (NLG) (pg. 124) - The use of AI to generate text from a computer database.

Regression (pg. 148) - A type of supervised learning task that involves predicting continuous outcomes based on input variables.

Reinforcement Learning (RL) (pg. 150) - Although typically an unsupervised learning paradigm, it can be adapted for supervised tasks, where the model is trained to make a sequence of decisions.

Supervised Learning (pg. 170) - A machine learning paradigm where models learn to predict outcomes based on input data that is paired with known output data (labels), allowing the model to be explicitly taught the relationships within the data.

Target Variable (pg. 172) - The variable that a supervised learning model is trained to predict, synonymous with "label" in the context of a dataset.

Train vs. Test (pg. 184) - Refers to the practice in supervised learning of dividing a dataset into a training set, used to train the model, and a test set, used to evaluate the model's performance on unseen data.

Video Data (pg. 200) - The use of video data in supervised learning tasks such as action recognition, object detection, and more.

Text and Language Processing

These terms encompass key concepts and methodologies in the field of text and language processing, illustrating the techniques and applications involved in understanding, interpreting, and generating human language using AI and machine learning models.

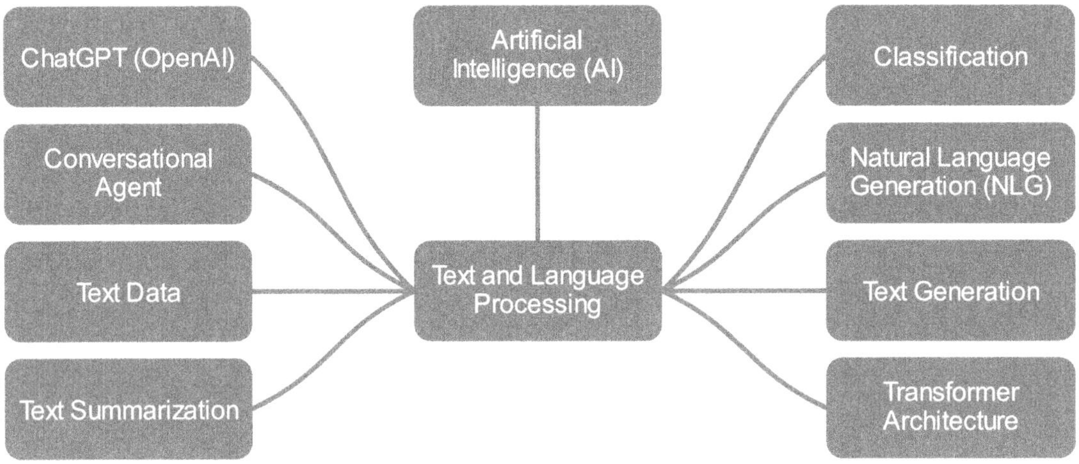

Figure 136: A simple mind map of "Text and Language Processing".

ChatGPT (OpenAI) (pg. 8) - A variant of the Generative Pretrained Transformer developed by OpenAI, specifically designed for generating human-like text based on given prompts, showcasing advancements in natural language processing and generation.

Classification (pg. 41) - In the context of text and language processing, this refers to categorizing text into predefined categories or classes, such as sentiment analysis, topic classification, or spam detection.

Conversational Agent (pg. 49) - AI systems designed to communicate with humans in natural language, relying heavily on natural language processing (NLP) to understand, process, and generate language-based responses.

Natural Language Generation (NLG) (pg. 124) - The process of using computers to generate natural language text from data, enabling applications like automated report writing, content generation, and chatbots.

Text Data (pg. 178) - Unstructured data in the form of sentences, paragraphs, or documents, which is the primary focus of text and language processing tasks.

Text Generation (pg. 180) - The task of automatically generating coherent text sequences, an important application in NLP for creating chatbot responses, content creation, and more.

Text Summarization (pg. 182) - The process of automatically creating a concise and coherent summary of a longer text document, important for quickly conveying the most important information in large texts.

Transformer Architecture (pg. 186) - A model architecture that has revolutionized natural language processing tasks due to its ability to handle sequences of data, such as text, with its self-attention mechanisms, forming the backbone of many state-of-the-art language models.

Unsupervised Learning

These terms highlight key areas and methodologies within unsupervised learning, illustrating how AI and ML models can infer patterns and make decisions from data without being given explicit instructions or labels.

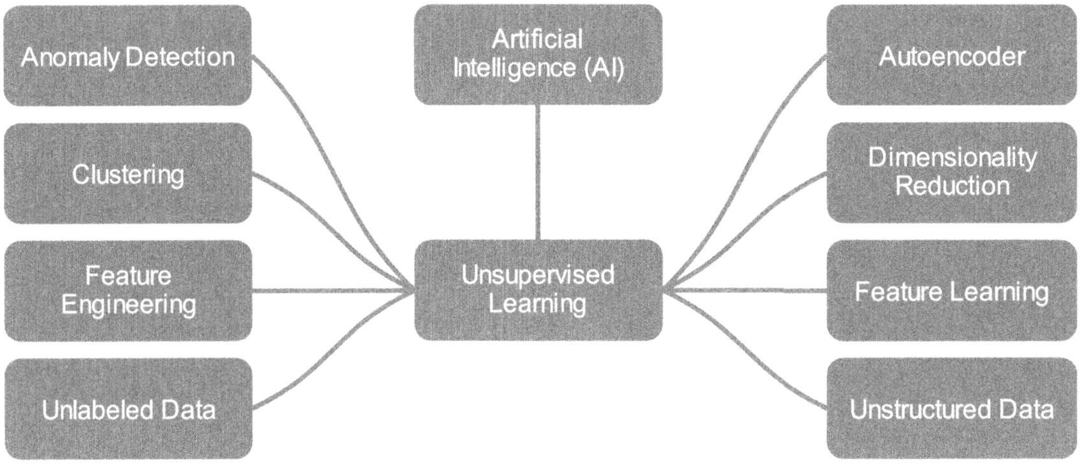

Figure 137: A simple mind map of "Unsupervised Learning".

Anomaly Detection (pg. 27) - The identification of rare items, events, or observations which raise suspicions by differing significantly from the majority of the data.

Autoencoder (pg. 35) - A type of artificial neural network used in unsupervised learning for tasks such as dimensionality reduction and feature learning by learning to encode the input data into a compact representation and then decoding it back to the original form.

Clustering (pg. 43) - A fundamental unsupervised learning technique where the algorithm groups a set of objects in such a way that objects in the same group (or cluster) are more similar to each other than to those in other groups.

Dimensionality Reduction (pg. 71) - A process used in unsupervised learning to reduce the number of random variables under consideration, by obtaining a set of principal variables, which can help in visualizing, compressing, and understanding the data better.

Feature Engineering (pg. 88) - The process of transforming raw data into features that better represent the underlying problem to the predictive models, resulting in improved model accuracy on unseen data.

Feature Learning (pg. 90) - A technique that allows a machine to automatically discover the representations needed for feature detection or classification from raw data.

Unlabeled Data (pg. 192) - Data that does not have explicit labels, making it ideal for unsupervised learning tasks where the algorithm tries to learn the patterns and the structure from the data itself without any external guidance or labels.

Unstructured Data (pg. 194) - Often the focus of unsupervised learning, this type of data does not follow a predefined data model, making it more complex and varied, encompassing formats like text, images, and more, where unsupervised learning can be applied to discover inherent patterns or groupings.

Video Processing

These terms highlight key concepts and methodologies in video processing, illustrating how AI and ML techniques are applied to analyze, understand, and generate insights from video data.

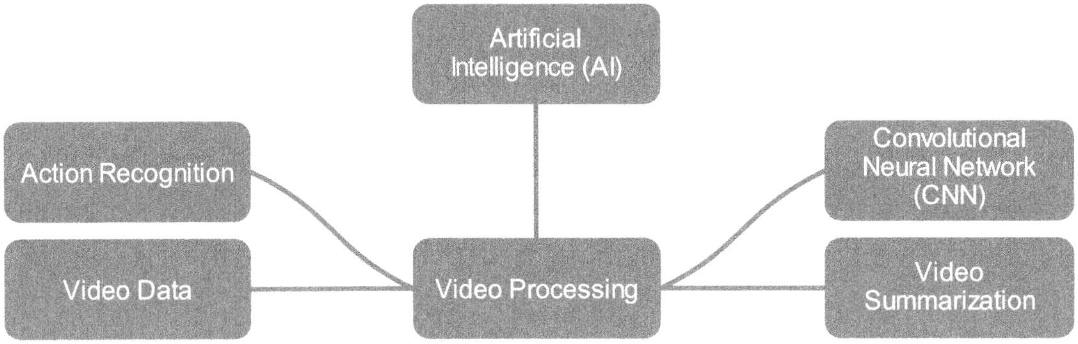

Figure 138: A simple mind map of "Video Processing".

Action Recognition (pg. 17) - Identifying and classifying different actions or activities within video sequences, a key task in video processing for applications like surveillance, sports analysis, and human-computer interaction.

Convolutional Neural Network (CNN) (pg. 51) - While commonly associated with image processing, CNNs are also extensively used in video processing, especially when frames are analyzed sequentially or in combination with Recurrent Neural Networks (RNNs) or 3D CNNs to capture temporal dynamics.

Video Data (pg. 200) - Refers to the use of video as input data for AI and machine learning models, which involves tasks such as classification, object detection, and activity recognition within video frames.

Video Summarization (pg. 202) - The process of creating a concise version of a video by retaining the most informative or important parts, making it easier to understand the content without watching the entire video.

Index

Printed in Great Britain
by Amazon

42085341R00172